KNOWLEDGE

Knowledge

A Human Interest Story

Brian Weatherson

https://www.openbookpublishers.com

©2024 Brian Weatherson

This work is licensed under a Creative Commons Attribution-NonCommercial 4.0 International (CC BY-NC 4.0). This license allows you to share, copy, distribute and transmit the text; to adapt the text for non-commercial purposes of the text providing attribution is made to the author (but not in any way that suggests that they endorse you or your use of the work). Attribution should include the following information:

Brian Weatherson, *Knowledge: A Human Interest Story*. Cambridge, UK: Open Book Publishers, 2024, https://doi.org/10.11647/OBP.0425

Further details about the CC BY-NC license are available at
http://creativecommons.org/licenses/by-nc/4.0/

All external links were active at the time of publication unless otherwise stated and have been archived via the Internet Archive Wayback Machine at https://archive.org/web

Any digital material and resources associated with this volume will be available at https://doi.org/10.11647/OBP.0425#resources

ISBN Paperback: 978-1-80511-394-2
ISBN Hardback: 978-1-80511-395-9
ISBN Digital (PDF): 978-1-80511-396-6
ISBN Digital eBook (EPUB): 978-1-80511-397-3
ISBN HTML: 978-1-80511-398-0

DOI: 10.11647/OBP.0425

Cover image: Golden Gate Bridge, San Francisco, California. Photo by Tj Kolesnik, https://unsplash.com/photos/silhouette-photography-of-mountain-beside-suspension-bridgeduring-golden-hour-Vnz7o7LeuDs.

Cover design: Jeevanjot Kaur Nagpal

Contents

Preface	1
1. Overture	7
2. Interests	25
2.1 Red or Blue?	25
2.2 Four Families	29
2.3 Against Orthodoxy	34
2.3.1 Moore's Paradox	34
2.3.2 Super-Knowledge to the Rescue?	38
2.3.3 Rational Credences to the Rescue?	42
2.3.4 Evidential Probability	43
2.4 Odds and Stakes	46
2.5 Theoretical Interests Matter	48
2.6 Global Interest-Relativity	50
2.7 Neutrality	52
2.7.1 Neutrality about Contextualism	52
2.7.2 Other Aspects of Neutrality	53
3. Belief	55
3.1 Beliefs and Interests	55
3.2 Maps and Legends	58
3.3 Belief and Stubbornness	60
3.4 Taking as Given	62
3.5 Blocking Belief	66
3.6 Questions and Conditional Questions	69
3.7 A Million Dead End Streets	75
3.7.1 Correctness	76
3.7.2 Impractical Propositions	77

3.7.3 Choices with More than Two Options	78
3.7.4 Hard Times and Close Calls	79
3.7.5 Updates and Modals	81
3.8 Ross and Schroeder's Theory	83
4. Knowledge	89
4.1 Ten Decision Commandments	90
4.2 Knowing Where the Ice Cream Goes	94
4.3 Other Answers	98
4.3.1 None of the Above	98
4.3.2 Evidence	100
4.3.3 Sufficiently High Probability	101
4.3.4 Wrapping Up	102
4.4 From KAE to Interest-Relativity	102
4.5 Theoretical Knowledge	103
4.6 Knowledge and Closure	112
4.6.1 Single Premise Closure	113
4.6.2 Multiple Premise Closure	116
4.7 Summary	123
5. Inquiry	125
5.1 Starting and Settling	127
5.1.1 Sensitivity Chasing	129
5.1.2 Rules	131
5.1.3 Understanding	131
5.1.4 Defragmentation	132
5.1.5 Public Reason	133
5.1.6 Evidence Gathering	135
5.1.7 Possible Responses	135
5.2 Using Knowledge in Inquiry	136
5.3 Independence	138
5.4 Double Checking	141
5.5 The Need to Inquire	144
5.6 Multiple Inquiries	147

6. Ties	153
6.1 An Example	154
6.2 Responding to the Challenge, Quickly	157
6.3 Back to Earth	159
6.4 I Have Questions	161
6.5 You'll Never Be Satisfied (If You Try to Maximise)	162
6.6 Deliberation Costs and Infinite Regresses	167
6.7 Ignorance is Bliss	176
7. Changes	179
7.1 Overview of Replies	180
7.2 So Long JTB	182
7.3 Making Up Knowledge	188
7.4 Every Theory is Interest-Relative	191
8. Rationality	195
8.1 Atomism about Rational Belief	195
8.2 Coin Puzzles	200
8.3 Playing Games	203
8.4 Puzzles for Lockeans	210
8.4.1 Arbitrariness	210
8.4.2 Correctness	212
8.4.3 Moorean Paradoxes	213
8.4.4 Closure and the Lockean Theory	213
8.5 Solving the Challenges	215
8.5.1 Coins	215
8.5.2 Games	215
8.5.3 Arbitrariness	215
8.5.4 Moore	216
9. Evidence	217
9.1 A Puzzle about Evidence	217
9.2 A Simple, but Incomplete, Solution	218
9.3 The Radical Interpreter	219
9.4 Risk-Dominant Equilibria	222
9.4.1 The Dominance Argument for Risk-Dominant Equilibria	226

9.4.2 Making One Signal Precise	230
9.5 Objections and Replies	231
9.6 Evidence, Knowledge, and Cut-Elimination	233
9.7 Basic Knowledge and Non-Inferential Knowledge	237
9.8 Holism and Defeaters	241
9.9 Epistemic Weakness	244
10. Power	247
References	253
List of Tables	267
Index	269

Preface

Over the years I've written many papers defending an idiosyncratic version of interest-relative epistemology. This book collects and updates the views I've expressed over those papers.

My original plan was not a collection of papers, that would hardly add much value over a well-designed webpage, but a book that was largely structured out of different sections of different papers. My thought was that I had something like a working theory between the papers, and what would be useful would be to blend the sentences, paragraphs, and even whole sections from them into a coherent narrative. Some of that plan has been retained. Most sections in Chapters 8 and 9 are very similar to sections in one or other previously published paper. But the bulk of the book is new. In putting the pieces together, I realised that I'd changed my mind about enough things, and needed to express myself very differently about enough other things, so as to make it worth rewriting much of what I had. The result is that this is about 60% a new book, 20% a heavily edited version of previous material, and 20% lightly edited republishing of previous material. Even that last 20% has some value I think—it helps to see those points in the context of an overall story—but this is mostly a new book.

Interest-relative epistemologies all start in roughly the same way. A big part of what makes knowledge important is that it rationalises action. But for almost anything we purportedly know, there is some action that it wouldn't rationalise. I know what I had for breakfast, but I wouldn't take a bet at billion to one odds about it. Knowledge has practical limits. The first idiosyncratic feature of my version of interest-relative epistemology is how those limits are identified. Other interest-relative philosophers typically say that the limits have to do with stakes; in *high-stakes* situations knowledge goes away. That's no part of my view. I think knowledge goes away in *long-odds* situations. High-stakes situations are almost always long-odds situations, for reasons to do with the declining marginal utility of money. But the converse isn't true. On my view, knowledge often goes away in cases where it is trivial to check before action. This idea, that interests matter in long-odds cases, and not just in high-stakes cases, is the main constant in what I've written on interest-relativity over the years.

But there are three other respects in which the view I'm going to set out and defend in this book is very different from the view I set out in older papers.

I used to say that knowledge went away in cases where replying on the purported knowledge would lead to the wrong answer. I focussed, that is, on the outputs of inquiry. Knowledge goes away if relying on it would lead one to make a mistake. I now think I was looking at the wrong end of inquiry. Knowledge goes away if the thinker starts conducting an inquiry where the purported knowledge is an inappropriate starting point, and inappropriate for the special reason that it might be false. One way to recognise a bad starting point is by realising that starting there will mean we end up at the wrong place. But it's not the only way. Sometimes a bad starting point will lead to the right conclusion for the wrong reasons. As the Nyāya philosophers argued, rational inquiry starts with knowledge. If it would be irrational to start this inquiry with a particular belief, that belief isn't knowledge.

Not all inquiries are practical inquiries, but many are. And practical inquiries are usually going to be at the centre of attention in this book. But what is someone trying to figure out when they conduct a practical inquiry? I used to think that they were trying to figure out which option maximised expected utility, and to a first approximation identified knowledge with those things one could conditionalise on without changing the option that maximised expected utility. As noted in the previous paragraph, I no longer think that we can identify knowledge with what doesn't change our verdicts. But more importantly, I no longer think that expected utility maximisation is as central to practical inquiry as I once did. There are theoretical reasons from game theory that raise doubts about expected utility maximisation being the full theory of rational choice. Weak dominance reasoning is part of our theory of rational choice, and can't be modelled as expected utility maximisation. Perhaps some kinds of equilibrium seeking are parts of practical inquiry, and can't be modelled as expected utility maximisation. There are also very practical reasons to think that practical inquiry doesn't aim at expected utility maximisation. When there are a lot of very similar options—think about selecting a can from a supermarket shelf—and it's more trouble than it's worth to figure out which of them maximises expected utility, it's best to ignore the differences between them and just pick. As I'll argue in Chapter 6, this makes a big difference to how interests and knowledge interact.

In the version of interest-relativity that I'm defending here, everything in epistemology is interest-relative. Knowledge, rational belief, and evidence are all interest-relative. But they are all interest-relative in slightly different ways. The main aim here is to defend the interest-relativity of knowledge. A common objection to interest-relative theories of knowledge is that they can't be extended into theories of all the things we care about in epistemology. Here I try to meet that challenge. The way I do so is a little messy. It would be nice if some part of epistemology were interest-invariant, as I once thought, or if all the interest-relative notions were interest-relative in the same way, as other interest-relative epistemologists argue. For better or worse, that's not the view I'm defending. Interests matter throughout epistemology, and we just have to go case by case to figure out how and why they matter.

The ideas from the last three paragraphs are totally absent from my earliest work—several times they are explicitly rejected—but become more prevalent as the years go on. This is the first time I've defended them all in one place. And I think they are all necessary to make the theory I want to defend hang together.

Here is a list of these papers on interest-relativity that I've mentioned a few times already.

- Can we do without pragmatic encroachment? *Philosophical Perspectives*, 19 (2005), 417–443.
- Defending interest-relative invariantism. *Logos and Episteme*, 2 (2011), 591–609.
- Games and the reason-knowledge principle. *The Reasoner*, 6 (2012), 6–7.

- Knowledge, bets and interests. In Jessica Brown and Mikkel Gerken (Eds.), *Knowledge Ascriptions* (75–103), Oxford University Press, 2012.
- Reply to Blackson. *Journal of Philosophical Research*, 46 (2016), 73–75.
- Games, beliefs and credences. *Philosophy and Phenomenological Research*, 92 (2016), 209–236.
- Reply to Eaton and Pickavance. *Philosophical Studies*, 173 (2016), 3231–3233.
- Interest-relative invariantism. In Jonathan Jenkins Ichikawa (Ed.), *Routledge Handbook of Epistemic Contextualism* (240–253), Routledge, 2017.
- Interests, evidence and games. *Episteme*, 15 (2018), 329–344.

I wrote most of this manuscript while on sabbatical at the Australian National University in the first half of 2019, and I'm very grateful for their hospitality while I was a visitor there.

Support for that sabbatical came from the Marshall M. Weinberg Professorship at the University of Michigan. And I'm once again incredibly grateful for the support Marshall has given to philosophy, and to many other disciplines, at the University of Michigan.

Many of the papers were drafted, and workshopped, while I was a Visiting Fellow at the Arché Research Centre at the University of St Andrews. You could probably fill a book this long with the mistakes I was talked out of in formal and informal meetings in St Andrews. And it was a real privilege to have been part of that community for a decade.

In Winter 2020 I taught a graduate seminar based off a draft of this manuscript at the University of Michigan. I received a lot of valuable feedback from the students in that seminar. I suspect I would have received even more valuable feedback had we not had to scramble to convert the course into a virtual event halfway through the semester. But I'm still very grateful for what I learned from them over that course.

I've presented this material at many departments and workshops, and am very grateful to the feedback I've received on each occasion. Most of the book was presented in one form or another at Arché. As well, parts have been presented at the 2012 Rutgers Epistemology Conference, the 2017 *Episteme* Conference, a workshop on pragmatic encroachment organised by Arizona State University in 2017, the University of Sydney, the Australian National University, and the 2020 Ranch Metaphysics Workshop. I've also had valuable feedback on ideas in the book over the years from Michael Almeida, Charity Anderson, Thomas Blackson, Jessica Brown, Stewart Cohen, Josh Dever, Tom Donaldson, Tamar Szabó Gendler, Peter Gerdes, Katherine Hawley, John Hawthorne, Jonathan Ichikawa, Jon Kvanvig, Jennifer Lackey, Barry Lam, Harvey Lederman, Matthew McGrath, Sarah Moss, Jennifer Nagel, Shyam Nair, Daniel Nolan, Ángel Pinillos, Jacob Ross, Mark Schroeder, Kieran Setiya, Ernie Sosa, Levi Spectre, Robert Stalnaker, Jason Stanley, and Matthew Weiner. Jonathan Ichikawa also read over the whole manuscript and provided many useful comments.

And of course I've got more feedback, and more useful feedback, from Ishani Maitra than from anyone, or any place, else. She's had to listen to, and often talk me out of, any number of dead ends, false leads, and outright mistakes, on this topic for the best part of two decades. If there's anything in what follows that manages to be true, useful, and new, it's thanks to her feedback, advice, and support.

1. Overture

The core thesis of this book is that what a person knows is sensitive to what their interests are, and in particular to what inquiries they are engaged in. The thesis is designed to resolve a puzzle about the nature of inquiry. Inquiry has to start somewhere, and a natural place to start is with what one knows. If one is planning a meal for friends, and choosing what to make, it's natural to start with what one knows about what ingredients are on hand or easily available, what the friends like, what dietary preferences and restrictions they have, and so on.

Now we face a puzzle. Either we identify knowledge with absolute certainty or we do not. If we do, then inquiry can barely get started. If one knows anything with absolute certainty, then it is at most trivialities like instances of the law of identity. That won't be enough to get going on planning dinner. So let's say we do not identify knowledge with absolute certainty, and instead pick some particular level of certainty below that. Then there will be propositions that are more certain than that threshold, but which one should not use in this particular inquiry. For instance, there will be cases where one's evidence that a particular friend is not allergic to peanuts is just above that threshold, but given the potentially lethal consequences of getting it wrong, this isn't something that should be taken as a starting point in inquiry.

The solution is to identify knowledge with a level of certainty which varies with the nature of the inquiry. In particular, it varies both with how important it is to get the inquiry right (very important in the case of the allergy), and with how hard it would be to get further information relevant to the inquiry.

I'm not the first to defend such a view; there is a thriving literature on interest-relative theories of knowledge like the one I'm defending here. But for a long time it was a remarkably curious literature. Interest-relative theories were discussed everywhere and endorsed virtually

©2024 Brian Weatherson, CC BY-NC 4.0   https://doi.org/10.11647/OBP.0425.01

nowhere. It's possible things changed around the time of the COVID-19 pandemic; after 2020 there were more positive discussions of interest-relativity.[1] Before then, interest-relative theories had a ratio of discussion to endorsement that philosophy hadn't seen since David Lewis put concrete modal realism on the agenda.

The terminology that is used to describe the debate about interest-relativity is striking. The interest-relative view is usually opposed to the 'purist' or 'traditionalist' view. I'm not going to dive into the literature on which views get described as 'pure' or 'impure', but I wanted to pause a bit over 'tradition'. This is a particularly curious choice of word, and I think its curiosity is related to the strange shape of the literature around interest-relativity.

The recent literature on interest-relativity was kick-started by three works in the early 2000s. First was Jeremy Fantl and Matthew McGrath's paper "Evidence, Pragmatics and Justification", published in *The Philosophical Review* in 2002. Then came two books from Oxford University Press: *Knowledge and Lotteries* by John Hawthorne in 2003, and *Knowledge and Practical Interests* by Jason Stanley in 2004. Now these works are, by standards of recent epistemology, from quite a long time ago. That is to say, two decades is a long time in epistemology. Compare, for instance, the literature on the idea that safety is central to the theory of knowledge. The idea that safety is important plays a crucial role in a series of works from the late 1990s and early 2000s by Lewis, Timothy Williamson, Ernest Sosa, and Duncan Pritchard.[2] And it became a central feature of a lot of epistemological theorising very quickly. But safety-relative epistemology is really only a few years older than interest-relative epistemology. So why is one of these traditional and the other not?

One possible answer is that while safety was a new idea, it struck epistemologists as similar to older ideas. Safety looks a lot like the sensitivity condition that Robert Nozick (1981) had argued plays a

---

1 See, for instance: Kim (2023), Gao (2023), Schmidt (forthcoming), Steglich-Petersen (2024), Wu (forthcoming), and Ye (2024). That's about as many people defending interest-relative theories in one year as defended them for the first 15 years since they were introduced in Fantl and McGrath (2002).
2 I'll discuss safety in more detail later. For now, a rough definition will suffice. A person's belief is considered safe if they couldn't easily have been wrong in forming that belief. According to safety-relative epistemology, only safe beliefs amount to knowledge, and this plays an important role in explaining knowledge.

central role in the theory of knowledge. Sosa (1999) plays up this similarity, framing safety as a kind of converse of sensitivity. And safety looks like a kind of reliability condition, so it is continuous with 20th-century work on reliabilism. So while safety theories are new, they have things that look like precursors. But to a lot of epistemologists, interest-relative theories seemed novel. It wasn't just that they offered a new account of what affects knowledge; it was that they offered a view that came out of nowhere.

If that was the impression that epistemologists had, it was mistaken. There are precursors to contemporary interest-relative views, and looking at them is helpful for thinking about why one might want to endorse an interest-relative view. I'm going to focus on two of these precursors, one from Hellenistic philosophy and one from medieval philosophy.[3]

Philo of Larissa lived from around 159 BCE to around 83 BCE, and was the last sceptical head of Plato's Academy.[4] He held a number of views over his life, but the one that's important here is his "mitigated scepticism" (Brittain and Osorio: §3.3). The sceptics faced a challenge: if no one knows anything, and indeed no one should believe anything, then it seems rational action is impossible. But surely some acts are rational, or at least more rational than other acts. What can be done?

Philo's response is to say that while it is true that nothing can be known, it can be rational to assent to certain "persuasive impressions" (Brittain and Osorio: §3.3). Action that is based in the right way on an impression that is really persuasive (and not just one that actually persuades) can be rational. Moreover, says Philo, how much evidence one needs to be properly persuaded can vary with differences in what's at stake with the action. As Peter Adamson puts it,

---

[3] A quick note on sources. This is not at all a work of historical scholarship, and I'm not in a position to write such a work. So everything I cite here is going to be a contemporary secondary (or tertiary) source. I do hope in the future there will be more work which looks at the relationship between these historically important figures and contemporary views, but that work will have to be done by someone with a different skill set to mine.

[4] My main sources here are the Stanford Encyclopedia of Philosophy entry on Philo (Brittain and Osorio, 2021) and the chapters on scepticism in Peter Adamson's book on Hellenistic philosophy (Adamson, 2015). I'm particularly drawing on section 3.3 of the SEP entry, and chapters 16 and 17 of Adamson's book.

> Like Arcesilaus, Philo suggests that these impressions will be used as a practical guide by the Skeptic. But he went further, observing that the standards we use will differ depending on how high the stakes are. In the normal course of affairs one bit of evidence will suffice. For instance, if I'm looking for the giraffes, I'll just ask another zoo-visitor and follow their directions. But what if it is really important—if, say, I need to be at the giraffe enclosure in five minutes to pay a ransom to the giraffe-nappers who are demanding £1 million for the safe return of Hiawatha, who just happens to be my favorite giraffe? Then I will want to make extra sure. (Adamson, 2015: 112)

Now Philo (probably) doesn't move from this to an interest-relative theory of knowledge. But look how close he gets. He thinks that the norm of belief, or at least the norm of the thing that plays the same role in his philosophical system as belief plays in ours, is interest-relative. All you have to add to get an interest-relative theory of knowledge is that knowledge is the norm of (the thing that plays the functional role of) belief.

Jumping ahead a millennium and a half, our next stop is with the epistemology of medieval philosopher Jean Buridan. I'm going to draw extensively here on Robert Pasnau's discussion of medieval epistemology in his *After Certainty*. Pasnau credits Buridan with introducing "what would become the canonical three-level distinction between absolute, natural, and moral certainty" (Pasnau, 2017: 32). The last of these, "moral certainty", is the most important one here. This isn't quite Buridan's phrase—he talks about moral evidentness—but he seems to be the causal origin of the introduction of the phrase "moral certainty" (or its equivalent in other languages) into western European discourse. And it's particularly interesting to the story here to see what kind of problem this notion is meant to solve.

> There is still another, weaker evidentness, which suffices for acting well morally. This goes as follows: if someone, having seen and investigated all the attendant circumstances that one can investigate with diligence, judges in accord with the demands of such circumstances, then that judgment will be evident with an evidentness sufficient for acting well morally—even if that judgment were false on account of invincible ignorance concerning some circumstance. For instance, it would be possible for a judge to act well and meritoriously by hanging an innocent man because through testimony and other documents it sufficiently appeared to him in accord with his duty that that good man was a bad murderer. (Buridan, as quoted in Pasnau, 2017: 34)

Note in particular the phrase "the demands of such circumstances". Buridan's notion here is clearly interest-relative. What it takes to properly judge a defendant guilty of murder is considerably more than what it takes to judge that someone broke a promise. The difference between the misdeeds, while in the first instance a moral difference, matters to the applicability of this epistemic concept.

Now Buridan does not have an interest-relative account of knowledge. After all, the very example he uses to introduce this interest-relative concept is one where the belief is false, and hence not knowledge. This would change over time. Eventually John Wilkins, writing in the 17th century, would take moral certainty to be the standard for knowledge (Pasnau, 2017: 218). Wilkins is important to the history of science as one of the founders of the Royal Society. And he is important to the history of epistemology because he starts the tradition of centring epistemology around attainable norms. Here is how Pasnau puts the point.

> Wilkins in particular, in his small way, takes what can retrospectively be seen as a decisive step, because he both rejects the principle of proportionality in favor of a broad scope for absolute belief and identifies the whole range of such belief with knowledge. For, even as he continues to associate knowledge with certainty, he allows that mere moral certainty is good enough, treating mathematical, physical, and moral as three different kinds of knowledge and thus locating the threshold for knowledge not at intellectual compulsion but at the absence of reasonable doubt: "that kind of assent which does arise from such plain and clear evidence as does not admit of any reasonable cause of doubting is called knowledge or certainty." (Pasnau, 2017: 43)

The "principle of proportionality" here is the idea that the better one's evidence for a proposition is, the stronger one's belief in that proposition should be. What's distinctive in Wilkins is that he thinks one can have absolute belief in a mere moral certainty. This violates proportionality because if one's belief is a mere moral certainty, then the evidence for it could be improved. But since it is an absolute belief, the belief couldn't get stronger.

What's distinctive about Wilkins is not the use of moral certainty in epistemology. That's there in Buridan three hundred years earlier. What's distinctive is the central role he gives it. And as Pasnau reads the situation, the approach taken by Wilkins becomes orthodox for the next three hundred years. The alternative option, one that Pasnau prefers, is to focus on what the epistemological ideal is, and on how close we can get to attaining that ideal. You can read at least some contemporary probabilists as working in the tradition—one that was common before Wilkins—of thinking that only maximally supported beliefs get the maximal level of belief. But this is definitely not the mainstream view for the last few centuries. The mainstream view is that there are these important, absolute, concepts that can be attained even though one's evidential situation could in principle improve further. And these concepts are closely tied to knowledge. And, most strikingly, the one that is mostly tied to knowledge is originally introduced as an interest-relative concept.

In both Philo of Larissa, and in the tradition that runs from Buridan to Wilkins and beyond, interest-relative epistemic concepts play central roles. There is no figure here who literally endorses every aspect of the contemporary interest-relative view. But the precursors are there. Indeed, they are there at some of the earliest sightings of what we might, in current terminology, call fallible epistemologies. If anything, I suspect the idea that an epistemology can be fallibilist and interest-invariant is the more recent innovation. Rather than dive too deeply into those historical waters, let's turn to a connection between Buridan's epistemology and (a particular strand in) Indian epistemology: the place of action theory in epistemology. What worries Buridan is whether a certain action, hanging an innocent man, can be given an epistemological defence. Buridan isn't the first philosopher to see a tight connection between epistemology and action theory.

The 5th century philosopher Vātsyāyana is known for his commentary on the 1st or 2nd century Nyāya-sūtra.[5] In this commentary he offers a number of anti-sceptical arguments. This one is most interesting to the story here.

> For Vātsyāyana, the purpose of knowledge is indeed crucially important. He begins his commentary by saying that knowledge is needed in order to secure any desired objective (artha). Each of us exerts effort only for the sake of achieving such an objective. Here one might think of an idea we encountered in Mīmāṃsā, that it is a sacrificer's desire that makes a ritual incumbent upon the sacrificer.

---

5   My source for everything here is Peter Adamson's and Jonardon Ganeri's *Classical Indian Philosophy* (Adamson and Ganeri, 2020).

> No desire, no action. Now Vātsyāyana adds: no knowledge, no result! After all, how can you get what you want when you literally don't know what you're doing? Vātsyāyana invokes the point again later on, when he responds to the standard skeptical argument that any means of knowledge must be ratified by some further means of knowledge, leading to a regress. Thus, the skeptic is suggesting, we cannot trust a pramāṇa like perception unless some further perception tells us that it is trustworthy. No, replies Vātsyāyana. If this were true then "the activities of practical life" would be impossible, since the only way we ever achieve anything that we want is by knowing how to get it. This applies to mundane goals like wealth and pleasure, and to more exalted goals too. Nyāya competes with the Buddhists not only on the epistemological front, by refuting skeptical arguments like the one just mentioned, but also on what we may, with apologies to Monty Python, call the liberation front. The elimination of suffering, promised by Buddhists and Naiyāyikas alike, is one more objective that can be achieved through knowledge and through knowledge alone. (Adamson and Ganeri, 2020: 170)

More bluntly, the argument is that some actions are rational, only actions based on knowledge are rational, and so we have some knowledge, contra scepticism. Unlike Vātsyāyana I'm not in the business of arguing against scepticism. But this is an excellent anti-sceptical argument. That's not just because it's sound, and persuasive, though it's both. It's because it derives anti-sceptical conclusions from the practical nature of knowledge. It grounds the anti-scepticism where is should be grounded, in the practical nature of knowledge.

The Nyāya philosophers, like Vātsyāyana, are relevant to this story for another reason. As well as closely connecting knowledge with action, they connect it closely with inquiry. And this book, like many contemporary philosophers, takes the same approach. Jane Friedman (2019a, 2019b, 2020, 2024b) has developed a detailed account of what inquiry is and how it relates to epistemology. Elise Woodard (2020) and Arienne Falbo (2021) have some persuasive criticisms of particular details of Friedman's views, but enough of the picture survives, and indeed is developed by both Woodard and Falbo, to be useful in theorising about knowledge. Guido Melchior (2019) has developed a detailed account of a special kind of inquiry, namely checking, and some of what he says about checking is very useful in resolving some tensions in the interest-relative picture.

Knowledge seems like it should be related to inquiry. But just what is the relationship? An inquiry, like any action, has a beginning, a middle, and an end. And it helps to think about ways in which knowledge can play a role at each of these three stages. In particular, the following three theses suggest ways in which knowledge plays a role at each stage in turn.

1. Inquiry should start with knowledge.
2. Inquiry should only be into things one does not know.
3. Inquiry should aim at knowledge.

All three of these are plausible, but I'm ultimately only going to accept 1. I'm going to accept a fairly strong form of it. On the version I accept, only knowledge is appropriate as a starting point for inquiry, and any knowledge could (in principle) be appropriate as a starting point. The latter claim has to be qualified in some ways—it isn't appropriate to start an inquiry into where the cat is with one's knowledge about early Roman history. But if, while inquiring into where the cat is, one knows which year Hannibal crossed the Alps, then that knowledge is certain enough for use in the inquiry. If it shouldn't be used, and it probably shouldn't be, that's on grounds of irrelevance, not on grounds of uncertainty.

But I'm going to reject 2 and 3. I'm disagreeing here with Friedman, whose theory of inquiry gives an important role to 2. And Woodard argues convincingly that the failure of 3 implies that 2 has to fail as well.[6] Inquiry might aim at knowledge, but it might aim at any number of other things: at understanding, or at sensitivity, or at developing reasons that convince others. (The latter aim plays an important role in the explanation Michael Strevens (2020) offers for some striking features of contemporary science.) Since one might want to understand something one knows, or have a more sensitive belief in what one knows, or convince others of what one knows, it can make sense to inquire into what one knows.

The next chapter presents a straightforward argument for interest-relative epistemology. Before I get to that, I want to offer two motivations

---

6   Note that Friedman (2024b) also rejects 3, but not because she thinks inquiry aims at something else; she is sceptical of the metaphor of aiming in this context. Note also that Falbo and Melchior developed similar arguments to Woodard's.

for the view. You could try to turn either of these motivations into a nice, clean, premise-conclusion argument for interest-relativity. I haven't done that because in both of these cases, the premise-conclusion format obscures more than it enlightens. The first motivation comes from the practical nature of belief, and the second from the thought that knowledge is a natural kind.

Think back to the problem facing Philo of Larissa. He wants to be a sceptic, so nothing is known. He also wants to be able to act in the world. Action requires a picture of what reality is like. So we need some mental state that aims to fit the world, and which can guide action. Once we have that state, you might well think that it's just belief. Hugo Mercier (2020) argues that people do not believe as many conspiracy theories as they say they do; these apparent endorsements he argues are moves in a complicated signaling game. His evidence that they don't actually believe the conspiracy theories is that they act nothing like how they would act were the theories true. Whether or not the details of Mercier's argument are right, the form of it seems right. Apparent belief that is out of sync with action is not really belief at all.

If belief is practical, the norms for belief should be practical too. This isn't a logically necessary conditional; it is easy to describe cases where we have non-practical norms for an essentially practical state. Still, you should expect that the norms of a practical state are typically practical. So you should expect that epistemology, the study of norms for belief, will be shot through with practical considerations. That's what the interest-relative theorist says is in fact the case.

The second motivation comes from reflection on what we're trying to do in epistemology, and how it relates to the importance of knowledge. I mentioned earlier that Pasnau regards the turn epistemology took after Wilkins, where a central focus is on clarifying sub-optimal notions like knowledge, to be a mistake. (By 'sub-optimal' here, I mean merely that they are standards one can meet while also being in a position to improve one's doxastic position.) He thinks this is a retreat into mere lexicography, and away from what was traditionally, and correctly, viewed as the primary task of epistemology, namely clarifying the nature of the epistemic ideal. I'm working in this post-Wilkins tradition, so I probably should say some words in defence of it. This defence ends up motivating an interest-relative approach.

Firstly, even if one didn't care about threshold standards like knowledge, the right thing to do isn't to focus on the ideal. We aren't going to attain the ideal. What we can do is get better and better. But knowing what the ideal is like is often very little help in figuring out how to do better. This is a general consequence of the Theory of the Second Best (Lipsey and Lancaster, 1956–1957). Very often, being like the ideal is a way of being worse rather than better. For example, the ideal inquirer doesn't forget anything, so they don't need to take notes while reading. Nevertheless, it's a good epistemic practice to take notes while reading. So even if what you ultimately care about is doing better, not meeting thresholds, it isn't obvious that exploring the ideal is the way to get there. If our aim is epistemic improvement, we're probably better off exploring tools that fallible humans have developed for helping other fallible humans, rather than striving for an unattainable ideal.

Secondly, and more importantly, the project here is not one of lexicography. I don't particularly care how the English word 'knows' is used. The fact that a phonologically indistinguishable word is used to talk both about knowing who won last night and knowing the players on the winning team is of no relevance to the project we're engaged in here. The fact that most languages have a word that is very close to synonymous to the English word 'knows' is more relevant. That's not because it makes the lexicography important. Rather, it's because it suggests that there is an important concept that English speakers are picking out with 'knows', that French speakers are picking out with 'savoir', and so on for all the other languages in the world. It could be that all these different language groups agreed to use one of their limited stock of words for this concept, and it was a mistake in every case. But as J. L. Austin frequently reminded us, that's not the way to bet.

The concept of knowledge is, among other things, scientifically important. Throughout the social sciences, there are theories that are grounded in patterns of human behaviour. Those patterns are, usually, best explained in terms of what those humans know. Consider the (stylised) fact that in a small, open, free market, competing suppliers of a common good will usually sell goods for the same price. We could offer an explanation of this in terms of the effective demand for a supplier's goods given their price and the price of competing suppliers. The demand curve facing this individual supplier will have a striking discontinuity; once the price goes above the price others are offering the good at, demand falls to 0.

Such an explanation will be good as far as it goes, but we can do better. We can note that there are mechanisms—in the sense of mechanism developed by Peter Machamer, Lindley Darden, and Carl Craver (2000)—that underlie this pattern of effective demand. The mechanisms are individual consumers who will change their purchasing patterns if they know that someone else is selling the same good more cheaply. Mechanisms, in this sense, are things that display a consistent pattern of activity. The activities have external triggers and reliable outputs given that trigger. Here the trigger is knowledge that someone else is offering the good more cheaply, and the output is buying the good elsewhere. The crucial thing for us is that here, like in many other social science applications, the trigger needs to be stated in terms of knowledge. It can't just be that the change in prices leads to a change in behaviour; a change in price that no one knows about won't plausibly bring about any behavioural change. It can't be that the trigger is stated in terms of what is absolutely certain because no one can be absolutely certain of contingent things like the price that a supplier is charging for a good. Nor can the trigger be stated in terms of high probability. No matter how probable I think it is that supplier B is cheaper than supplier A, it might still be rational to buy from supplier A if the rest of the probability goes to possibilities where B is much more expensive.

Knowledge alone seems to do the trick. The generalisation that people buy from suppliers they know to be cheaper seems both to be true and to rationalise their purchasing behaviour. What's important for us is that this places knowledge at the centre of our understanding of how this social arrangement works. That is going to be the general case; you just can't do social science without talking about how people behave when they come to know things.

So we have two reasons for thinking knowledge is a reasonably natural kind: there are more or less synonymous terms for it across languages, and it plays a key role in scientific explanations. Most fallibilist theories of knowledge won't make it be particularly natural. (I'll expand on this point in Section 8.4.1.) Most such theories say that to know something is to have a belief that's good enough along some dimension. So the belief must be justified enough, or safe enough, or produced by a reliable enough mechanism. Concepts that just pick out points high enough up some or other scale are not particularly natural. We should expect that we could do better.

Some fallibilist theories, or at least theories that make knowledge 'sub-optimal' in the sense I used above, do seem to be reasonably natural. The sensitivity theory that Nozick (1981) develops, for instance, plausibly makes knowledge into a natural kind. Whether a belief would be retained were its content false is not a matter of how well the belief performs on some scale. Alternatively, one could hold that knowledge is primitively natural, not natural in virtue of its analysis or parts.[7] That's not completely implausible; it isn't obvious that the naturalness of social kinds has to be explained by the same things that metaphysically explain why individuals fall into those kinds. Still, it would be nice to have a better explanation of why knowledge is natural.

On the view defended here, a person knows a proposition if and only if they properly take it to be settled. What one properly takes to be settled is interest-relative, hence knowledge is interest-relative. I'm not putting forward this biconditional as an analysis of knowledge, or an explanation of knowledge. It could be that the direction of explanation here runs from knowledge to proper settling. What I am claiming is that this biconditional is true, and is part of the explanation of why knowledge is a natural kind. The way to finish that explanation is to develop a theory where knowledge is interest-relative.

So those are the two big motivations for the interest-relative view: the practicality of belief and the naturalness of knowledge. Belief is a practical notion, so the norms of it should be practical. Knowledge is, at its most essential, a norm of belief. Knowledge is a natural kind, as evidenced by its cross-linguistic prevalence and its role in science. This raises a challenge, since knowledge often feels like it requires the knower do 'well enough' along one or other scale, and there is nothing particularly natural about choosing this point on the scale rather than that point. The interest-relative theory has an answer to this problem: a believer has knowledge when their evidence is good enough to properly settle the inquiries the believer is engaged in, and that's more than an arbitrary point on a scale.

---

7   Such a view might be inspired by the 'knowledge first' program of Williamson (2000).

While these are motivations, neither of them is strictly speaking an argument. The main argument in this book for the interest-relative theory is developed in Chapter 2. It is that in some fairly simple situations, there is a choice between four options.

1. Accepting scepticism about all contingent knowledge.
2. Denying some very simple principles connecting knowledge and action—and in particular denying that it is rational to take the action one knows to be best.
3. Denying some very strong intuitions about which actions are rational in these simple situations.
4. Saying that knowledge is interest-relative.

Since the first three options are implausible, the fourth is correct. That is, knowledge is interest-relative.

The argument does not turn on intuitions about who knows what in what situations. The only cases where the interest-relative theory disagrees with its rivals are ones where intuitions about knowledge seem to me to be very weak. For what it's worth, and it isn't worth much, I think the interest-relative theory says the more intuitive thing about most cases. Ultimately though, I don't particularly care about intuitions about knowledge, at least in these relatively borderline cases. I will spend some time defending my version of the interest-relative theory against the frequently voiced complaint that interest-relative theories get some clear cases incorrect. When the cases are indeed clear, I'll show that my version of the theory matches the intuitions, but curve-fitting around case intuitions will not be my priority.

To know something is to properly take it to be settled. There are two kinds of practical considerations that might make it improper to take something to be settled even if the evidence in favour of settling is strong enough for everyday purposes. The first is that the cost of being wrong is very high. The second is that the cost of checking whether one is wrong is very low. The previous literature on interest-relativity has primarily focussed on the first kind of reason. So the literature is replete with discussion of 'high-stakes' cases, where someone stands to lose a lot if something they have excellent evidence for turns out to be false. Knowledge is often lost in these cases. There is somewhat less discussion, however, about how knowledge is also lost in 'easy checking' cases, or about how (as Mark Schroeder (2012) notes), knowledge might not be lost in cases where the stakes are high but checking is impossible. As I'll put it in Section 2.4, what matters is not the stakes, but the odds one faces in a particular situation.

Humans engage in both practical and theoretical inquiries. For that matter, they often engage in inquiries which mix the practical and the theoretical. A lot of the focus in the literature on interest-relativity has been on how knowledge interacts with practical inquiry. Indeed the title of Stanley's defence of an interest-relative account is *Knowledge and Practical Interests*. I don't impose any such restriction here. If p can't be properly taken to be settled in a purely theoretical inquiry that someone is engaged in, they don't know that p. This has one striking implication. Let's say the person is trying to figure out as precisely as possible the probability of p. If they can take p as settled in that inquiry, then the answer to the inquiry will be 1. Unless the correct answer to this inquiry is actually 1, it won't be proper to take p as settled. So in general one easy way to lose knowledge that p is true is to launch an inquiry into precisely how probable p is. I've set this out using the ideology of probability, but this is unnecessary. Any inquiry into how well supported p is by one's overall evidence will usually not be allowed to take p as a starting point. So engaging in that inquiry will lead to loss of knowledge. This is what is right in scepticism, and infallibilism. The Cartesian meditator does, on this view, lose knowledge in anything when they seriously reflect on how good their evidence is for it. Happily, this knowledge comes back when they return to their normal life.

In the middle of the discussion about knowledge and probability there is a little inference: from the premise that taking p as settled would lead to an incorrect answer, it follows that it is improper to take p as settled. That's a good inference; that taking p as settled leads to a mistaken conclusion is indeed compelling evidence that it is improper to take p as settled. But it's not the only reason that it could be improper to take p as settled. Among other things, taking p to be settled might get to the right answer for the wrong reasons. So this principle of 'don't take something to be settled if it will lead to the wrong answer' might be good advice, but it isn't a full account of when not to take something as settled. I will go over this point in much more detail in Sections 3.4 to 3.6.

What one can properly take as given is a function of one's evidence. This should be common ground between evidentialists, who think that one's evidence determines what can be properly taken for granted, and non-evidentialists, who deny this. (On certain coherentist pictures, for example, it will make sense to talk about someone's evidence, but the fact that they have some evidence will be ultimately explained by patterns of coherence among their other beliefs, and will not be analytically prior to facts about rationality.) It would be convenient for several purposes if we could have an interest-invariant notion of evidence that explained why interests caused people to sometimes lose knowledge. Unfortunately, that's not a viable position. As I'll argue in Chapter 9, the arguments that knowledge is interest-relative generalise into arguments that evidence itself can be interest-relative.

So far, I've sketched in the very broadest outlines the kind of theory I'm going to propose. Here's the plan for how that theory will be laid out, and defended, over the coming chapters, as well as some more details on how the chapters relate to previously published work.

In Chapter 2, I'll set out the main argument for the interest-relative theory. The argument turns on how to think about a particular low-stakes bet. I argue that every option other than the interest-relative theory says very implausible things about this case.

The next two chapters set out the fundamentals of the theory. In Chapter 3 I lay out the interest-relative theory of belief, and how that view differs from the view I developed in "Can We Do without Pragmatic Encroachment?". Then in Chapter 4 I extend that to a theory of knowledge, and introduce a problem that will come up more in later chapters—how this theory interacts with closure principles.

The following three chapters are, in one way or another, responses to various objections to interest-relative theories. They are also the most novel parts of the book; very little of these three chapters draws on previously published work. Indeed, some of the key arguments build on work that was unpublished at least when I started work on this book. Chapter 4 draws heavily on work by Woodard (2020) and Chapter 7 draws heavily the doctoral dissertation of Nilanjan Das (2016).

In Chapter 5 I discuss the role that the concept of inquiry plays in my theory. In my theory, if something is known, it is available to use as a starting point in inquiry. I used to think this meant I was committed to agreeing with Friedman (2019b) that it is incoherent to inquire into something one knows. I've come to see that this isn't right; depending on what one wants to do in an inquiry one may want to deliberately set aside some premises. That might mean inquiry into what one already knows is reasonable. This fact is used to respond to an influential objection by Jessica Brown (2008) to the style of argument I use in Chapter 2.

In Chapter 6 I respond to an objection that theories like mine are committed to implausible closure failures in cases where choosers have very similar options to choose between. There is a proof in "Can We Do without Pragmatic Encroachment?" that the theory developed there is immune to closure failures in these types of cases, so the objection can't be right as stated. It turns out that the reason the theory of that paper respects closure is that it has absurdly sceptical consequences in cases where there are similar objects to choose between. That's hardly better than a closure failure. In this chapter I aim to do better.

I show that the objection relies on the assumption that the chooser aims to maximise expected utility, and this isn't the right criteria of correctness for decisions in close call situations. It isn't true that when one is selecting cans off the supermarket shelf, one's selection is rational if and only if (henceforth, iff) it is utility maximising. Rather, the rational chooser in such a situation will adopt a strategy that has the best long-run consequences. In this case, the strategy will probably be something like the strategy of picking arbitrarily unless it is clear that one of the choices is defective. Given a theory of rational choice that emphasises the importance of decision-making strategies, rather than the importance of utility maximisation, my preferred epistemological theory gets the right answers. There are two traps to avoid here: closure failure and scepticism. And the focus on strategies lets us avoid both.

In Chapter 7 I respond to the frequently voiced objection that interest-relative theories lead to implausible verdicts about pairs of situations where knowledge is lost or gained due to what looks like an irrelevant feature of a situation. I have two responses to these objections. One was first offered in "Defending Interest-Relative Invariantism" (Weatherson, 2011). I argue that the intuitions are about what makes it the case that a person does or doesn't know something, and the argument from these examples moves too quickly from a claim about modal variation to a claim about what knowledge is made of. The second response is, I think, more compelling, and it's essentially a point that Das makes which I borrow. These objections over-generate. Every modern theory of knowledge leads to pairs of cases where a person gains or loses knowledge depending on factors that seem 'irrelevant'. So it's not an objection to my view that it has the same consequences as every plausible theory of knowledge.

The last two long chapters go into relatively technical details of my theory of knowledge. I've put them at the end partially because they are technical—I don't want to lose readers until as late as possible! But also partially because they are the least changed from earlier work.

Chapter 8 goes over my theory of rational belief. Surprisingly, and in contrast to the view defended by Jeremy Fantl and Matthew McGrath (2009), interests affect rational belief in a very different way to how they affect knowledge. On my view, but not theirs, someone who has mistaken, and irrational, beliefs about what practical situation they are facing can easily have a rational, true belief that is not knowledge. This chapter also tidies up some loose ends from Chapter 3 concerning the so-called 'Lockean' theory of belief.

Chapter 9 sets out my interest-relative theory of evidence. I argue that one's evidence is what a Radical Interpreter would say one's evidence is. In some cases, this means we end up playing a kind of coordination game with The Radical Interpreter. What our evidence is turns on what the right solution to that game is. The solution is interest-relative, but not in the same way as knowledge, nor in the same way as rational belief.

Chapter 10 ends with a short note connecting interest-relativity to the familiar saying *Knowledge is Power*. I argue that this saying only makes sense given an interest-relative view of knowledge. If interest-relative theories were flawed for one reason or another, then we'd have to simply concede that the saying is false. We shouldn't concede that; the saying is true, and interest-relative epistemology explains why it is true.

2. Interests

2.1 Red or Blue?

The key argument that knowledge is interest-relative starts with a puzzle about a game. Here are the rules of the game, which I'll call the Red-Blue game.

1. Two sentences will be written on the board, one in red, one in blue.
2. The player will make two choices.
3. First, they will pick a colour, red or blue.
4. Second, they say whether the sentence in that colour is true or false.
5. If they are right, they win. If not, they lose.
6. If they win, they get $50, and if they lose, they get nothing.

Our player is Anisa. She has been reading some medieval history, and last night was reading about the Battle of Agincourt. She was amused to see that it took place on her birthday, October 25, and in 1415, precisely six hundred years before her own birthday. The book says all these things about the Battle of Agincourt because they are actually true, and when she read the book, Anisa believed them. She believed them because she had lots of independent evidence that the book was reliable (it came from a respected author and publisher, it didn't contradict her well-grounded background beliefs), and she was sensitive to that evidence of its reliability. These beliefs were correct; the book was reliable and accurate on this point. The Battle of Agincourt was indeed on October 25, 1415, and everything else the book says about the battle without qualification is also true.

Anisa comes to know that she is playing the Red-Blue game, and that these are its rules. She does not come to know any other relevant fact about the game.[1] When the game starts, the following two sentences are written on the board, the first in red, the second in blue.

- Two plus two equals four.
- The Battle of Agincourt took place in 1415.

Anisa looks at this, thinks to herself, "Oh, my book said that the Battle of Agincourt was in 1415, so (given the rules of the game) playing Blue-True will be as good as any other play, so I'm playing Blue-True. Playing Red-True would get the same amount, since obviously two plus two is four, but I'm going to play Blue-True instead". That's what she does, and she wins the $50.

Intuitively, Anisa's move here is irrational, because it creates a needless risk. There was a simple safe option that she should have taken, and she declined it. Now it wasn't that much money; it's $50. To be sure, she doesn't actually lose it; she gets the answer correct. The worlds where the risk is costly are somewhat distant; they are worlds where either she has misremembered something that seems vivid, or where a book that is clearly reliable has gone wrong. Still, it's sometimes true that books, even good ones, make mistakes, and memory falters. She took a risk, one that she didn't have to take, and got no compensation for taking it. That's irrational.

I'm going to argue, at some length, that the best explanation of why it is irrational for Anisa to play Blue-True is that knowledge is interest-relative. When she was at home reading the book and just thinking about

---

[1] When presenting this material, some people have been puzzled about how this could be possible. It's implausible that Anisa knows nothing else about the game; if she didn't know who was putting the money up she could hardly trust that she would be paid out iff she was correct. More importantly, this extra knowledge might tell her something about the sentences. I think it helps assuage these worries to imagine this as one round of a repeated game Anisa is playing. Every round two sentences from a large stock are drawn at random to be the red and blue sentences. Anisa will play 20 such rounds, and get paid something between $0 and $1000 at the end, depending on how many she gets right. Why is she playing this? It could be the prize round of a game show that she was the nightly winner on. With something like this background, it's plausible that what I said in the text is true; she knows 1–6, and nothing else relevant. At least, this backstory should be enough to make it plausible that the setup is indeed possible.

medieval history, Anisa knew that the Battle of Agincourt took place in 1415. When she was playing the game, and thinking about winning as much money as possible, Anisa did not know this. When she is moved into the game situation, she loses some knowledge she previously had.

In the recent literature, arguments for and against interest-relativity to date have not focussed on examples like Anisa's, but on examples involving high-stakes choices. I'll present one example, involving a character I'll call Blaise, presently. The example involving Anisa does, however, have a handful of notable predecessors. Its structure is similar to the examples of low-cost checking that Bradley Armour-Garb (2011) discusses (though he draws contextualist conclusions from these examples, not interest-relative ones). And it is similar to some of the cases of three-way choice that Charity Anderson and John Hawthorne deploy in arguing against interest-relativity (2019a, 2019b). Still, these are outlier cases. Most of the literature has focussed on high-stakes cases. Let's have one on the table.

Last night, Blaise was reading the same book that Anisa was reading. He too was struck by the fact that the Battle of Agincourt took place on October 25, 1415. Today he is visited by a representative of the supernatural world, and offered the following bet. (Blaise knows these are the terms of the bet, and doesn't know anything else relevant.) If he declines the bet, life will go on as normal. If he accepts, one of two things will happen.

- If it is true that the Battle of Agincourt took place in 1415, an infant somewhere will receive one second's worth of pure joy, of the kind infants often get playing peek-a-boo.
- If it is false that the Battle of Agincourt took place in 1415, all of humanity will be cast into The Bad Place for all of eternity.

Blaise takes the bet. The Battle of Agincourt was in 1415, and he can't bear the thought of a lovable baby missing that second of pure joy.

Again, there is an intuition that Blaise did something horribly wrong here, and one possible explanation of this wrongness is that knowledge is interest-relative. However, the argument that the interest-relativity of knowledge is the very best explanation of what's going on is somewhat weaker in Blaise's case than in Anisa's. It's not that I don't accept the interest-relative explanation of the case; I do accept it. It's rather that plausible interest-invariant explanations of the intuitions about Blaise's case exist. Because these competing explanations exist, it's hard to argue that interest-relativity is the best explanation of why Blaise's action is wrong. Without that argument, it's hard to infer from Blaise's case that knowledge is interest-relative by inference to the best explanation. So I'll focus on Anisa, not Blaise.

This choice of focus occasionally means that this book is less connected to the existing literature than I would like. I occasionally infer what a philosopher would say about cases like Anisa's from what they have said about cases like Blaise's. I'll probably get some of those inferences wrong. But I want to set out the best argument for the interest-relativity of knowledge that I know, and that means going via the example of Anisa.

Though I am starting with an example, and with an intuition about it, I am not starting with an intuition about what is known in the example. I don't have any clear intuitions about what Anisa knows or doesn't know while playing the Red-Blue game. The intuition that matters here is that her choice of Blue-True is irrational. It's going to be a matter of inference, not intuition, that Anisa lacks knowledge.

That inference will largely be by process of elimination. In Section 2.2 I will set out four possible things we can say about Anisa, and argue that one of them must be true. (The argument won't appeal to any principles more controversial than the Law of Excluded Middle.) But all four of them, including the interest-relative view I favour, have fairly counterintuitive consequences. So something counterintuitive is true around here. This puts a limit on how we can argue. At least one instance of the argument *this is counterintuitive, so it is false* must fail. That casts doubt over all such arguments. This is a point that critics of interest-relativity haven't sufficiently acknowledged, but it also puts constraints on how one can defend interest-relativity.

When Anisa starts playing the Red-Blue game, her practical situation changes. You might think I've gone wrong in stressing Anisa's interests, not her practical situation. I've put the focus on interests for two reasons. One is that if Anisa is totally indifferent to money, then there is no rational requirement to play Red-True. We need to posit something about Anisa's interests to even get the data point that the interest-relative theory explains. The second reason, which I'll talk about more in Section 2.5, is that sometimes we can lose knowledge due to a change not in our practical situation, but our theoretical interests.

In the existing literature, views like mine are sometimes called versions of **subject-sensitive invariantism**, since they make knowledge relevant to the stakes and salient alternatives available to the subject. This is a bad name; of course whether a knowledge ascription is true is sensitive to who the subject of the ascription is. I know what I had for breakfast and you (probably) don't. The distinctive feature of theories like mine is that a particular fact about the subject's situation is relevant: their interests. That should be reflected in the name. In the past, I've called this view **interest-relative invariantism**, or IRI. For reasons I'll say more about in Section 2.7, I'm not committed to *invariantism* in this book. So in this book, I will refer to it simply as the interest-relative theory of knowledge (IRT).

2.2 Four Families

A lot of philosophers have written about cases like Anisa's and Blaise's over the last couple of decades. Relatedly, there are a huge number of theories that have been defended concerning these cases. Rather than describe them all, I'm going to start with a taxonomy of them. The taxonomy has some tricky edge cases, and it isn't always trivial to classify a philosopher from their statements about the cases. It is, nevertheless, a helpful way to start thinking about the available moves.

Our first family of theories are the **sceptical** theories. They deny that Anisa ever knew that the Battle of Agincourt was in 1415. The particular kind of sceptic I have in mind says that if someone's epistemic position is, all things considered, better with respect to q than with respect to p, that person doesn't know that p. The core idea for this sceptic, which perhaps they draw from work by Peter Unger (1975), is that knowledge is a maximal epistemic state, so any non-maximal state is not knowledge. The sceptics say that for almost any belief, Anisa's belief that two plus two is four will have higher epistemic standing than that belief, so that belief doesn't amount to knowledge.

Our second family of theories are what I'll call **epistemicist** theories. The epistemicists say that Anisa's reasoning is perfectly sound, and perhaps Blaise's is too. They both know when the Battle of Agincourt took place, so they both know that the choices they take are optimal, so they are rational in taking those choices. The intuitions to the contrary are, say the epistemicist, at best confused. There is something off about Anisa and Blaise, perhaps, but it isn't that these particular decisions are irrational.

It's not essential to epistemicism, but one natural form of epistemicism takes on board Maria Lasonen-Aarnio's point that act-level and agent-level assessments might come apart.[2] On this version of epistemicism, taking the bet reveals something bad about Blaise's character, and arguably manifests a vice, but the act itself is rational. It's that last claim, that actions like Blaise's are rational, that is distinctive of epistemicism.

The third family is the family of **pragmatist** theories, and this family includes the interest-relative theory that I'll defend. The pragmatists say that yesterday Anisa knew when the Battle of Agincourt was, but now she doesn't. The change in her practical situation, combined with her interest in getting more money, destroys her knowledge.

And the final family are what I'll call, a little tendentiously, the **orthodox** theories. Orthodoxy says that Anisa knew when the Battle of Agincourt was last night, since her belief satisfied every plausible criterion for testimonial knowledge. Orthodoxy also says she knows it today, since changing practical scenarios or interests like this doesn't affect knowledge. On the other hand, orthodoxy says that the actions that Anisa and Blaise take are wrong; they are both irrational, and Blaise's is immoral. Moreover, it says that they are wrong because they are risky. So knowing that what one is doing is for the best is consistent with one's action being faulted on epistemic grounds.

My reading of the literature is that a considerable majority of philosophers writing on these cases are orthodox. (Hence the name!) But I can't be entirely sure, because a lot of these philosophers are more

---

2 See Lasonen-Aarnio (2010, 2014) for more details on her view. In *Normative Externalism*, I describe the difference between act-level and agent-level assessments as the difference between asking whether what Anisa does is rational, and whether Anisa's action manifests wisdom (Weatherson, 2019: 124–125). The best form of epistemicism, I'm suggesting, says that Anisa and Blaise are rational but unwise. This isn't Lasonen-Aarnio's terminology, but otherwise I'm largely adopting her ideas.

vocal about opposing pragmatist views than they are about supporting any particular view. There are some views that are clearly orthodox in the sense I've described, and I really think most of the people who have opposed pragmatist treatments of cases like Anisa's and Blaise's are orthodox, but it's possible more of them are sceptical or epistemicist than I've appreciated.

Calling this last family orthodox lets me conveniently label the other three families as heterodox. This lets me state what I hope to argue for in this book: the interest-relative treatment of these cases is correct; and if it isn't, then at least some pragmatist treatment is correct; and if it isn't, then at least some heterodox treatment is correct.

It's worth laying out the interest-relative case in some detail, because we can only properly assess the options holistically. Every view is going to have some very counterintuitive consequences, and we can only weigh them up when we see them all laid out. For instance, here are the claims made by each of these views:

- Sceptical theories say that when Anisa is reading her book, she doesn't gain knowledge even though the book is reliable and she believes it because of a well-supported belief in its reliability.
- Epistemicist theories say that Anisa and Blaise make rational choices, even though they take what look like absurd risks.
- Pragmatist theories say that offering someone a bet can cause them to lose knowledge and, presumably, that withdrawing that offer can cause them to get the knowledge back.
- Orthodox theories say that it is irrational to do something that one knows will get the best result simply because it might get a bad result.

I'm going to mostly focus on the orthodox theories throughout the book, and in particular I'll go into much more detail on this last point in Section 2.3.

Much of the argumentation in this book, like much of what's in this literature, will fall into one of two categories. Either it will be an attempt to sharpen one of these implausible consequences, so the view with that consequence looks even worse than it does now. Or it will be an attempt to dull one of them, by coming up with a version of the view that doesn't have quite as bad a consequence. Sometimes this latter task is sophistry in the bad sense; it's an attempt to make the implausible consequence of the theory harder to say, and so less of an apparent flaw on that ground alone. Sometimes, though, it is a valuable drawing of distinctions. That is, it is scholasticism in the good sense. It turns out that the allegedly plausible claim is ambiguous. On one disambiguation we have really good reason to believe it is true, on another the theory in question violates it, but on no disambiguation do we get a violation of something really well-supported. I hope that the work I do here to defend the interest-relative theory is more scholastic than sophistic, but I'll leave that for others to decide.

Still, if all of the theories are implausible in one way or another, shouldn't we look for an alternative? Perhaps we should, but we won't find one. At least if we define the theories carefully enough, the truth is guaranteed to be among them. Let's try placing theories by asking three yes/no questions.

1. Does the theory say that Anisa knew last night that the Battle of Agincourt was in 1415? If no, the theory is sceptical; if yes, go to question 2.
2. Does the theory say that Anisa is rational to play Blue-True? If yes, the theory is epistemicist; if no, go to question 3.
3. Does the theory say that Anisa still knows that the Battle of Agincourt was in 1415, at the time she chooses to play Blue-True? If no, the theory is pragmatist; if yes, the theory is orthodox.

That's it—those are your options. There are two points of clarification that matter, but I don't think they make a huge difference.

The first point of clarification is really a reminder that these are families of views. It might be that one member of the family is considerably less implausible than other members. Indeed, I've changed my mind a fair bit about what is the best kind of pragmatist theory since I first started writing on this topic. There are a lot of possible orthodox theories. Finding out the best version of these kinds of theories, especially the last two kinds, is hard work, but it is worth doing. That doesn't mean that it will lessen the implausibility of endorsing a view from that family; some of the implausibility flows directly from how one answers the three questions.

The second point of clarification is that what I've really done here is classify what the different theories say about Anisa's case. They may say different things about other cases. A theory might take an epistemicist stand on Anisa's case, but an orthodox one on Blaise's case, for example. Or it might be orthodox about Anisa, but would be epistemicist if the blue sentence was something much more secure, such as that the Battle of Hastings was in 1066. If this taxonomy is going to be complete, it needs to say something about theories that treat different cases differently. So here is the more general taxonomy I will use.

The cases I'll quantify over have the following structure. Our hero, called Hero, is given strong evidence for some truth p, and they believe it on the basis of that evidence. There are no defeaters, the belief is caused by the truth of the proposition in the right way, and in general all the conditions for knowledge that people worried about in the traditional (i.e., late 20th century) epistemological literature are met. Then they are offered a choice, where one of the options will have an optimal outcome if p, but will not be the best choice according to normal theories of decision unless the probability of p is incredibly close to one. While Hero's evidence is strong, it isn't maximally strong. Despite this, Hero takes the risky option, using the fact that p as a key part of their reasoning. Now consider the following three questions.

1. In cases with this form, does the theory say that when Hero first forms the belief that p, they know that p? If the answer is that this is *generally* the case, then restrict attention to those cases where they do know that p, and move to question 2. Otherwise, the theory is sceptical.

2. In the cases that remain, is Hero rational in taking the option that is optimal iff p? If the answer is yes in *every* case, the theory is epistemicist. Otherwise, restrict attention to cases where this choice is irrational, and move to question 3.

3. In *any* of the cases that remain, does the fact that Hero was offered the choice destroy their knowledge that p? If yes, the theory is pragmatic. If no, the theory is orthodox.

So I'm taking epistemicism to be a very strong theory—it says that knowledge always suffices for action that is optimal given what's known, and that offers of bets never constitute a loss of knowledge. The epistemicist can allow that the offer of a bet may cause a person to 'lose their nerve', and hence their belief that p, and hence their knowledge that p. Still, if they remain confident in p, they retain knowledge that p.

Pragmatism is a very weak theory—it says sometimes the offer of a bet can constitute a loss of knowledge. The justification for defending such a weak theory is that so many philosophers are aghast at the idea that practical considerations like this could ever be relevant to knowledge. So even showing that the existential claim is true—that sometimes practical issues matter—would be a big deal.

Orthodoxy is a weak claim on one point, and a strong claim on another. It says there are some cases where knowledge does not suffice for action, though it might take these cases to be very rare. It is common in defences of orthodoxy to say that the cases are quite rare and use this fact to explain away intuitions that threaten orthodoxy. The key thing is that it says that pragmatic factors never matter—so it can be threatened by a single case like Anisa.

2.3 Against Orthodoxy

The orthodox view of cases like Blaise's is that offering him the bet does not change what he knows, but still he is irrational to take the bet. In this section, I'm going to run through a series of arguments against the orthodox view. The reason I am making so many arguments is not that I lack confidence in any one of them. Rather, it is because the orthodox view is so widespread that we need to appreciate how many strange consequences it has.

2.3.1 Moore's Paradox

Start by thinking about what the orthodox view says a rational person in Blaise's situation would do. Call this rational person Chamari. According to the orthodox view, offering someone a bet does not make them lose knowledge. So Chamari still knows when the Battle of Agincourt was fought. Chamari is rational, so despite having this knowledge, Chamari will decline the bet. Think about how Chamari might respond when you ask her to justify declining the bet.

> You: When was the Battle of Agincourt?
> Chamari: October 25, 1415.
> You: If that's true, what will happen if you accept the bet?
> Chamari: A child will get a moment of joy.
> You: Is that a good thing?
> Chamari: Yes.
> You: So why didn't you take the bet?
> Chamari: Because it's too risky.
> You: Why is it risky?
> Chamari: Because it might lose.
> You: You mean the Battle of Agincourt might not have been fought in 1415.
> Chamari: Yes.
> You: So the Battle of Agincourt was fought in 1415, but it might not have been fought then?
> Chamari: Yes, the Battle of Agincourt was fought in 1415, but it might not have been fought then, and that's why I'm not taking the bet.

Chamari has given the best possible answer at each point. Yet she has ended up assenting to a Moore-paradoxical sentence. In particular, she has assented to a sentence of the form *p, but it might be that not p*. It is very widely held that sentences like this cannot be rationally assented to. Since Chamari was, by stipulation, the model for what the orthodox view thinks a rational person is, this shows that the orthodox view is false.

There are three ways out of this puzzle, and none of them seems particularly attractive.

One is to deny that there's anything wrong with where Chamari ends up. Perhaps in this case the Moore-paradoxical claim is perfectly assertable. I have some sympathy for the general idea that philosophers over-state the badness of Moore-paradoxicality (Maitra and Weatherson, 2010). Still, it does seem very unattractive to end up precisely here.

Another is to deny that the fact that Chamari knows something licences her in asserting it. I've assumed in the argument that if Chamari knows that *p*, she can say that *p*. Maybe that's too strong an assumption. The conversation, says this reply, goes off the rails at the very first line. From this perspective, it is hard to determine the point of knowledge. If knowing something isn't a strong enough reason to assert it, then it is unclear what would be.

The orthodox theorist has a couple of choices here, neither of them good. One is to say that although knowledge is not interest-relative, the epistemic standards for assertion are interest-relative. Basically, Chamari meets the epistemic standard for saying that p only if Chamari knows that p according to the (false!) interest-relative theory. At this point, given how plausible it is that knowledge is closely connected with testimony, it seems we would need an excellent reason to not simply identify knowledge with this epistemic standard. The other is to say that there is some interest-invariant standard for assertion. By running through varieties of cases like Anisa's and Blaise's, we can show that such a standard would have to be something like Cartesian certainty. So most everything we say, every single day, would be norm violating. Such a norm is not plausible.

So we get to the third way out, one that is only available to a subset of orthodox theorists. We can say that 'knows' is context-sensitive, that in Chamari's context the sentence "I know when the Battle of Agincourt was fought" is actually false, and those two facts explain what goes wrong in the conversation with Chamari. Armour-Garb (2011), who points out how much trouble non-contextualist orthodox theorists get into with these Moore-paradoxical claims, suggests a contextualist resolution of the puzzles. While this is probably the least bad way to handle the case, it's worth noting just how odd it is.

It's not immediately obvious how to get from contextualism to a resolution of the puzzle. Chamari doesn't use the verb 'to know' or any of its cognates. She does use the modal 'might', and the contextualist will presumably want to say that it is context sensitive. That doesn't look like a helpful way to solve the problem though, since her assertion that the battle might have been on a different day seems like the good part of what she says. What's problematic is the unqualified assertion about when the battle was, in the context of explaining her refusal to bet. We need some way of connecting contextualism about epistemic verbs to a claim about the inappropriateness of this assertion.

The standard move by contextualists here is to simply deny that there is a tight connection between knowledge and assertion (Cohen, 2004; DeRose, 2002). (So this is really a sophisticated form of a response I just rejected.) What they say instead is that there is a kind of meta-linguistic standard for assertion. It is epistemically responsible to say that p iff it would be true to say *I know that p*. Since it would not be true for Chamari to say she knows when the Battle of Agincourt was fought, she can't responsibly say when it was fought.³

The most obvious reason to reject this line of reasoning is that it is implausible that meta-linguistic norms like this exist. Imagine we were conversing with Chamari about her reasons for declining the bet in Bengali rather than English, and at every line a contribution with the same content was made. Would the reason her first answer was inappropriate be that some English sentence would be false if uttered in her context, or that some Bengali sentence would be false? If it's an English sentence, it's very weird that English would have this normative force over conversations in Bengali. If it's Bengali, then it's odd that the standard for assertion changes from language to language.

If there were a human language that didn't have a verb for knowledge, then that last point could be made with particular force. What would the contextualists say is the standard for assertion in such a language? Somewhat surprisingly, no such language exists (Nagel, 2014). It's still somewhat interesting to think about possible languages that do allow for assertions, but do not have a verb for knowledge. Just what the contextualists would say is the standard for assertion in such a language is a rather delicate matter.

Rather than thinking about these merely possible languages, let's return to English, and end with a variant of the conversation with Chamari. Imagine that she hasn't yet been offered any bet, and indeed that when the conversation starts, we're just spending a pleasant few minutes idly chatting about medieval history.

> You: When was the Battle of Agincourt?
> Chamari: October 25, 1415.
> You: Oh that's interesting. Because you know there's this bet that someone offered my friend Blaise, and I bet I could get them to offer it to you. If you were to accept it, and the Battle of Agincourt was in 1415, then a small child would get a moment of joy.
> Chamari: That's great, I should take that bet.

---

3   The objection I'm making here is really targeted at orthodox forms of contextualism. Other forms of contextualism are not subject to it. The kind of contextualism I will describe in Section 2.7.1, for instance, can agree with IRT about what's wrong with Chamari's utterances. For more on this kind of view, see Ichikawa (2017: §1.9).

You: Well, wait a second, I should tell you what happens if the Battle turns out to have been on any other date. [You explain what happens in some detail.]
Chamari: That's awful, I shouldn't take the bet. The Battle might not have been in 1415, and it's not worth the risk.
You: So you won't take the bet because it's too risky?
Chamari: That's right, I won't take it because it's too risky.
You: Why is it risky?
Chamari: Because it might lose.
You: You mean the Battle of Agincourt might not have been fought in 1415.
Chamari: Yes.
You: Hang on, you just said it was fought in 1415, on October 25 to be precise.
Chamari: That's true, I did say that.
You: Were you wrong to have said it?
Chamari: Probably not; it was probably right that I said it.
You: You probably knew when the battle was, but you don't now know it?
Chamari: No, I definitely didn't know when the battle was, but it was probably right to have said it was in 1415.

And you can probably see all sorts of ways of making Chamari's position sound terrible. The argument I'm giving here is a version of an argument against contextualism given by John MacFarlane (2005). He notes that contextualists have a particular problem with retraction; Chamari's position sounds much worse than it should if contextualism is right. Still, I don't want to put too much weight on how she sounds. Every position in this area ends up claiming some strange things. The very idea that the epistemic standard for assertion could be meta-linguistic, either in the version which says some English word determines the appropriateness conditions for assertions in every language, or that the appropriateness conditions change from language to language, is even more implausible than the idea that we should end up where Chamari does.

2.3.2 Super-Knowledge to the Rescue?

Let's leave Blaise and Chamari for a little and return to Anisa. The orthodox view agrees that it is irrational for Anisa to play Blue-True. So it needs to explain why this is so. IRT offers a simple explanation. If she plays Red-True, she knows she will get $50; if she plays Blue-True, she does not know that—though she knows she will get at most $50. So Red-True is the weakly dominant option; she knows it won't do worse than any other option, and there is no other option that she knows won't do worse than any other option.

The orthodox theorist can't offer this explanation. They think Anisa knows that Blue-True will get $50 as well. So what can they offer instead? There are two broad kinds of explanation that they can try. First, they might offer a structurally similar explanation to the one IRT gives, but with some other epistemic notion at its centre. So while Anisa knows that Blue-True will get $50, she doesn't *super-know* this, in some sense. Second, they can try to explain the asymmetry between Red-True and Blue-True in probabilistic, rather than epistemic, terms. I'll discuss the first option in this subsection, and the probabilistic notion in the next subsection.

What do I mean here by *super-knows*? I mean this term to be a placeholder for any kind of relation stronger than knowledge that could play the right kind of role in explaining why it is irrational for Anisa to play Blue-True. So super-knowledge might be iterated knowledge. Anisa super-knows something iff she knows that she knows that ... she knows it. She super-knows that two plus two is four, but not that the Battle of Agincourt was in 1415. Or super-knowledge might be (rational) certainty. Anisa is (rationally) certain that two plus two is four, but not that the Battle of Agincourt was in 1415. Or it might be some other similar relation. My objection to the super-knowledge response won't be sensitive to the details of how we understand super-knowledge.

If a super-knowledge solution is going to work, it had better be that Anisa does not in fact super-know that the Battle of Agincourt was in 1415. That already rules out some versions of the super-knowledge solution. In normal versions of the case, Anisa does know that she knows the Battle of Agincourt was in 1415. She knows that she read this in a book, that the book had a lot of indicators of reliability, and (at least according to the orthodox theorist), that what she read was correct. If she was asked to sort people into whether they do or don't know that the battle was in 1415, she would (in normal versions of the case) be fairly good at doing this, and would sort herself into the group that does know.[4] So she passes all the standard tests for knowing that she knows when the battle was.

For most versions of what super-knowledge is, it looks like in ideal cases it should be closed under conjunction. That is, Anisa super-knows a conjunction (that she is considering) iff she super-knows each of the conjuncts. I'll come back to one important exception to this, that super-knowledge is credence above a threshold, in the next subsection. For now, assume that super-knowledge is closed under conjunction in this way.

Given that assumption, the fact that Anisa doesn't super-know when the Battle of Agincourt was can't explain the asymmetry between Red-True and Blue-True. In particular, it can't explain why Anisa rationally must choose Red-True. This is because she doesn't super-know that playing Red-True will win the $50. If super-knowledge is demanding enough that she doesn't know when the battle was, it's demanding enough that she doesn't know the rules of the game. That implies that she doesn't know that playing Red will win the $50. She has ordinary testimonial knowledge of the rules, just like she has ordinary testimonial knowledge about the Battle of Agincourt. It's just as realistic that she has misunderstood the rules of the game as that a reliable history book has gotten a key date wrong. It's not just in evil demon situations that someone misunderstands a rule. In a very ordinary sense, she can't be completely certain that she has the rules correct. If testimony from careful historians can't generate super-knowledge, neither can testimony from game-show hosts.

In fact, her knowledge of the rules of the game, in the sense that matters, is probably weaker than her knowledge of history. It is not unknown for game shows to promise prizes, then fail to deliver them, either because of malice or incompetence. Knowledge of the game rules, in particular knowledge that she will actually get $50 if she selects a true sentence, requires some knowledge of the future. That seems harder

---

4   To be sure, she presumably doesn't know for most people what they know about medieval history. What I'm imagining is that if she was presented with a bunch of people, asked if they know when the Battle of Agincourt was, and was allowed to say "Yes", "No", or "Don't Know", then most of the "Yes" and "No" answers would be correct, and she would say "Yes" about herself.

to obtain than knowledge of what happened in history. After all, she has to know that there won't be an alien invasion, or a giant asteroid, or an incompetent or malicious game organiser. (The last two being considerably more important considerations in normal cases.)

So there is no way of understanding 'super-knows' such that 1 is true and 2 is false.

1. Anisa super-knows that if she plays Red-True, she'll win $50.
2. Anisa does not super-know that if she plays Blue-True, she'll win $50.

If the super-knowledge based explanation of why she should play Red-True worked, there should be some sense of super-knowledge where 1 is true and 2 is false. There isn't, so the explanation doesn't work.

The point I'm making here, that in thinking about these games we need to attend to the player's epistemic attitude towards the game itself, is not original. Dorit Ganson (2019) uses this point for a very similar purpose, and in turn quotes Robert Nozick (1981) making a similar point. I've belaboured it here because it is so easily overlooked. It is easy to take things that one is told about a situation, such as the rules of a game that are being played, as somehow fixed and inviolable. They aren't the kind of thing that can be questioned. In any realistic case, the rules will not have such an exalted practical or epistemic status—at least if one assumes that only what is super-known can be taken as fixed.

This is why I rest more weight on Anisa's case than on Blaise's. I can't appeal to your judgment about what a realistic version of Blaise's case would be like, because there are no realistic versions of cases like Blaise's. Anisa's case, on the other hand, is very easy to imagine and understand. We can ask what a realistic version of it would be like. That version would be such that the player would know what the rules of the game are, but would also know that sometimes game shows don't keep their promises, sometimes they don't describe their own games accurately, sometimes players misinterpret or misunderstand instructions, and so on. This shouldn't lead us to scepticism: Anisa knows what game she's playing. But she doesn't super-know what game she's playing, which means she doesn't super-know she'll win if she plays Red-True.

2.3.3 Rational Credences to the Rescue?

So imagine the orthodox theorist drops super-knowledge, and looks somewhere else. A natural alternative is to use credences. Assume that the probability that the rules of the game are as described is independent of the probabilities of the red and blue sentence. Assume also that Anisa must, if she is to be rational, maximise expected utility. Then we get the natural result that Anisa should pick the sentence that is more probably true.[5] And that can explain why she must choose Red-True, which is what the orthodox theorist needed to explain.

This kind of approach doesn't really have any place for knowledge in its theory of action. One should simply maximise expected utility; since doing what one knows to be best might not maximise expected utility, we shouldn't think knowledge has any particularly special role.

There are many problems with this kind of approach. Several of these problems will be discussed elsewhere in this book at more length. I will point to where those problems are discussed rather than duplicate the discussion here. Some other problems I'll address straight away.

Like the view discussed in Section 2.3.1 that separates knowledge from assertion, separating knowledge from action leads to strange consequences. As Timothy Williamson (2005) points out, once we break apart knowledge from action in this way, it becomes hard to see the point of knowledge. It's worth pausing a bit more over the bizarreness of the claim that Blaise knows that taking the bet will work out for the best, but he shouldn't take it—because of its possible consequences.

If one excludes knowledge from having an important role in one's theory of decision, one ends up having a hard time explaining how dominance reasoning works. It is, however, a compulsory task for a theory of decision to explain how dominance reasoning works. Among other things, we need a good account of how dominance reasoning works in order to handle Newcomb's problem, and we need to handle Newcomb's problem in order to motivate, or even to state, a careful version of expected utility maximisation. That little argument was very

---

5   Strictly speaking, we need one more assumption—namely that for any unexpected way for the game to be, the probability of it being that way is independent of the truth of both the red and blue sentences. This feels like a safe assumption for the orthodox theorist to make.

compressed. I'm not going to expand upon it just yet because there will be so much more discussion of dominance reasoning throughout this book; a sketch will do for now.

Probabilistic models of reasoning and decision have their limits, and what we need to explain about the Red-Blue game goes beyond those limits. So probabilistic models can't be the full story about the Red-Blue game. To see this, imagine for a second that the Blue sentence is not about the Battle of Agincourt, but is instead a slightly more complicated arithmetic truth, like *Thirteen times seventeen equals two hundred and twenty one*, or a slightly complicated logical truth, like $\neg q \to ((p \to q) \to \neg p)$. If either of those are the blue sentence, then it is still uniquely rational to play Red-True, even though the probability of each of those sentences is one. So rational choice is more demanding than expected utility maximisation. In Sections 8.2 and 8.3 I'll go over more cases of propositions whose probability is 1, but which should be treated as uncertain even it is certain that two plus two is four. The lesson is that we can't just use expected utility maximisation to explain the Red-Blue game.

Finally, we need to understand the notion of probability that's being appealed to in this explanation. It can't be some purely subjective notion, like credence, because that couldn't explain why some decisions are rational and others aren't. If Anisa was subjectively certain that the Battle of Agincourt was in 1415, she would still be irrational to play Blue-True. It can't be some purely physical notion, like chance or frequency, because that won't even get the cases right. (What is the chance, or frequency, of the Battle of Agincourt being in 1415?) It needs to be something like evidential probability. That will run into problems in versions of the Red-Blue game where the Blue sentence is arguably (but not certainly) part of the player's evidence. I'll end my discussion of orthodoxy with a discussion of cases like these.

2.3.4 Evidential Probability

No matter which of these explanations the orthodox theorist goes for, they need a notion of evidence to support them.[6] Let's assume that we

---

6   This subsection is based on Weatherson (2018: §2).

can find some doxastic attitude D such that Anisa can't rationally stand in D to *Play Blue-True*, and that this is why she can't rationally play Blue-True. Then we need to ask the further question, why doesn't she stand in relation D to *Play Blue-True*? And presumably the answer will be that she lacks sufficient evidence. After all, if she had optimal evidence about when the Battle of Agincourt was, she could play Blue-True.

The orthodox theorist also has to have an interest-invariant account of evidence. I guess although it's logically possible to have evidence be interest-relative, but knowledge be interest-neutral, it is very hard to see how one would motivate such a position.

Now we run into a problem. Imagine a version of the Red-Blue game where the blue sentence is something that, if known, is part of the player's evidence. If it is still irrational to play Blue-True, then any orthodox explanation that relies on evidence sensitive notions (like super-knowledge or evidential probability) will be in trouble. The aim of this subsection is to spell out why this is.

Let's imagine a new player for the Red-Blue game. Call her Parveen. She is playing the game in a restaurant near her apartment in Ann Arbor, Michigan. Just before the game starts, she notices an old friend, Rahul, across the room. Rahul is someone she knows well, and can ordinarily recognise, but she had no idea he was in town. She actually thought Rahul was living in Italy. Still, we would ordinarily say that she now knows Rahul is in town; indeed, that he is in the restaurant. As evidence for this, note that it would be perfectly acceptable for her to say to someone else, "I saw Rahul here". Now the game starts.

3. The red sentence is *Two plus two equals four*.
4. The blue sentence is *Rahul is in this restaurant*.

On the one hand, there is only one rational play for Parveen: Red-True. She hasn't seen Rahul in ages, and she thought he was in Italy. A glimpse of him across a crowded restaurant isn't enough for her to think that *Rahul is in this restaurant* is as likely as *Two plus two equals four*. She might be wrong about Rahul, so she should take the sure money and play Red-True. So playing the Red-Blue game with these sentences makes it the case that Parveen doesn't know where Rahul is. This is another case where knowledge is interest-relative, and at first glance it doesn't look very different to the other cases we've seen.

But take a second look at the story for why Parveen doesn't know where Rahul is. It can't be just that her evidence makes it certain that two plus two equals four, but not certain that Rahul is in the restaurant. At least, it can't be that unless it is not part of her evidence that Rahul is in the restaurant. If evidence is not interest-relative, then it is part of Parveen's evidence that Rahul is in the restaurant. This isn't something she infers; it is a fact about the world she simply appreciates. Ordinarily, it is a starting point for her later deliberations, such as when she deliberates about whether to walk over to another part of the restaurant to greet Rahul. That is, ordinarily it is part of her evidence.

So the orthodox theorist has a challenge. If they say that it is part of Parveen's evidence that Rahul is in the restaurant, then they can't turn around and say that the evidential probability that he is in the restaurant is insufficiently high for her to play Blue-True. After all, its evidential probability is one. If they say that it is no part of Parveen's evidence that Rahul is in the restaurant because she is playing this version of the Red-Blue game, they give up orthodoxy. So they have to say that our evidence never includes things like Rahul is in the restaurant.

This can be generalised. Take any proposition such that if the red sentence was that two plus two is four and that proposition was the content of the blue sentence, then it would be irrational to play Blue-True. Any orthodox explanation of the Red-Blue game entails that this proposition is no part of your evidence—whether you are playing the game or not. Once we strip all these propositions out of your evidence, you don't have enough evidence to rationally believe, or even rationally make probable, very much at all.

Descartes, via a very different route, walked into a version of this problem. His answer was to (implicitly) take us to be infallible observers of our own minds, and (explicitly) offer a theistic explanation for how we can know about the external world given just this psychologistic evidence. Nowadays, most people think that's wrong on both counts: we can be rationally uncertain about even our own minds, and there is no good path from purely psychological evidence to knowledge of the external world. If we side with the moderns on these questions, i.e., that we do not have infallible access to our own minds, and that there is no theistic proof of the external world, Descartes's position is intolerably sceptical. The orthodox position ends up being just as badly off.

2.4 Odds and Stakes

If orthodox views are wrong, then it is important to get clear on which heterodox view is most plausible.[7] I'm defending a version of the pragmatic view, but it's a different version to the most prominent versions defended in the literature. The difference can be most readily seen by looking at the class of cases that have motivated pragmatic views.

The cases involve a subject making a practical decision. The subject has a safe choice, which has a guaranteed return of S. They also have a risky choice. If things go well, the return of the risky choice is $S + G$, so they will gain G from taking the risk. If things go badly, the return of the risky choice is $S - L$, so they will lose L from taking the risk. What it takes for things to go well is that a particular proposition p is true. All of this is known by the subject facing the choice. It's also true (but not uncontroversially known by the subject) that they satisfy all the conditions for knowing p that would have been endorsed by a well-informed epistemologist circa 1997. (That is, by a proponent of the traditional view.) So p is true, and things won't go badly for them if they take the risk. Still, in a lot of these cases, there is a strong intuition that they should not take the bet, and as I've just been arguing, that is hard to square with the idea that they know that p. So assuming the traditional view is right about the subject as they were before facing the practical choice, having this choice in front of them causes them to lose knowledge that p.

But what is it about these choices that triggers a loss of knowledge? There is a familiar answer to this, one explicitly endorsed by Hawthorne (2004) and Jason Stanley (2005). It is that they are facing a 'high-stakes' choice. Now what it is for a choice to be high-stakes is never made entirely clear, and Anderson and Hawthorne (2019a) show that it is hard to provide an adequate definition in full generality. In the simple cases described in the previous paragraph, however, it is easy enough to say what a high-stakes case is. It just means that L is large. So one gets the suggestion that practical factors kick in when faced with a case where there is a chance of a large loss.

---

7 This section is based on Weatherson (2016a: §3).

The version of IRT defended in this book does not care about whether a subject faces a high-stakes bet. Instead, it says that L matters, but only indirectly. What is (typically) true in these cases is that the subject should maximise expected utility relative to their evidence.[8] And taking the risky choice maximises expected utility only if this equation is true.

$$\Pr(p) / (1 - \Pr(p)) > L / G$$

The left-hand side expresses the odds that p is true. The right-hand side expresses how high those odds have to be before the risk is worth taking. If the equation fails to hold, then the risk is not worth taking. If the risk is not worth taking, then the subject doesn't know that p.

Since the numerator of the right-hand side is L, then one way to destroy knowledge that p is to present the subject with a situation where L is very high. It isn't, however, the only way. Since the denominator of the right-hand side is G, another way to destroy knowledge that p is to present the subject with a situation where G is very low.

In effect, we've seen such a situation with Anisa. To make the parallel to Anisa's case even clearer, consider the following case, involving a character I'll call Darja. Darja has been reading books about World War One, and yesterday read that Franz Ferdinand was assassinated on St Vitus's Day, June 28, 1914. She is now offered a chance to play a slightly unusual quiz game. She has to answer the question *What was the date of Franz Ferdinand's assassination?* If she gets it right, she wins $50. If she gets it wrong, she wins nothing. Here's what is strange about the game. She is allowed to Google the answer before answering. So here are the two live options for Darja. In the table, and in what follows, p is the proposition that Franz Ferdinand was indeed assassinated on June 28, 1914.

---

[8] This simplifies the relationship between rational choice and expected utility maximisation. Later in the book I'll have to be much more careful about this relationship. See Chapter 6 for many more details.

Table 2.1 Darja's choice between answering the question, and checking Google.

	p	$\neg p$
Say "June 28, 1914"	50	0
Google the answer	$50 - ε	$50 - ε

If Darja has her phone near her, and has cheap easy access to Google, then ε might be really low. In that case she should take the safe option; it's the one that maximises expected utility. That means she doesn't know that p, even if she remembers reading it in a book that is actually reliable. Facing a long-odds bet can cause knowledge loss, even in low-stakes situations.

So I'm committed to the view that Darja loses knowledge in her relatively low-stakes situation, and indeed I think that's true. That's not because I have any kind of intuition that she loses knowledge. I don't have any clear intuition about her case, and I'm certainly not taking any intuition about the case as a premise. What I am taking as a premise is that Darja should Google the answer in cases like this one; doing otherwise is taking a bad risk. The best explanation of why this is a bad risk is that she doesn't know when Franz Ferdinand was assassinated. So practical interests can matter even in relatively low-stakes cases.

I'm not the first to focus on these long-odds/low-stakes cases. Jessica Brown (2008: 176) notes that these cases raise problems for the stakes-centric version of IRT. Anderson and Hawthorne (2019a) argue that once we get beyond the simple two-state/two-option choices, it isn't at all easy to say what situations are and are not high-stakes choices. These cases are not problems for the version of IRT that I defend, since this version gives no role to stakes.

2.5 Theoretical Interests Matter

When explaining why I called my theory IRT, one of the reasons I gave was that I wanted theoretical, and not just practical, interests to matter to knowledge.[9] This is also something of a break with the existing

---

9   This section is based on Weatherson (2017: §4).

literature. After all, Stanley's book on interest-relative epistemology is called *Knowledge and Practical Interests*. He defends a theory on which what an agent knows depends on the practical questions they face. There are strong reasons to think that theoretical reasons matter as well.

In Section 2.4, I suggested that someone knows that p only if the rational choice to make would also be rational given p. That is, someone knows that p only if the answer to the question *What should I do?* is the same unconditionally as it is conditional on p. My preferred version of IRT generalises this approach. Someone knows that p only if the rational answer to a question she is interested in is the same unconditionally as it is conditional on p. Interests matter because they determine just what it is for the person to be interested in a question. Are the questions, in this sense, always practical questions, or do they also include theoretical questions? There are two primary motivations for allowing theoretical interests as well as practical interests to matter.

The first comes from what Jeremy Fantl and Matthew McGrath call the Unity Thesis (Fantl and McGrath, 2009: 73–76). They argue that whether p is a reason for someone is independent of whether they are engaged in practical or theoretical deliberation. The intuition supporting this is quite clear. Consider two people with the same background thinking about the question *What to do in situation S*. One of them is in S, the other is just thinking about it as an idle fantasy. Any reasoning one can properly do, the other can properly do. Since one is facing a theoretical question, and the other a practical question, the difference between theoretical and practical questions can't be relevant.

Let's make that a little less abstract. Imagine Anisa is not actually faced with the choice between Red-True, Blue-True, Red-False and Blue-False with these particular red and blue sentences. In fact, she has no practical decision to make that turns on the date of the Battle of Agincourt. Instead, she is idly musing over what she would do if she were playing that game. (Perhaps because she is reading this book.) If she knows when the battle was, then she should be indifferent between Red-True and Blue-True. After all, she knows they will both win $50. Intuitively she should think Red-True is preferable, both in the abstract setting and when she's actually making the decision. This seems to be the totally general case.

The general lesson is that if whether one can take p for granted is relevant to the choice between A and B, it is similarly relevant to the theoretical question of whether one would choose A or B, given a choice. Since those questions should receive the same answer, if p can't be known while making the practical deliberation between A and B, it can't be known while musing on whether A or B is more choice-worthy.

There is a second reason for including theoretical interests in what's relevant to knowledge. There is something odd about reasoning from the premise that the probability of p is precisely x, to the conclusion that p, in any case where $x < 1$. It is a little hard to say, though, why this is problematic. We often take ourselves to know things on grounds that we would admit, if pushed, are probabilistic. The version of IRT that includes theoretical interests explains this oddity. If we are consciously thinking about whether the probability of p is x, then that's a relevant question to us. Conditional on p, the answer to that question is clearly no, since conditional on p, the probability of p is 1. So anyone who is thinking about the precise probability of p, and not thinking it is 1, is not in a position to know p. That's why it is wrong, when thinking about p's probability, to infer p from its high probability.

Putting the ideas so far together, we get the following picture of how interests matter. Someone knows that p only if the evidential probability of p is close enough to certainty for all the purposes that are relevant, given their theoretical and practical interests. Assuming the background theory of knowledge is non-sceptical, this will entail that interests matter.

2.6 Global Interest-Relativity

IRT was introduced as a thesis about knowledge. I'm going to argue in Chapter 8 that it also extends to rational belief. We need not stop there. At the extreme, we could argue that every epistemologically interesting notion is interest-relative. Doing so gives us a global version of IRT. That is what I'm going to defend here.

Stanley (2005) comes close to defending a global version. He notes that if one has both IRT, and a "knowledge first" epistemology (Williamson, 2000), then one is a long way towards global IRT. Even if one doesn't accept the whole knowledge first package, but just accepts the thesis that evidence is all and only what one knows, then one is a long way towards globalism. After all, if evidence is interest-relative, then probability, justification, rationality, and evidential support are interest-relative too.

That's close to the path I'll take to global IRT, but not exactly it. In Chapter 9 I'm going to argue that evidence is indeed interest-relative, and so all those other notions are interest-relative too. That's not because I equate knowledge and evidence. The version of IRT I defend implies that evidence is a subset of knowledge, and which subset it is turns out to be interest-relative.

There is a deep puzzle here for IRT. On the one hand, the arguments for IRT look like they will generalise to arguments for the interest-relativity of evidence.[10] On the other hand, the simplest explanation of cases like Anisa's presupposes that we can identify Anisa's evidence independent of her interests. That simple explanation says that Anisa shouldn't play Blue-True because the evidential probability of the blue sentence being true is lower than the evidential probability of the red sentence being true. Since she can't rationally play Blue-True, it follows that she mustn't know that the blue sentence is true. If evidence is identified independently, this looks like it might generalise into a nice story about when changes of interests lead to changes of knowledge. The story looks much less nice if evidence is also interest-relative, and it is.

The aim of Chapter 9 is to tell a story that avoids the worst of these problems. In the story I'll tell, evidence is indeed interest-relative, so we can't tell a simple story about precisely when changes in interests will lead to changes in knowledge. Still, it will be true that people lose knowledge when the evidential probability of a proposition is no longer high enough for them to take it for granted with respect to every question they are interested in.

---

10 I was first convinced of this by conversations with Tom Donaldson some years back. The earlier example of Parveen in the restaurant grew out of these conversations.

2.7 Neutrality

This book defends, at some length, the idea that knowledge is interest-relative. I am, however, staying neutral on a number of other topics in the vicinity.

2.7.1 Neutrality about Contextualism

Most notably, I'm not taking any stand on whether contextualist theories of knowledge are true or false. If you think that contextualism is true, then what I'm defending is that the view that 'knowledge' picks out in this context, and in most other contexts, is interest-relative.

Contextualist theories of knowledge have a lot in common with interest-relative theories. The kind of cases that motivate the interest-relative theories, cases like Anisa's and Blaise's, also motivate contextualism. They might even be seen as competitors, since they are offering rival explanations of similar phenomena. They are not, however, strictly inconsistent. Consider principles A and B below.

A. A's utterance that *B knows that p* is true only if for any question *Q?* in which A is interested, the rational answer for B to give is the same unconditionally as it is conditional on *p*.

B. A's utterance that *B knows that p* is true only if for any question *Q?* in which B is interested, the rational answer for B to give is the same unconditionally as it is conditional on *p*.

I endorse principle B, and that's why I endorse an interest-relative theory of knowledge. If I endorsed principle A, then I would be (more or less) committed to a contextualist theory of knowledge. And principle A is not inconsistent with principle B.[11]

It isn't hard to see why cases like Anisa and Blaise can move one to endorse principle A, and hence contextualism. It would be very odd for Anisa to say "This morning, I knew the Battle of Agincourt was in 1415." That's odd because she can't now take it as given that the Battle of Agincourt was in 1415, and in some sense she wasn't in any better

---

11 There is a technical difficulty in how to understand one person answering an infinitival question that another person is asking themselves. The points I'm making in this section aren't sensitive to this level of technical detail.

or worse evidential position this morning with respect to the date of the battle. Perhaps, and this is the key point, it would even be false for Anisa to say this now. The contextualist, especially the contextualist who endorses principle A, has a good explanation for why that's false. The interest-relative theorist doesn't have anything to say about that. Personally I think it's not obvious whether this would be false for Anisa to say, or merely inappropriate, and even if it is false, there may be decent explanations of this that are not contextualist. (For instance, maybe knowledge is sensitive to what interests one will have. Or maybe some kind of relativist theory is true.) But there is clearly an argument for contextualism here, and it isn't one that I'm going to endorse or reject.

One reason I'm not rejecting contextualism is that I'm not sure really what it is. Here's a theory about 'knows' that I think is interesting, and I don't know whether it is contextualist. The word 'knows' is polysemous. It has three possible meanings. One of them is something like Cartesian certainty. In this sense, most knowledge claims are false. Another is something like information possession. In this sense, my car might know lots of things, since its systems do quite reliably store a lot of information. Finally, there is a moderate sense, which is what we most commonly use. The difference between the three might even be marked phonologically; the Cartesian sense is often somewhat drawn out or otherwise emphasised. Is this contextualist? I don't know. Sort of, I guess. It agrees with the standard contextualist account of the appeal of scepticism. On the other hand, it denies that 'knows' has the kind of continuous variation that is typical in comparative adjectives like 'rich'. Since I think this kind of polysemy theory might be true, and (independently) that it might be contextualist, I'm not in a position to deny contextualism.

2.7.2 Other Aspects of Neutrality

As I've already noted, I'm making heavy use of the principle that Brown calls K-Suff. I'm going to defend that at much greater length in what follows. What I'm not defending is the converse of that principle, what she calls K-Nec.

K-Nec
An agent can properly use p as a reason for action only if she knows that p.

The existing arguments for and against K-Nec are intricate and interesting, and I don't have anything useful to add to them. All I will note is that the argument of this chapter doesn't rely on K-Nec, and I'm mostly going to set it aside.

I'm obviously not going to offer anything like a full theory of knowledge. I am just defending a particular necessary condition on knowledge. That condition entails that knowledge is interest-relative given some common-sense assumptions about how widespread knowledge is.

I will be making one claim about how interests typically enter into the theory of knowledge. I'll argue that there is a certain kind of defeater. A person only knows that p if the belief that p coheres in the right way with the rest of their attitudes. What's 'the right way'? That, I argue, is interest-relative. In particular, some kinds of incoherence are compatible with knowledge if the incoherence concerns questions that are not interesting.

So the impact of interests is (typically) very indirect. Even if the other conditions for knowledge are satisfied, someone might fail to know something because it doesn't cohere well with the rest of their beliefs. What turns out to be most important here is an exception to this exception clause. Incoherence with respect to uninteresting questions is compatible with knowledge.

This is going to matter because it affects how we think about what happens when interests change. It is odd to think that a change in interests could make one know something. It isn't as odd to think that a change in interests could block or defeat something that was potentially going to block or defeat an otherwise well-supported belief from being knowledge. This is something I will return to repeatedly in Chapter 7.

3. Belief

3.1 Beliefs and Interests

One core premise of this book is that someone knows something only if they properly take it to be settled. Taking something to be settled is what we might call believing it. Or, at least, it's a philosophically significant precisification of the notion of belief. Since belief and settling will play such an important role in the rest of this book, I'm going to discuss them here before we turn to knowledge.

The theory in this chapter owes a lot to proposals by Dorit Ganson (2008, 2019). Like her, I'm going to develop a theory where we first say what it is to have a belief in normal cases, then include an exception clause for what happens in special cases, such as high-stakes or long-odds cases. The details will differ in some respects, but the underlying architecture will be the same.

And it also owes a lot to work by Jonathan Weisberg (2013, 2020). Believing something is a matter of being willing to use that thing as an input to deliberation.[1] If we assume perfect rationality, it will often be possible to compute what inputs a thinker is using from the outputs of their deliberation. But it's a bad idea to assume perfect rationality in the general case, and without that assumption the inputs and outputs to deliberation can be arbitrarily far apart. And when they are, it's the inputs that matter to what someone believes. Here's how Julia Staffel puts the idea.

---

1 In earlier work I'd identified beliefs with something that we computed from the outputs of deliberation. This was a mistake; I should have been focussing on the inputs not the outputs. I'll say much more in Chapter 7 about how my views on this point have changed.

> One of the most important differences between outright beliefs and credences is how they behave in reasoning. If someone relies on an outright belief in p in reasoning, the person takes p for granted, or treats p as true. The possibility that $\neg p$ is ruled out. By contrast, if someone reasons with a high credence in p, they don't take p for granted. The possibility that p might be false is not ruled out. (Staffel, 2019: 939)

What's essential to belief is that to believe something is to be willing to use it as a starting point in deliberation. That slogan needs a lot of qualification to be a theory, but as a slogan it isn't a bad starting point.

Before we get too deep into this, I need to pause over a terminological point. When I talk about belief here, I mean to talk about the psychological aspect of knowledge. Roughly, that is, I'm talking about the mental state which is such that when things go well the thinker has knowledge, and which is indistinguishable from knowledge from the thinker's perspective. I'm not interested here in how closely this notion tracks the notion we pick out in ordinary language with words like 'believes' or 'thinks'.

This caveat is important because of a notable recent argument that belief is *weak* (Hawthorne, Rothschild, and Spectre, 2016). Imagine that some panellists on a TV show are discussing the upcoming Champions League season. They are asked who will win the League this year, and one of them says "I think Tranmere will win". And without theorising about this too much, assume this is an appropriate thing to say given their credal states and the situation they are in. Now see what happens to this case when we adopt two more premises. First, this is an honest and sincere self-report: they do, as we'd ordinarily say, think that Tranmere will win. Second, 'think' in English means *believes*. So this person believes Tranmere will win. Note though that in the circumstances of the TV show, they could say "I think Tranmere will win" even if they think Tranmere is merely the most likely team to win, which might happen even if they think the probability of that is very low. (If there are n teams in the Champions League, and who knows what value n will be when you're reading this, their credence that Tranmere will win could be maximal even if it is above 1 in n by an arbitrarily small amount.) Yet surely this person would not, at least responsibly, take Tranmere's winning to be a starting point in deliberation.

3. Institutional Systems

Now there are a lot of things we could say about that argument. I wouldn't want to sign up for either of the two premises that I mentioned in the middle of the paragraph. I'm sympathetic to the criticisms of the argument that Timothy Williamson makes in "Knowledge, Credence, and the Strength of Belief" (Williamson, forthcoming). For now, though, I just want to note that this is a discussion of a separate topic to the one I'm discussing. And in identifying the topic as I have, I'm working within a very standard, and very long, tradition. Here's Robert Pasnau, responding to a similar kind of challenge in the context of interpreting historical figures.

> I do not know of any historical figure who resists the idea that we can identify a kind of mental state, in the vicinity of assent, which can serve as a component in analyzing what it is to be in some more exalted epistemic state, in the vicinity of knowledge. What that component state gets called varies from century to century and from author to author. For Buridan, for instance, it will not be called *opinio*, because "*opinio* signifies a defect from scientia in some way" (Summulae VIII.4.4, trans. p. 710). But this is just a point about that Latin word, as it gets used at that moment in time, and goes no deeper than the analogous observation today that a *guess* cannot count as *knowledge*, no matter what gets added to it. Accordingly, throughout these lectures, I use 'belief' to pick out the mental state that is a constituent in the epistemically ideal state of *scientia* and so on, without fussing over whether 'belief' corresponds to *assensus, credere, opinio*, and so on. (Pasnau, 2017: 219)

I agree with all of that except possibly for the claim that belief is strictly speaking a constituent of *scientia*, or of knowledge. I want to leave open, at least at this stage, a knowledge-first account where belief is something like attempted knowledge. If that's right, knowledge would be a constituent of belief, and not vice versa. What's crucial is that there are close, even analytic, ties between belief as it's being used here and knowledge. Since our TV panellist can't know, and can't reasonably think they know, that Tranmere will win, their expression can't be an expression of belief, in this philosophically significant sense, that Tranmere will win.

Here's another way to put the point. It's a starting point in a lot of work in action theory that there is a true principle somewhere in the vicinity of the following idea.

> Zach intends to do some action, *A*. And he believes that to do *A*, he must do *B*. Zach bears an interesting and important normative relationship to *B*. It is an action that he believes to facilitate his intended end, and something is going wrong, if he intends *A*, believes *B* to be necessary for *A*, has reflected clear-headedly on this fact, and yet still fails to intend to do *B*. (Schroeder, 2009: 223)

There are challenges about how to make this principle quite right in cases where Zach shouldn't intend to do *A*. If the 'belief is weak' thesis is correct, however, the whole tradition in action theory that Schroeder is here joining is fundamentally mistaken. From the intention to do *A*, and the best guess that the only way to do *A* is *B*, it does not follow at all that coherence requires intending to do *B*. Since I don't think that the entire literature on means-end coherence was based on fundamentally misunderstanding the nature of belief, I'm going to assume that we have a strong notion of belief. Just how it relates to the English words 'guess', 'think', and even 'believes' is left as an issue for another day.

3.2 Maps and Legends

Beliefs, Frank Ramsey famously said, are maps by which we steer (Ramsey, 1990: 146). This can be turned into an argument that belief should be interest-relative as well. This argument isn't quite right (contrary to my earlier views), but it's instructive to see why it goes wrong. First let's explore Ramsey's analogy a bit more closely.[2]

When I was growing up in car-dependent, suburban Melbourne, the main street directory that was used was the *Melways*. This was a several-hundred-page-thick book that most people kept a copy of in their car. It largely consisted of page after page of 1:20,000 scale maps of the Melbourne suburbs, plus more detailed maps of the inner city, and then progressively less detailed maps of the rural areas around Melbourne, the rest of Victoria, and finally of the rest of the country. And it was everywhere. It was common for store advertisements, party

---

[2] The picture I'm sketching about the map-like nature of belief is similar to the one that Seth Yalcin has defended in two articles (2018 and, especially, 2021). That's not to say he would endorse any of the conclusions here, but simply to note that he has set out the the idea that belief is less like a map and more like an atlas, and put that idea to philosophical work.

invitations and event announcements to include the *Melways* page and grid coordinates of the location. In fact I was a little shocked when I moved to America and I found it was socially expected (in those pre-Google Maps days) that you would give people something like turn-by-turn directions to a location. I was used to just telling people where something was, i.e., giving them the *Melways* grid coordinates, and letting them use the map to get themselves there. The *Melways* really was, collectively, the map by which we steered.

But you wouldn't want to use it for everything. You wouldn't want to use it as a hiking map, for example. For one thing, it was much too heavy. For another, it was patchy on which walking trails it even included, and had almost no usable topographical information. You steer yourself by one map when you drive, and another map (or set of maps) when you hike. What one steers by should be a function of one's interests. And the same is true of belief. For most people, beliefs are interest-relative because to believe something is to steer yourself by a map that represents the world as being that way, and which map one will steer by is sensitive to one's interests.

Maybe you think this argument leans too heavily on Ramsey's analogy of beliefs and maps. But once you see the structure of the case, you can get more purely cognitive examples. (And this in turn helps us see the brilliance of Ramsey's metaphor.) If you or I were in Anisa's position, then we would not include the fact that the Battle of Agincourt was in 1415 on the map by which we steer through the Red-Blue game, even if we would typically include it on our map. When I'm reading the morning papers and thinking about the effects of some economic policy, such as a proposed minimum price for alcohol, I'll steer myself by the maps given in introductory economics texts. That is, I'll just use simple supply-demand graphs to predict the effects of the policy. Still, I won't always do that. For example, I won't do it when thinking about changes in the minimum wage, because systematic changes like that push simple models beyond their breaking point.[3] Or we can mix and

---

[3] I've said in the text that I believe that simple supply-demand models are right for some purposes. At least, I implied that when I said I steer by them, and that beliefs are maps by which we steer. Some philosophers think this is wrong, and that one only ever accepts these simple models, rather than believes them. Once we allow beliefs to be interest-relative, this role for the belief/acceptance distinction seems

match the practical and the theoretical. If there is a proposed price floor on something widely traded (like electricity), and my predictions about the effects of this change have even a small practical significance (e.g., I'm thinking about whether my small business should lock in the price it purchases electricity at for three years), then I might not use the simple model. In this case the combination of theoretical and practical interests will change which map I steer by, i.e., what I believe, even if neither interest on their own would have been enough to bring about a change.

So it looks like belief is interest-relative, and that's for deep reasons about the role that belief plays in our cognitive economy. To believe something is to steer by a map that represents it as true. To steer by it, in this sense, is to take it as given in our inquiries. For normal people, what is taken as given is dependent on what question one is interested in. So for normal people, belief is interest-relative. I used to think that this could be extended to an argument that it was part of the metaphysics of belief that it was interest-relative. But as we'll see in the next section, that isn't quite right. The restriction to 'normal people' a couple of sentences back turns out to be essential, and this creates complications.

3.3 Belief and Stubbornness

Things get complicated when we stop focussing on what normal (or normal-ish) people do, and think about less common reactions. So consider a person, call them Stubbie, who uses the same maps and models for every task. He uses the *Melways* for hiking, he makes macro-economic forecasts using simple supply-demand models, he takes ordinary knowledge for granted in high-stakes and long-odds cases, and so on. And he does this even though he knows full well that there are excellent reasons to be more flexible. What should we say about Stubbie?

I think we should say that Stubbie is irrationally stubborn, and part of his irrationality consists in steering by the same map, in holding onto the same beliefs, in situations where this is uncalled for. Stubbie acts as if simple supply-demand models are predictive in complicated

---

to go away. A lot of what are commonly called acceptances are, in my theory, beliefs that are highly sensitive to changes in interests.

situations, and as if the *Melways* has all the information a hiker needs. Neither of these things are true, and Stubbie should know they aren't, but our theory of belief had better allow for some irrational practices that could only be rationalised by false assumptions.

Stubbie's example shows that while one's beliefs should be interest-relative, they need not be. One should steer by a map suitable to the circumstances. If one stubbornly steers by the same map come what may, the fact that it would be advisable to steer by different maps at different times does not affect what one believes. Stubbie really is steering himself by the *Melways* when hiking, and he really believes the simple economic model he uses.

This shows that one can be a believer, without having those beliefs be sensitive to one's interests. That suggests that the interest-relativity of belief comes from the norms—how one should believe—not the metaphysics—what belief itself is.

There is another complicated variant of this example that raises deeper questions about the relationship between belief and interests. Imagine that Stubbie is disposed to keep taking what history books say about Agincourt for granted. Now he is faced with a decision where a lot rides on this practice. Perhaps he is playing a version of the Red-Blue game where the prize is $50,000, not $50. And the shock of having that much at stake causes him to reconsider. So he goes back to thinking it merely probable that the Battle of Agincourt was in 1415. This is not a case of interest-relativity of belief. Rather, it is like the kind of case Jennifer Nagel (2010) discusses, when she talks about beliefs being causally sensitive to interests. And this shows we have to be careful in order to be sure that a case of interest-sensitivity is really a case where belief is constitutively, and not merely causally, sensitive to interests.[4]

This version of Stubbie's case opens up the possibility that no beliefs are really interest-relative. Sometimes a change in circumstances might cause someone to change the map they steer by, but that's the only way that interests matter. I don't think this is right, but I'm much less confident of this than I am of most of the other claims in this book.

There are three significant differences between the way that interests change the beliefs of normal people to how they change Stubbie's beliefs.

---

4   In earlier work I was not careful on exactly this point. I'll say more about this in Chapter 7.

First, they are reversible. Someone who switches to a more complicated model, or to thinking that a source provides probability rather than knowledge, can easily switch back. Second, they are predictable. For a reasonably well-functioning thinker, we can say when they will switch maps. It will be when the stakes are high, or the odds are long, or the question pushes on the limitations of their models. Third, they are not emotionally loaded. The natural way to tell this variant of Stubbie's story involves shock; he feels the change in his attitude. But when you or I play the Red-Blue game, we switch from thinking something is true to thinking it is probable without any significant phenomenology. I think these three differences are enough to justify saying that in the normal case, the change of interests constitutes a change of beliefs, while in Stubbie's case, the change of interests merely causes a change of beliefs. And if that's right, the belief itself is interest-relative, in normal cases.

But whether we accept the argument of the last paragraph or not, it won't affect what we say about Anisa. She believes the Battle of Agincourt was in 1415. This belief is irrational; she should have switched to thinking it is merely probable that the battle was in 1415. The change in the rational status of her belief is constituted by, and not merely caused by, her change in interests. So interests can be constitutively relevant to rational belief, even when they don't affect belief.

The next two sections aim to turn these Ramseyan observations about the relationship between beliefs and interests into a theory of belief.

3.4 Taking as Given

To start towards a positive theory of belief, it helps to think about the following example, featuring a guy I'll call Sully. (This example is going to resemble the examples involving Renzo in Ross and Schroeder (2014), and at least for a while, my conclusions are going to resemble theirs as well.) Sully is a fan of the Boston Red Sox, and one of the happiest days of his life was when the Red Sox broke their 86-year-long curse, and won baseball's World Series in 2004. He knows, and hence believes, that the Red Sox won the World Series in 2004. He likes their chances to win again this year, because in Sully's heart, hope always springs eternal.

It's now the start of a new baseball season, and Sully is offered, for free, a choice between the following two bets.

- Bet A wins $50 if the Red Sox win the World Series this year, and nothing otherwise.
- Bet B wins $60 if the same team wins the World Series this year as won in 2004, and nothing otherwise.

For Sully, this choice is a no-brainer. If the Red Sox win this year, he wins more money taking B than A. If the Red Sox don't win this year, he gets nothing either way. So it's better to take B than A, and that's what he does.

What Sully has done here is use dominance reasoning, in particular weak dominance reasoning. One option weakly dominates another if it might have a better return, and can't have a worse return. Weak dominance is used as an analytical tool in game theory. It is also a form of inference that non-theorists, like Sully, can use. (Though unless they've taken a game theory course they might not use this phrase to describe it.)

Sully's case can be distinguished from that of his more anxious friend Mack. Mack is also a big Red Sox fan, and also looks back on that curse-busting World Series win with fondness. But if you offer Mack the choice between these two bets, he'll hesitate a bit. He'll wonder if he's really sure it was 2004 that the Red Sox won. Maybe it was 2005, he thinks. He'll eventually think that even if he's not completely sure that it was 2004, it was very likely 2004, and so it is very likely that bet B will do better, and that's what he will take.

Even if Sully and Mack end up at the same point, they have used very different forms of reasoning. Sully uses weak dominance reasoning, while Mack uses probabilistic reasoning. Sully takes the fact that the Red Sox won in 2004 as given, while Mack just takes it to be very likely. The big thing I want to rely on here is that these are very different psychological processes. Neither of these guys is doing something that approximates, or simplifies, the other; they both take bet B, but they get to that conclusion via very different routes.

There is a theoretical analogue to this psychological point. Many game theorists, perhaps most, think that weak dominance reasoning can be iterated more or less indefinitely. (That's not to say that they are right; I'm trying to make a point about conceptual distinctiveness here, not game theory.) But few if any think that likelihood reasoning can be iterated indefinitely. This reflects the fact that they are very different kinds of reasoning. Dominance reasoning is pre-probabilistic.

Sully's reasoning isn't just dominance reasoning. It's dominance reasoning that relies on a contingent assumption, namely that the Red Sox won the World Series in 2004. When Sully reasons that A can't do better than B, he's not drawing any kind of logical or metaphysical point. It's logically and metaphysically possible that the Red Sox lost in 2004. For that matter, and this is a point Ganson (2019) stresses, it's logically and metaphysically possible that the payouts for A and B are other than what Sully thinks they are.

And though he might not make it explicit, at some level Sully surely knows this. If pushed, he'd endorse the conditional "If I've misremembered when the curse-busting World Series win was, and the Red Sox didn't win in 2004, then bet A might do better than bet B". So while he is disposed to use dominance reasoning in deciding whether to take A or B, this disposition rests on taking some facts about the world for granted.

Recall the disjunctive way that Sully reasoned. Either the Red Sox will win this year or they won't. Either way, I won't do better taking bet A, but I might do better taking bet B. So I'll take bet B. This reasoning—not just the reasons Sully has but his reasoning—can be appropriately represented by the kind of decision table that is familiar from decision theory or game theory.

Table 3.1 Betting on the Red Sox.

	Red Sox Win	Red Sox Don't Win
Take Bet A	$50	$0
Take Bet B	$60	$0

Focus for now on the columns in this table. Sully takes two possibilities seriously: that the Red Sox win this year, and that they don't. The 'possibilities' here are possibilities in the sense described by Humberstone (1981). They have content—in one of them the Red Sox win, in the other they don't, but they don't settle all facts. In the right-hand column, there is no fact of the matter about which other team wins the World Series. In neither column is there a fact of the matter about what Sully will have for lunch tomorrow. If you want to think of these in terms of worlds, they are both very large sets of worlds, and within those sets there is a lot of variability.[5]

But there is more to the content of each column than what is explicitly represented in the header row. In each column, for example, the Red Sox won in 2004. That's why Sully can put those monetary payoffs into the cells. And in each column, the terms of the bet are as Sully knows that they are. In sets of worlds terms, the sets that are represented by the columns are exclusive, but far from exhaustive.

Consider those propositions which are true according to all of the columns in this table. Say a proposition is *taken as given* in a decision problem when it the decider treats one option as dominating another, and does so in virtue of a table in which that proposition is true in every column. Then here is one principle about belief that seems to be very plausible.

Given
S believes that p only if there is some possible decision problem such that S is disposed to take p as given when faced with that problem.

Given is logically weak in one respect, and strong in another. It only requires that S be willing to take p for granted in one possible choice. It doesn't have to be a likely, or even particularly realistic choice. Sully is unlikely to have strangers offer him these free money bets. Given how representationally sparse decision tables are, for something to be true in all columns of a decision table is a very strong claim. It doesn't suffice, for instance, for p to be true in some columns and false in none. Each column has to take a stance on p, and endorse it.

I will have much more to say about the relationship between decision tables like Table 4.1. First, however, I need to say more about belief. I used to think that Given, or something like it, could be strengthened into a biconditional, and from there we could get something like a functionalist analysis of belief. That turns out not quite to be right. Being disposed to sometimes take p as given is not sufficient for belief. If Anisa had played the Red-Blue game rationally, she would have lost any belief

---

5   Analysing these possibilities as sets of worlds is unhelpful when we want to use a model like this to represent modal or logical uncertainty. Still, it's often a helpful heuristic, and there isn't anything wrong with using a model that breaks down when applied outside its appropriate zone.

about when the Battle of Agincourt was. To explain cases like that, we need to expand our theory of belief.

3.5 Blocking Belief

Imagine a person, call him Erwin, who is made the offer Blaise is made, but declines it. He declines on the very sensible grounds that the Battle of Agincourt might not have been in 1415, and he does not want to run the risk of sending everyone to The Bad Place. If we stop our theory of belief with Given, then we have to say that Erwin has some kind of weird pragmatic incoherence. He believes that p, and wants what is best for everyone, but won't do the thing that will, given his beliefs, produce what is best for everyone. Declining the bet is not practically incoherent in this way. So Erwin does not believe that the Battle of Agincourt was in 1415. At least, he doesn't believe that at the time he is declining the bet.

So a theory of belief with any hope of being complete needs some supplementation. The idea I'll use is one that seems *prima facie* like it might apply without restriction. A little reflection, however, shows that it will ultimately need to be restricted, and the most natural restrictions are pragmatic.

Imagine that we don't ask Erwin whether he is prepared to bet the welfare of all of humanity on historical claims, but instead ask him a simple factual question H.

> H. How many (full) centuries has it been since the Battle of Agincourt?

Erwin will think to himself, "Well, the Battle of Agincourt was in 1415, and that's a bit over six hundred years ago, so that's six centuries. The answer is six." Now compare what happens if we ask him this slightly more convoluted question.

> I. If the Battle of Agincourt was in 1415, how many (full) centuries has it been since the Battle of Agincourt?

Erwin will give the same answer, i.e., six. And he will give it for basically the same reasons. Indeed, apart from the date of the Battle being one of his reasons in answering H, and not needed to answer I, he has the same reasons for answering the two questions with six. I mean that both in the sense that what justifies giving the answer six is the same for the two questions, and in the sense that what causes him to answer six is the same for the two questions. (With the exception that the date of the battle is a reason in answering H, but not in answering I.)

Say that a person answers the questions $Q?$ and $If\ p,\ Q?$ in the same way if they offer the same answer to the two questions, and their reasons (in both senses) for these answers are the same except only that p is one of the reasons for their answer to $Q?$. Then here is a plausible principle about belief—albeit one that isn't going to be quite right.

Unrestricted Conditional Questions
If S believes that p, then for any question $Q?$, S is disposed to answer the questions $Q?$ and $If\ p,\ Q?$ the same way.

Note that in saying these questions are answered the same way, I really don't just mean that they get the same answers. I will offer the same answer to the questions *What is one plus one?* and *What is the largest n such that xn + yn = zn has positive integer solutions?*, but I don't answer these questions the same way. My reasons for the first answer are quite closely related to the fact that one plus one does equal two. My reasons for the second answer are almost wholly testimonial. So in the sense relevant to Unrestricted Conditional Questions, I do not answer each question the same way.

I'm understanding what a conditional question is in a particular way, one I'll describe in the next paragraph. I think this is how conditional questions usually work in English, so the shorthand *If p, Q?* that I'm using is not misleading. But I don't intend to defend a particular claim about the way natural language conditionals work. That would be another whole book (or more.) So I intend to use this shorthand *If p, Q?* somewhat stipulatively, as follows.

If p, Q? is the question $Q?$ asked under the assumption that p can be taken as given. So the question *If p, how probable is q?* is asking for the conditional probability of q given p. The question *If p, which option is most useful?* is asking for a comparison of the conditional utilities of the various options. And the question *If p, must it be that q?* gets an affirmative answer if all the (salient) possibilities where p is true are ones where q is true. (So it becomes very close to asking if the material implication $p \supset q$ must be true.) Now it is notoriously difficult to connect these conditional questions with questions about the truth of any conditional.[6] But I'm setting all those issues aside here. Everything that I say about conditional questions I could say, more verbosely, by making it explicit that they are to be understood as questions about conditional probability, conditional utility, conditional modality, and so on.

Now thinking about a few simple cases might make it seem that Unrestricted Conditional Questions is true. After all, there is something very odd about a counterexample to it. It would have to be a case where S believes that *p*, and there is a way they are disposed to get answer *If p, Q?*, i.e., to get from *p* to an answer to *Q?*, but they are not disposed to use that to answer *Q?*. That seems at best rather odd.

There is one potential counterexample that I don't think ultimately undermines Unrestricted Conditional Questions. There could be a case where I believe *p*, and *p* is relevant to *Q?*, but I don't realise its relevance. On the other hand, when I am explicitly asked *If p, Q?*, being reminded of *p* makes me see the connection, so I follow the natural path from *p* to an answer to *Q?*. These kinds of one-off performance errors are, sadly, easy to make. As long as they are one-off, they don't threaten the principle connecting dispositions.

A bigger problem comes from the two cases that I started the book with. If the Battle of Agincourt was in 1415, then Anisa maximises expected utility by playing Blue-True, and Blaise maximises expected utility by taking the bet. So answers to the conditional questions *If the Battle of Agincourt was in 1415, what options of Anisa's maximise expected utility?* and *If the Battle of Agincourt was in 1415, what option of Blaise's maximises expected utility?* are different to the answers to the corresponding unconditional questions. Or at least so say I, and hope you do too. So if Unrestricted Conditional Questions is true, then none of us have ever believed that the Battle of Agincourt was in 1415. That can't be right, so there must be some restriction on the principle.

Happily, a restriction isn't too hard to find. The principle just needs to be restricted to questions that the subject is currently taking an interest in. When we're thinking about questions like H and I, then we do have

---

6 See Lewis (1976, 1986) on the issues about conditional 'how probable' questions; Lewis (1988, 1996) on the issues about conditional 'how useful' questions; and Gillies (2010) on issues about modals in the consequent of conditional questions.

beliefs about when the Battle of Agincourt was. Were we to be placed in Anisa or Blaise's situation, or arguably when we even think about their situation, we lose this belief. So I suggest the following principle is true, and explains a lot of the cases that have been discussed so far.

Relevant Conditional Questions
If S believes that p, then for any question $Q?$ that S is currently taking an interest in, S is disposed to answer the questions $Q?$ and *If p, $Q?$* the same way.

As I argued in Section 2.5, whether one is interested in a question isn't just a matter of one's practical situation. One can be interested in a question because one is thinking about what to do should it arise, or because one is just naturally inquisitive. Many of the questions we're interested in are practical questions, but not all of them are.

I've argued that Given and Relevant Conditional Questions are necessary conditions on belief. Very roughly, I think they are jointly sufficient for belief. I say 'roughly' because I don't mean to take a stance on, say, whether animals have beliefs, or whether one can have singular thoughts about things one is not acquainted with. A more accurate claim is that if it is plausible that S is the kind of thing that can have beliefs, and p is the kind of thing it could in principle have beliefs about, and both Given and Relevant Conditional Questions are satisfied, then S believes that p.

Obviously neither Given nor Relevant Conditional Questions would be particularly helpful principles to use in providing a reductive physicalist account of mental content. They say something about necessary conditions for belief, but the statement of those conditions makes a lot of assumptions about other content-bearing states of the agent. So even if these conditions are individually necessary and jointly sufficient for belief, they wouldn't be any kind of analysis or reduction of belief.[7] But they could be part of a theory of belief, and the theory they are part of is helpful for seeing how beliefs and interests fit together.

---

7   Compare: One can consistently deny that any analysis or reduction of *knowledge* is possible and say that the condition *p is part of S's evidence* is both necessary and sufficient for S to know that p.

3.6 Questions and Conditional Questions

In the previous section I defended this principle:

Relevant Conditional Questions
If S believes that *p*, then for any question *Q?* that S is currently taking an interest in, S is disposed to answer the questions *Q?* and *If p, Q?* the same way.

To spell out what that principle amounts to, I need to say something about what questions are, and what conditional questions are. I'm going to say just enough about questions to understand the principle. This won't be anything like a full theory of questions. While much of what I say will draw on insights from theorists who have worked on questions in natural language, I'm not primarily interested in how questions are expressed in natural language. Rather, I'm interested in the contents of these questions. These contents are interesting because they can be the contents of mental states. For example, a cat can wonder where a mouse is hiding. There are deep and fascinating issues about how we can and do talk about the cat, and the cat's attitudes, but I'm more interested in the cat's relationship to the question *Where is the mouse hiding?* than I am in our talk about the cat.[8]

The simplest questions are true/false questions, like *Did the Boston Red Sox win the 2018 World Series?* These won't play a huge role in what follows, but they are important to have on the table. I am going to assume that whenever someone considers a proposition, and they don't take its truth value to be settled, they are interested in the question of whether it is true.

Next, there are quantitative questions, where the answer is some number or sequence of numbers.[9] One tricky thing about quantitative questions is that they may admit of imprecise answers, but need not. If

---

[8] A useful introduction to ways in which questions are relevant to philosophy of language is the Stanford Encyclopedia article by Cross and Roelofsen (2018). A canonical text on the role of questions is Roberts (2012). Roberts originally circulated that paper in 1996. Since then it has influenced a huge range of works, including this one.

[9] I'm including here any question that could be answered with a number or sequence of numbers, even if that would not be the most usual, or the most helpful, way to answer them. So *Where is Fenway Park?* is a quantitative question, because 42.3467° N, 71.097° W is an answer, even if *The corner of Jersey St and Van Ness St* is a better answer.

I ask, "When does tonight's Red Sox game start?", an answer of "Seven" would usually be acceptable, even if the game actually starts at a few minutes after seven. That's because, I take it, the truth conditional content of the utterance "Seven" in this context is that tonight's Red Sox game starts at approximately seven, and I'm asking a question that admits of an approximate answer. I could have been asking a question where the only acceptable answer would be the time that the Red Sox game starts to the nearest minute, or even to the nearest second. And I could even have asked that question using those exact same words. (Though if I intended to ask the question about seconds, using these words would be extremely unlikely to result in communicative success.)

The main thing that matters for the purposes of this book is that the questions with different appropriate answers are different questions. Even if one would normally use the same words in English to express the questions, the fact that they have different acceptable answers shows that they are different questions. And as noted above, what really matters for this book is the mental representation of the contents of questions. There could be two people who we could report as wondering when tonight's Red Sox game starts, but one of them will cease wondering if they find out that it starts around seven, and the other still wonders which minute near seven it will start at. These people are wondering about different questions.

The more precise a numerical question one is considering, the fewer things one can rationally take for granted in trying to answer it. So the version of IRT I defend implies that the more precise a numerical question one is considering, the fewer things one knows. Or, to put the same point another way, the less precise a numerical question one is considering, the less impact interest-relativity has on knowledge. This will matter when thinking about how the theory applies to various examples. If we ascribe to a thinker an interest in an unrealistically precise question, we might draw implausible conclusions about what IRT says about them. But this isn't a consequence of IRT; it's a consequence of not getting clear about which question a thinker is considering.

Next, there are questions that ask to identify an individual or a class of individuals. A striking thing about these questions is that they often have so-called 'mention-some' readings. To understand what this means, compare these two little exchanges.

1. a. Who was in the Beatles?
   b. John Lennon was in the Beatles.
2. a. Where can I get good coffee in Melbourne?
   b. You can get good coffee at Market Lane.

There is something wrong with 1b as an answer to 1a. It's true that John Lennon was in the Beatles. But an ordinary use of 1a will be to ask for the names of everyone in the Beatles, not just one person in them. (There are exceptions, and it's a fascinating task for another day to work out when they occur.) On the other hand 2b is a perfectly good answer to 2a. (Or so I think, but my knowledge of Melbourne coffee is a little out of date.) It is definitely not necessary to properly answer 2a that one list every place in Melbourne where one can get good coffee. That could take some time. Moreover, 2b does not (on its most natural reading) imply that Market Lane is the only place in Melbourne to get good coffee.

An answer is a 'mention-some' answer when it does not imply exhaustivity in this sense. And a question admits of mention-some answers when it is properly answered with a mention-some answer. Lots of questions asking for individuals will be mention-some questions in this sense, but not all of them will. And, again, it is important to understand what kind of question is being asked to think about whether it is satisfactorily answered by an answer that does not imply completeness or exhaustiveness.

Next, there are questions with infinitivals, such as the following.

- When to visit Venice?
- How to climb Ben Nevis?
- What to do?

In most dialects of English, it is rare to use these to simply ask questions.[10] But they can be the complements of any number of verbs. Any of the three questions above, like any number of other questions with infinitivals, can complete sentences like:

- A doesn't know ...
- B is wondering ...

---

10 My hunch is that there is quite a bit of dialectical variation here; I would need to do much more empirical research to back this up.

- C wants D to tell him ...

Mixing and matching the sentence fragments from the last two lists produces nine different sentences. Some examples of these are:

- C wants D to tell him how to climb Ben Nevis.
- A doesn't know what to do.
- B is wondering whether to visit Venice.

The philosophical work on these kinds of sentences has been almost exclusively focussed on just one of the nine sentences I just described: the one combining a knowledge verb with a 'how to' question. I suspect this is a mistake; what to say about 'know how' reports is going to have a lot in common with what to say about 'wondering when' reports. (Here I'm agreeing with Stanley (2011), though I'm about to disagree with him on a related point.)

There is a puzzle about why, in English, we cannot use these questions to complete sentences like:

- E believes ...
- F suspects ...
- G wants H to guess ...

I'm going to set that puzzle aside, as interesting as it is, and just focus on the sentences we can produce in English.

I'm going to call these questions with infinitivals *practical questions*. One thing to note about them is that they are usually mention-some. When I am wondering what to buy in the supermarket, and I resolve this by choosing one particular carton of eggs, I don't thereby imply that there is anything defective about the other cartons. I just choose some eggs.

For related reasons, answering a practical question like this is distinct from answering any question, or questions, about the modal status of different actions. Imagine that in the grip of choice-phobia I am stuck staring at the cartons of eggs, unable to decide which one to buy because they are all just alike. In that situation I might know that there is no carton such that it is what I should buy, and also that there are many cartons such that I could (rationally, morally) buy any one of them. But there are so many, and they are so alike and I can't decide, so I don't know what to buy.[11]

Resolving this indecision will not involve accepting any modal proposition like *I should buy this carton in particular*. It had better not, because I really have no reason to accept any such proposition. Rather, it involves accepting a proposition like *I will buy this carton in particular*. I can accept that by simply buying the eggs. There were many other answers I could equally well have accepted, since there were many other cartons I could buy.[12]

Practical questions are distinct from questions about modals or utilities, but there will usually be a correlation between their answers. Usually, if someone asks you when to visit Venice, and there is one time in particular such that visiting then maximises expected utility, that's what you should tell them. That's when they should visit, and that's what to say when they ask you when to visit. Relatedly, practical questions can come in conditional form. We can utter sentences like the following in English.

- J asks K what to do if his patient has hepatitis.

And there is one feature of these sentences that needs noting. I don't know what to do if one's patient has hepatitis, so let's just say that K tells J to do X. What that means is not that in any situation where the patient has hepatitis, do X. If the patient's symptoms are confusing, it might be best to run more tests before doing X. What it does mean is that if the fact that the patient has hepatitis is taken as given, then do X. As always,

---

[11] This discussion will probably remind many readers of the story of Buridan's ass, who was stuck between two equally appetising bales of hay. As Peter Adamson (2019: 453ff) points out, the connection of this example to Buridan is not the one philosophers usually assume. That is, it's not Buridan's example. An example of roughly this kind was earlier given by al-Ghazālī. And the example involving the ass was not given by Buridan at all, but by his opponents, objecting to Buridan's own equation of choice with judgment that something is best to do. That's the role the example will play a few times in this book, as a critique of theories that equate choice with formation of a belief about goodness. My earlier versions of IRT, which equated that choosing to do something with judging it has highest expected utility, will be among the theories thus targeted.

[12] I'm here mildly disagreeing with Stanley (2011: Ch. 5) when he says that these questions with infinitival complements can be paraphrased using modals like 'should'. If 'will' just is the modal that gets used in the paraphrase, as Bhatt (1999) suggests, the spirit of Stanley's view is preserved, even if the letter isn't.

conditional questions should be understood as questions about what happens in scenarios where the condition in question is taken as given. And the constraint expressed by Relevant Conditional Questions is that whatever is known can be taken as given in just this sense.

3.7 A Million Dead End Streets

As I've noted already, the view I'm defending here is somewhat different from my earlier view. And it's helpful to understand the view of this book to lay out, in one place, the ways in which time has changed my views. Here is a somewhat simplified version of the view from "Can We Do without Pragmatic Encroachment?". Assume that S is interested in some quantitative questions and some alethic (i.e., yes/no) questions. Then the view was that S believes that p if and only if these two conditions are met.

1. For any quantitative question $Q?$ that S is interested in, and any alethic question A that S is interested in, S's answers to the question *If A, Q?* and *If A and p, Q?* are the same.
2. S's credence in p is greater than 0.5.

It was assumed that S is always 'interested' in the null question *Is a tautology true?*, so one special instance of this is that S answers $Q?$ and *If p, Q?* the same way. And it was assumed that S is an expected utility maximiser, so the practical question of what to do becomes just the quantitative question *Which of these options has the highest expected utility?*. There are bells and whistles, especially in thinking about the level of precision that goes along with the quantitative questions that S is interested in. (Draw these too fine, and S doesn't have beliefs, so you have to be a little careful here.) Even without those complications, I've said enough that you can see the basic view, and perhaps see its problems.

The biggest change from that view to the one I'm defending here concerns propositions that are not relevant to any question S is considering. I used to say in that case belief required credence above 0.5; I now say that S must be willing, at least sometimes, to take p for granted.

There are other changes too. I no longer presuppose that questions about what to do just are questions about expected utility. I've stopped focussing exclusively on answers to (conditional) questions, and moved to talking about both answers and ways that questions are answered. And I dropped the requirement that we look at these potentially quite abstruse questions, such as how to answer Q? assuming both A and p. The last two changes offset each other; the reason for including these doubly conditional questions was, in effect, to look at how S was willing to get to answers about questions with more practical import.

There are many reasons, most of them due to perceptive critics of my earlier work, for making these changes. I'll just focus here on the five that have been most significant.

3.7.1 Correctness

Jacob Ross and Mark Schroeder (2014) note that my earlier theory doesn't have a good story about why false beliefs are incorrect.[13] I think that's right. Even if p is false, there is nothing necessarily mistaken about either having credence in p above 0.5, or in having unconditional preferences match preferences conditional on p.

But surely false beliefs are, in a way, incorrect. They may be rational, they may be well-supported, and so on, but still if you believe that p, and p turns out not to be the case, you got it wrong. There are other mental states that have truth as a correctness condition. Guesses are correct or incorrect, even if there need be nothing at all irrational about making a false guess. Indeed, any mortal who doesn't make false guesses from time to time isn't playing the guessing game well. Not all mental states are like this. Hoping for something that doesn't turn out to happen is unfortunate, but not incorrect. To say that a false belief is incorrect is not to just make the trivial point that it is false. It is also to say that the belief failed to meet one important standard of evaluation for beliefs—correctly representing the world. Credences do not have these correctness conditions, so the relatively simple reduction I proposed of belief to credence must be mistaken.

---

13 Fantl and McGrath (2009) make a similar argument, targeted at Lockean theories of belief more than at my theory. I'll come back to how this is a problem for Lockean theories in Section 8.4.2.

The new theory does not have this problem. Doing dominance reasoning where all of the situations one considers are non-actual is a mistake. It's not a mistake because it will inevitably lead to an irrational decision. Rather, it's a mistake because one draws a conclusion that is not supported by the premises it is based on. Those premises only say that one option is better than another conditional on one or other condition obtaining. That's a bad reason to say the first option is simply better if there is some extra option that might obtain. And whatever does obtain, might obtain.

This way of explaining the incorrectness of false belief suggests a central role for knowledge in norms of beliefs. False beliefs are mistaken because they lead one to treat the actual situation as one that could not obtain, yet the actual situation might obtain. One can make the same mistake by treating a situation that doesn't obtain, but might, as one that could not obtain. Believing something one doesn't know will (typically) lead to doing that.

3.7.2 Impractical Propositions

The second clause in my earlier theory was designed to rule out trivial belief in irrelevant propositions. The first clause on its own has some absurd consequences. Imagine that I'm relaxing by a stream watching the ripples without a care in the world. All of the very few questions that I'm currently interested in have the same answer unconditionally as they do conditional on the Battle of Agincourt having been fought in 1415. So according to clause 1, I believe the Battle of Agincourt was in 1415. That's good, because I do believe that. It's also true that all of the very few questions that I'm currently interested in have the same answer unconditionally as they do conditional on the Battle of Agincourt having been fought in 1416. So if clause 1 was the full theory of belief, then I would also believe that the Battle of Agincourt was in 1416, which I do not.

I added clause 2 to the theory in order to try to fix this problem, but it turned out only to fix a special case. Here's a case it doesn't fix. Let p be the proposition that the next die I roll will land 1, 2, 3 or 4. My credence in that is two-thirds, so it satisfies clause 2. And conditionalising on it doesn't change the answer to any of the very few problems that I'm interested in while the ripples float down the stream. So I believe p. That's absurd, since I know it is just 2/3 likely. (This objection is also due in important parts to Ross and Schroeder (2014), though my presentation differs from theirs to emphasise just which parts of the objections most worry me.)

The new theory handles this case easily. There is no context where I would simply ignore the possibility that this next die roll will land 5 or 6 for the purposes of doing dominance reasoning. So I don't believe that p, as required.

Is there anything we can rule out on purely probabilistic grounds? It's a little interesting to think this kind of case through. Imagine there is some salient very large number, and it matters what the remainder is when that large number is divided by 1000, or 1000000. Could we get to a point where a choice that is better than some alternative unless that remainder is, say 537, could feel like a dominating choice? I'm not sure whether that would ever happen. It does seem plausible to say that whether such a choice ever feels like a dominating choice correlates with whether we could ever unqualifiedly believe that the remainder is not precisely 537 on purely probabilistic grounds.

3.7.3 Choices with More than Two Options

Consider this variant of the Red-Blue game. As well as the four options Anisa has in the original version of the game, she has a fifth option. This option presents her with a question (as well as the red and blue sentences), and says that if she answers the question correctly, she wins $100. And in this case, the question is, "Who was the first American woman to win an Olympic gold medal?".

Imagine that Anisa just skim-reads the red and blue sentences, and doesn't think about which of them she'd pick, because she knows the answer to this question. It was, she knows, Margaret Abbott. So she promptly gives that answer, and wins $100.

Now she clearly takes an interest in the options Red-True and Blue-True. She has reasons for preferring to answer the question than take one of those two options. And she could give those reasons without any reflection. So Red-True and Blue-True should be in the range of things that we quantify over when thinking about options she is interested in.

Moreover, she has a stable disposition to choose Red-True over Blue-True; I think that stable disposition is a strict preference. That strict preference does not survive conditionalising on the proposition that the Battle of Agincourt was in 1415. So my earlier theory says that even in this revised version of the game, Anisa does not believe that the Battle of Agincourt was in 1415.

This now seems mistaken to me. In any deliberation Anisa does, her regular disposition to take it for granted that the Battle of Agincourt was in 1415 survives. There is a very nearby deliberation where it does not survive, namely the deliberation about whether Red-True or Blue-True is better. But, crucially, she does not have to take an interest in that question in order to take an interest in the two options Red-True and Blue-True. If they are both (clearly) suboptimal options in her current situation, she can simply settle for concluding that they are suboptimal, and leave it at that.

So I think my old theory made it too easy to lose belief in cases where one has to choose between many options. Being interested in some options, because you want to choose the best one of them, does not mean being interested in all questions about preferences between pairs of them. The problem was that I'd been focussing largely on two-way choices, so the distinction between being interested in some choices and being interested in which of those two is better got elided. That distinction matters, and the hybrid pragmatic theory handles it better than my old theory.

3.7.4 Hard Times and Close Calls

In my earlier theory, any practical deliberation was modelled as an inquiry into which option had the highest expected utility. This was wrong for a number of reasons, not least that it gives implausible results in cases involving choices between very similar options. I'll briefly describe one example that illustrates the problem, and the start of how I plan to solve it. It turns out to be rather tricky to get the details right, and I'll come back to this in Section 4.6.1 and again in Chapter 6. The details of the example are new, but it's a very minor modification of a kind of example that is discussed in Matthew McGrath and Brian Kim (2019) and credited to a talk by John Hawthorne "circa 2007". Similar examples are also discussed by Alex Zweber (2016) and by Charity Anderson and John Hawthorne (2019b), and I'm drawing on their insights in describing this one.

David is doing the weekly groceries. He needs a can of chickpeas, so he walks to where the chickpeas are and looks at the shelf. There are two cans, call them c_1 and c_2, that are equally easy to reach and get from the shelf. Call the actions of taking them t_1 and t_2. David simply assumes, partially on inductive grounds and partially on grounds of what he knows about supermarkets, that neither can has passed its expiry date. While it is wildly implausible that either can has, the probability is not zero. Let e_i be that can i has expired, and assume that $Pr(e_1)$ and $Pr(e_2)$ are low and equal. Call this probability e. Let h be the utility of choosing an unexpired can, and l the utility of choosing an expired can, where obviously $h > l$. Then both t_1 and t_2 have utility $(1-e)h + el$. Conditional on $\neg e_1$, the utility of t_1 is h, which is greater than $(1-e)h + el$ as long as $e > 0$ and $h > l$. So unconditionally, t_1 and t_2 have the same utility, but conditional on $\neg e_1$, they have different utilities. So, according to the theory I used to defend, when David is making this choice, he does not believe, and hence does not know $\neg e_1$. This seems wrong, and there are even worse consequences one can draw my thinking about minor variants of the case.

The key part of my response to this will be distinguishing between the questions *Which can to choose?* and *Which choice of can has maximal expected utility?* If David is thinking about the latter question, then it turns out he really doesn't know $\neg e_1$. That's a somewhat surprising result, and I'll turn to defending it in Chapter 6. But as long as he is focussing solely on the former question, the argument of the previous paragraph doesn't go through.

So the big move here is to move from somewhat quantitative questions, like *Which choice maximises expected utility?*, to practical questions like *What to do?* Once we do that, the problem that Zweber, and Anderson and Hawthorne, raise ceases to be a problem. I don't intend these brief remarks to be a convincing case that I've got a good solution to these problems. Rather, the point is to flag that the theory I'm defending here is distinct from the theory I used to defend, and this gives me some more resources to handle cases like David and the chickpeas.

3.7.5 Updates and Modals

The version of IRT that I defend here gives a big role to conditional attitudes.[14] That's something that it has in common with everything I've written about IRT. I used to have a particular pair of views about how to understand conditional attitudes. In particular, I took the following two claims to be at least close approximations to the truth about conditional attitudes.

1. An attitude conditional on p is (usually) the same as the attitude one would have after updating on p.
2. The way to update on p is to conditionalise.

The first is at best an approximation for familiar reasons. I can think that no one knows whether p is true, and even think that this is true conditional on p. But after updating on p, I will no longer think that. So we have to be a bit careful in applying principle 1; it has counterexamples. Still, it is a useful enough heuristic to work with.

What wasn't originally obvious to me was that there are counterexamples to principle 2 as well. They are more significant for the way IRT should be understood. I used to describe the picture of belief I was defending as the view that to believe something is to have a credence in it that's close enough to 1 for current purposes. That's still a decent heuristic, but it isn't always right. When someone is interested in modal questions, credence 1 might be insufficient for belief. To see how this might be so, it helps to start with some points Thony Gillies (2010) makes about the relationship between modals, conditionals, and updating.

When modal questions are on the table, updating will not be the same as conditionalising. This is shown by the following example. (A similar example is in Kratzer (2012: 94).)

> I have lost my marbles. I know that just one of them – Red or Yellow – is in the box. But I don't know which. I find myself saying things like ..."If Yellow isn't in the box, the Red must be." (Gillies, 2010: 4:13)

---

14 This subsection is based on Weatherson (2016a: §1).

What matters for the purposes of this book is not whether this conditional is true, but whether its truth is consistent with the Ramsey test view of conditionals. And Gillies argues that it is.

> The Ramsey test – the schoolyard version, anyway – is a test for when an indicative conditional is acceptable given your beliefs. It says that (if p)(q) is acceptable in belief state B iff q is acceptable in the derived or subordinate state B-plus-the-information-that-p. (Gillies, 2010: 4:27)

And he notes that this can explain what goes on with the marbles conditional. Add the information that Yellow isn't in the box, and it isn't just true, but must be true, that Red is in the box.

Note though that while we can explain this conditional using the Ramsey test, we can't explain it using any version of the idea that probabilities of conditionals are conditional probabilities. The probability that Red must be in the box is 0. The probability that Yellow isn't in the box is not 0. So conditional on Yellow not being in the box, the probability that Red must be in the box is still 0. Yet the conditional is perfectly assertable.

There is, and this is Gillies's key point, something about the behaviour of modals in the consequents of conditionals that we can't capture using conditional probabilities, or indeed many other standard tools. And what goes for consequents of conditionals goes for updated beliefs too. Learn that Yellow isn't in the box, and you'll conclude that Red must be. But that learning can't go via conditionalisation; just conditionalise on the new information and the probability that Red must be in the box goes from 0 to 0.

Now it's a hard problem to say exactly how this alternative to updating by conditionalisation should work. Very roughly, the idea is that at least some of the time, we update by eliminating worlds from the space of possibilities. This affects dramatically the probability of propositions whose truth is sensitive to which worlds are in the space of possibilities.

All this matters when we are considering modal questions. For example, if we are considering the question *Must q be true?*, then it is plausible that unconditionally the answer is no, and indeed the unconditional probability that q must be true is 0, but that conditional on p, q must be true.

We don't even have to be considering modals directly for this to happen. Assume that actions A and B have the same outcome conditional on q, but A is better than B in every $\neg q$ possibility. Then if we are considering the question *Is A better than B?*, it will matter whether it must be the case that q.

Assume that q could have probability 1 without it being the case that q must be true. (This is controversial, but I'll offer arguments in Sections 8.2 and 8.3 that it is possible.) Then unconditionally, A is better than B, even though they have the same expected utility. That's because weak dominance is a good principle of practical reasoning: if A might be better than B and must not be worse, then A is better than B. But by hypothesis, conditional on p, A is not better than B. So in this case p will not be believed; conditional on p the question *Is A better than B* gets a different answer to what it gets unconditionally.

Note though that all I said to get this example going is that p rules out $\neg q$, and q has probability 1. That means p could have any probability at all, up to probability 1. So it's possible that conditional on p, some relevant questions get different answers to what they get unconditionally, even though p has probability 1. So belief can't be a matter of having probability close enough to 1 for practical purposes; sometimes even probability 1 is insufficient.

3.8 Ross and Schroeder's Theory

Jacob Ross and Mark Schroeder (2014) have what looks like, on the surface, a rather different view to mine.[15] They say that to believe p is to have a "default reasoning disposition" to use p in reasoning. Here's how they describe their view.

> What we should expect, therefore, is that for some propositions we would have a *defeasible* or *default* disposition to treat them as true in our reasoning–a disposition that can be overridden under circumstances where the cost of mistakenly acting as if these propositions are true is particularly salient. And this expectation is confirmed by our experience. We do indeed seem to treat some uncertain propositions as true in our reasoning; we do indeed seem to treat them as true automatically, without first weighing the costs and benefits of so

---

15 This section is based on Weatherson (2016a: §3).

> treating them; and yet in contexts such as High where the costs of mistakenly treating them as true is salient, our natural tendency to treat these propositions as true often seems to be overridden, and instead we treat them as merely probable.
>
> But if we concede that we have such defeasible dispositions to treat particular propositions as true in our reasoning, then a hypothesis naturally arises, namely, that beliefs consist in or involve such dispositions. More precisely, at least part of the functional role of belief is that believing that p defeasibly disposes the believer to treat p as true in her reasoning. Let us call this hypothesis the *reasoning disposition account* of belief. (Ross and Schroeder, 2014: 9–10)

There are, relative to what I'm interested in, three striking characteristics of Ross and Schroeder's view.

1. Whether you believe p is sensitive to how you reason; that is, your theoretical interests matter.
2. How you would reason about some questions that are not live is relevant to whether you believe p.
3. Dispositions can be masked, so you can believe p even though you don't actually use p in reasoning now.

The view I'm defending here agrees with them about 1 and 2, though my theory manifests those characteristics in a quite different way. But point 3 is a cost of their theory, not a benefit, so it's good that my theory doesn't accommodate it. (For the record, the theory I put forward in Weatherson (2005a) did not agree with them on point 2, and I changed my view because of their arguments.)

I agree with 1 because, as I've noted a few times above, I think theoretical interests as well as pragmatic interests matter for the relationship between credence and belief. I agree with 2 because I think that whether someone is disposed to use p as a premise matters to whether they believe p. Let p be some ordinary proposition about the world that a person believes, such as that the Florida Marlins won the 2003 World Series. And let q be a lottery proposition that is just as probable as p. (That is, let q be a lottery proposition such that if the person were to play the Red-Blue game with p as red and q as blue, they would be rationally indifferent between the choices.) Then on my theory the person believes p but not q, and this isn't due to any features of their credal states. Rather, it is due to their dispositions to use p as a premise in reasoning. (For example, they might use it in figuring out how many World Series were won by National League teams in the 2000s.)

Ross and Schroeder argue, and I basically agree, that interest-relative theories of belief that only focus on practical interests have trouble with folks who use odd techniques in reasoning. This is the lesson of their example of Renzi. The details of that case are unimportant; here's the structure of it. An agent knows that X is better to do if p, and Y is better to do if $\neg p$. They could work out the relative benefit of each option in these two circumstances, and how that interacts with the probability of p to determine which option is best in expectation. They do not in fact do that. Instead, for some proposition q which is not relevant to the case, and very strongly supported by their evidence, they divide into four possibilities: $p \wedge q, p \wedge \neg q, \neg p \wedge q$ and $\neg p \wedge \neg q$. They then calculate the expected utility of X and Y given that these are the four possibilities.

This is bad reasoning. Adding this extra division to the possibility space is a waste of time, and increases the chances of making a mistake. They should just use two 'small worlds': p and $\neg p$. The problem we face as theorists is what to say about someone who makes this kind of mistake.

Ross and Schroeder say that such an agent should not be counted as believing that q. If they are consciously calculating the probability that q, and taking $\neg q$ possibilities into account when calculating expected utilities, they regard q as an open question. Regarding q as open in this way is incompatible with believing it.

I agree. The agent was trying to work out the expected utility of X and Y by working out the utility of each action in each of four 'small worlds', then working out the probability of each of these. Conditional on q, the probability of two of them ($p \wedge \neg q, \neg p \wedge \neg q$), will be 0. Unconditionally, this probability won't be 0. So the agent has a different view on some question they have taken an interest in unconditionally to their view conditional on q. So they don't believe q.[16]

So far I agree with Ross and Schroeder. The disagreement starts with a principle they endorse, which they call Stability.

---

16 For the record, the theory I defended at the time Ross and Schroeder wrote their paper did not have the resources to make this reply; I've changed my view in light of their arguments.

Stability
A fully rational agent does not change her beliefs purely in virtue of an evidentially irrelevant change in her credences or preferences. (2014: 20)

Stability is motivated by cases like this one.

> Suppose Stella is extremely confident that steel is stronger than Styrofoam, but she's not so confident that she'd bet her life on this proposition for the prospect of winning a penny. PCR [their name for my old view] implies, implausibly, that if Stella were offered such a bet, she'd cease to believe that steel is stronger than Styrofoam, since her credence would cease to rationalize acting as if this proposition is true. (2014: 20)

Ross and Schroeder's own view is that if Stella has a defeasible disposition to treat as true the proposition that steel is stronger than Styrofoam, that's enough for her to believe it. They say that can be true if the disposition is not only defeasible, but actually defeated in the circumstances Stella is in. This all strikes me as just as implausible as the failure of Stability. Let's go over its costs.

The following propositions are clearly not mutually consistent, so one of them must be given up. We're assuming that Stella is facing, and knows she is facing, a bet that pays a penny if steel is stronger than Styrofoam, and costs her life if steel is not stronger than Styrofoam.

1. Stella believes that steel is stronger than Styrofoam.
2. Stella believes that if steel is stronger than Styrofoam, she'll win a penny and lose nothing by taking the bet.
3. If 1 and 2 are true, and Stella considers the question of whether she'll win a penny and lose nothing by taking the bet, she'll believe that she'll win a penny and lose nothing by taking the bet.
4. Stella prefers winning a penny and losing nothing to getting nothing.
5. If Stella believes that she'll win a penny and lose nothing by taking the bet, and prefers winning a penny and losing nothing to getting nothing, she'll take the bet.
6. Stella won't take the bet.

It's part of the setup of the problem that 2 and 4 are true. It's common ground that 6 is true, at least assuming that Stella is rational. So we're left with 1, 3 and 5 as the possible candidates for falsehood.

Ross and Schroeder say that it's implausible to reject 1. After all, Stella believed it a few minutes ago, and hasn't received any evidence to the contrary. Now I agree that rejecting 1 isn't the most intuitive philosophical conclusion one has ever seen. But the alternatives are worse.

If we reject 3, we must say that Stella will simply refuse to infer r from p, q and $(p \land q) \to r$. Now it is notoriously hard to come up with a general principle for closure of beliefs. Still, it is hard to see why this particular instance would fail. Further, it's hard to see why Stella wouldn't have a general, defeasible, disposition to conclude r in this case, so by Ross and Schroeder's own lights, it seems 3 should be acceptable.

That leaves 5. It seems on Ross and Schroeder's view, Stella simply must violate a very basic principle of means-end reasoning. She desires something, she believes that taking the bet will get that thing, and come with no added costs. Yet, she refuses to take the bet. And she's rational to do so! Attributing this kind of practical incoherence to Stella is much less plausible than attributing a failure of Stability to her.

4. Knowledge

In Chapter 3, I argued that to believe something is to take it as given in all relevant inquiries, and in at least one possible inquiry. I explained what it was to take something as given in terms of how one answers conditional and unconditional questions. In this chapter I'm going to argue that whatever is known can be properly taken as given in all relevant inquiries, where a relevant inquiry is one that one either is or should be conducting. Since some things that are usually known cannot be properly taken as given in some inquiries, this implies that knowledge is sensitive to one's inquiries and hence to one's interests.

There is an easy argument for the conclusion of this chapter.

1. To believe something is to, inter alia, take it as given for all relevant inquiries.
2. Whatever is known is correctly believed.
3. So, whatever is known is correctly taken as given in all relevant inquiries.

I think this argument is basically sound, but both premises are controversial. Further, it isn't completely obvious that it is even valid. So I'm not going to rely on this argument. Rather, I'll argue more directly for the conclusion that whatever is known is correctly taken as given in all relevant inquiries. This will provide indirect evidence that the theory of belief in Chapter 3 was correct, since we can now take that theory of belief to be an explanation for the claim that whatever is known is correctly taken as given in all relevant inquiries, rather than as part of the motivation for it.

The argument here will be in two parts. First, I'll focus on practical inquiries, i.e., inquiries about what to do, and argue that what is known can be taken as given in all practical inquiries. Then I'll extend the discussion to theoretical inquiries, and hence to inquiries in general. Finally, with the argument complete, I'll look at two possible objections to the argument. One objection is that it has implausible consequences about the role of logical reasoning in extending knowledge, and the other is that it leads to implausible results when a source provides both relevant and irrelevant information.

4.1 Ten Decision Commandments

A practical inquiry can often be represented by the kind of decision table that we use in decision theory courses.[1] Table 4.1, for instance, is a table for the problem faced by a person, call him Ragnar, choosing how to get to work.

Table 4.1 Ragnar's trip to work

	Rain	Dry
Walk	0	5
Bus	3	4

If we tell the students that the probability of rain is 0.4, we expect them to figure out that the expected utility of walking is 3, while the expected utility of taking the bus is 3.6. Therefore, taking the bus is the better choice. And that's a little surprising, since it probably won't rain, and if it doesn't, it is better to walk. The key point is that walking is risky, and in this case expected utility theory suggests that the risk isn't worth taking.

Table 4.1 can serve two related philosophical purposes, which we can helpfully distinguish using terminology from Peter Railton (1984). The table can provide a *criterion of rightness* for Ragnar's actions. It is rational for him to take the bus because of the expected utility calculation. The table can do more than that though. In simple cases like this one, it can provide a *deliberation procedure*. Ragnar can, in theory and in simple cases, use a table like this to decide what to do. There are limits to when tables can be used in this way, and as I'll argue in Chapter 6, those limits

---

[1] This section and the next are loosely based on Weatherson (2012: §1.1).

end up suggesting limits to how often the tables even provide criteria of rightness. In simple cases though, the table isn't just something the theorist can use to understand Ragnar, it is something Ragnar himself can use to deliberate. This is especially true in cases where one of the options is dominated, either strictly or weakly, by another.[2] I've appealed to the fact that the tables can be deliberation procedures, and not just criteria of rightness, already, in the discussion of Sully and Mack in Section 3.4. There the focus was on how tables like these related to belief; here I want to relate them to knowledge.

There are (at least) ten ways in which Table 4.1 could misrepresent Ragnar's situation. To put the same point another way, there are (at least) ten ways in which it could correctly represent his situation. One way to think about the core project of this book is to say what it means for a table to correctly represent a decision situation in one of these ten respects. It is a little easier to think about the misrepresentations, so I'll start with them.

First, the numbers in the table might be wrong. The table says that, conditional on catching the bus, Ragnar is better off if it is dry than if it rains. Maybe that isn't true. The theory of well-being (Crisp, 2021) addresses, among other things, when the numbers in the cells of tables like this are accurate. That's a big topic, and not one I'm going to have anything to say about here.[3]

Second, the probabilities might be wrong. Maybe it isn't the case that the probability of rain is 0.4, and in fact it is 0.2. There is an enormous question here about what it even means for one to misrepresent the probabilities. Is the correct representation one that tracks objective

---

[2] An option is strictly dominated by another if it does worse than that option in every state. It is weakly dominated by another if it does worse than that option in some states, and never does better than it.

[3] As well as questions about well-being, there are also questions here about what one should do in cases where the outcome is itself a kind of gamble. Imagine that the chooser is trying to decide whether to bet on a basketball game, and it is known how much money they will win or lose in the four states. The value to the chooser of those outcomes depends on any number of further things, like the rate of inflation in the near term, and the "position of wealth holders in the social system" (Keynes, 1937: 214) some years hence. Just how these uncertainties should be accounted for is a difficult question, especially for any theorist who deviates in any way from orthodox expected utility theory. I would like to have a better theory of how the account of decision making with deliberation costs, as discussed in Chapter 6, interacts with this question.

chances, or Ragnar's evidence, or Ragnar's beliefs, or something else, or some combination of these? One upside of focussing on dominance arguments is that these questions can be temporarily set aside.

The next four questions concern the rows, and here we have less philosophical work to draw on. Brian Hedden (2012) has a paper arguing that the options should all be decisions, rather than actions. So the first row should say "Ragnar decides to walk" rather than "Ragnar walks". This would be a fairly radical change from practice in decision theory, though one worth taking seriously. The more conservative option would be to link the rows to some or other philosophical theory of abilities (Maier, 2022). In some sense it seems right to say that there should be a row for all and only the actions that Ragnar is able to perform. The details are going to be tricky though. This book is focussed on the columns rather than the rows, but I want to briefly mention four important topics about the rows, which will constitute our third through sixth ways the table might misrepresent Ragnar's situation.

Third, the table might leave off an option that should be there. Perhaps Ragnar should, or at least should consider, driving to work. Or perhaps it should include the option of quitting his job immediately, and hence not going to work.

Fourth, the table might include an option that should not be there. If the bus route near Ragnar's house has just been cancelled, perhaps the table should not include a row for the bus.

Fifth, the table might have merged multiple options that should be separated. Perhaps it should have separate rows for walking with an umbrella, and walking without an umbrella. This differs from the third point, because it does not say that Ragnar should do (or consider) something wholly distinct from what is already there, but rather that it should separate out different ways of bringing about something that is considered.

Sixth, the table might have separated multiple options that should be merged. It's hard to see how Table 4.1 could have made this mistake, but if we had separate rows for walking while wearing a red shirt, and walking while wearing a blue shirt, it would be arguable that this is too fine a grain, and the right table would not distinguish these.

The final four questions concern the columns, and they mirror the four questions about the rows. These questions will be central to the narrative of this chapter, and of this whole book.

Seventh, the table might leave off a state that should be there. Perhaps Ragnar should consider the possibility that it will snow, or that there will be an ice storm. Taking the only two states to be rain and dry excludes those possibilities,[4] and perhaps they should be included.

Eighth, the table might include a state that should not be there. If it is bucketing down as Ragnar is preparing to leave, including a state where it is dry might be a mistake.

Ninth, the table might have merged states that should be separated. Perhaps the column that simply says "Dry" should have been split into two: one being "Dry and Sunny", the other being "Dry and Cloudy".

Tenth, the table might include separate states that should be merged. It's unlikely that a two state table will do this, but if we had made the split suggested in the previous paragraph, one could easily argue that it was a mistake, and that Ragnar should have treated these as a single state.

That gives us ten ways that the table could go wrong. It's helpful to have them in a simple list.

1. The values could be wrong.
2. The probabilities could be wrong.
3. An option could be improperly excluded.
4. An option could be improperly included.
5. The options might be too coarse-grained.
6. The options might be too fine-grained.
7. A state could be improperly excluded.
8. A state could be improperly included.
9. The states might be too coarse-grained.
10. The states might be too fine-grained.

For every one of these ten possible mistakes, there is a prior philosophical question about what it means for the table to have made, or not made, that mistake. Every one of those ten questions is, at least to my mind, incredibly philosophically important. Even someone who thought, like Herbert Foxwell, that books should only be written for "grave cause"

---

4   As noted back in Section 3.4, I'm using 'possibilities' here in the sense described by Humberstone (1981).

(Keynes, 1936: 599), should concede that a clear answer to any one of the ten would be sufficient grounds to warrant a scholarly monograph.

This book is primarily concerned with the seventh, though the argument touches to some extent on the eighth as well. It is proper to exclude a possibility from the table if the chooser knows that possibility does not obtain. If that conditional could be turned into a biconditional, we'd have an answer to the eighth question, too, but that is a more delicate question.[5] In any case, the conditional will be enough.

4.2 Knowing Where the Ice Cream Goes

The aim of this section is to argue for the following principle.

> **Knowledge Allows Exclusion (KAE)**
> If a chooser knows that a possibility does not obtain, then it is permissible to use a decision table where that possibility is excluded, i.e., is incompatible with the possibilities in each of the columns.

Knowledge Allows Exclusion is Jessica Brown's principle K-Suff applied to practical decision making using tables. That's a fairly central case for K-Suff, so if KAE is true, then it seems plausible that K-Suff will be true too. I'll come back to the more general case for K-Suff in later sections, though; here the focus is KAE. I'm going to build up to KAE in stages; first I'm going to talk about ice cream.

The contemporary theory of duopoly starts with Harold Hotelling's paper "Stability in Competition" (1929). Hotelling describes how a duopoly that does not maximise consumer welfare can be stable if the two parties have the ability to differentiate their product along one dimension. Surprisingly, the equilibrium is that they do not in fact take advantage of this ability, and instead provide the very same product. Hotelling's observation is that if both parties could differentiate, neither party has the incentive they would normally have to reduce prices to the point where consumer surplus is maximised. Hotelling is interested in possible equilibria, and he doesn't focus on how the parties might calculate the equilibria. (The impression one gets from the paper is that it will involve a good chunk of trial-and-error.) Subsequent work revealed that it turns

---

5   Back in Section 2.7 I said I was staying neutral on that question, and I'm not changing that position here.

out that in some duopoly situations, not much is needed to get to the equilibrium; just iterated deletion of dominated strategies.

Here is the standard way Hotelling's model is introduced in textbooks.[6] Imagine that two ice cream trucks have to choose (simultaneously) where they will be located on a beach. The beach has seven locations, numbered 1 to 5. The distance between location m and location n is $|m - n|$. Assume for simplicity that the price of ice cream is fixed, the trucks just compete on location. There are two beach-goers at each of locations 1 to 5, so 10 in total. Each beach-goer will buy an ice cream from the nearest truck. If two trucks are equidistant from a location, the two people there will head off in either direction, one buying from each truck. Question: Where should the two trucks go, assuming that it is common knowledge that each truck owner is rational, and simply wants to maximise their own sales?

This puzzle can be solved using just the idea that strictly dominated strategies can be iteratively deleted. Table 4.2 shows how many sales each truck will make for each choice of location. The choice of the first truck determines which row of the table we're in, the choice of the second truck determines which column of the table we're in, and the resulting cell lists first the sales of the first truck, then the sales of the second truck. (So we'll call the first truck Row, and the second truck Column.)

Table 4.2 Payouts in the Hotelling game.

	1	2	3	4	5
1	5,5	2,8	3,7	4,6	5,5
2	8,2	5,5	4,6	5,5	6,4
3	7,3	6,4	5,5	6,4	7,3
4	6,4	5,5	4,6	5,5	8,2
5	5,5	4,6	3,7	2,8	5,5

---

[6] This particular example isn't in Hotelling, but it is in so many textbooks that I haven't been able to find out where it was first introduced. It differs from his examples in that the parties do not have the capacity to compete on price.

Assume that it is common knowledge, in the sense of David Lewis (1969), that Table 4.2 is the payout table, and that each player will not make choices that are strictly dominated. That is, for each n, the proposition we get by having n iterations of *each player knows* in front of *this is the game table, and each player is rational*, is true. Then the theorist, and each player, can reason as follows.

Row's option 1 is strictly dominated by option 2; option 2 gets 1 more sale in three possible states, and 3 more sales in the other two, so it should be excluded. The same goes for option 5, which is strictly dominated by option 4. Since the game is symmetric, the same goes for Column's options 1 and 5. By the common knowledge assumption, this means we can delete those rows, and columns, from the table. The result is Table 4.3.

Table 4.3 The Hotelling game after one iteration.

	2	3	4
2	5,5	4,6	5,5
3	6,4	5,5	6,4
4	5,5	4,6	5,5

For both players, option 3 dominates the other two options, so it will be chosen. Moreover, the reasoning here generalises. If there are seven options to start with, we need to do two rounds of deleting dominated options to get the players to the middle of the beach. If there are nine options to start with, we need to do three rounds of deletion. In general, if there are $2k+1$ options, we get the players to the middle of the beach after k rounds of deletion. Since common knowledge licences all these iterations, the players will always end up in the middle of the beach if there are an odd number of options.

At this point you might be worried for two reasons. Practically, this seems like it proves too much. Contra the conclusion of Hotelling's paper, it's not true that shoes, churches, and cider mills are as homogenous as this argument would suggest. Theoretically, there are plenty of reasons to be worried about common knowledge as Lewis understood it. Harvey Lederman (2018) shows that assuming common knowledge, in Lewis's sense, of dominance avoidance leads to paradoxes. Let's see whether we can get by with less.

Assume that it is not common knowledge, but merely mutual knowledge that the payout table is as in Table 4.2, and the players do not take dominated options. That is, each player knows both those things. That is all we'll assume. Since knowledge is factive, we can still rule out the extreme options, i.e., 1 and 5. Given that each player knows the other will not take dominated options, each player knows that it is only options 2 through 4 that are relevant. So given just the mutual knowledge assumption, we can show that from each player's perspective, they are playing the game depicted in Table 4.3. In that game, option 3 is strictly dominant. So this assumption is enough to get us back to the middle of the beach. Note, however, that this reasoning does not generalise. Given merely mutual knowledge of non-dominance, we can show that neither player will take options 1 or 2, or the second-last or last options, but we can't show any more than that. So in the seven-option game, we can only show that they will both end up somewhere between options 3 and 5. In the games with much larger numbers of options, we can't show much at all. That seems both empirically and theoretically more plausible.

The argument of the last paragraph is meant to serve two distinct, but related, philosophical purposes.[7] First, it is meant to show that we theorists can deduce what the players will in fact do, given their evidence, and the assumptions about rationality. Second, it is meant to show that it would be rational for the players themselves to get to that conclusion via just that reasoning. It is important, in general, to distinguish between what is entailed by some assumptions, and what can be reasonably inferred from those assumptions (Harman, 1986). In this case, though, I want to claim that the reasoning I've set out in that paragraph plays both roles. As theorists, we can tell that the players will not play either the extreme, or the next to extreme, option, and no more. The players themselves will not go to any of those 4 spots, given our assumptions, but we can't know more about their actions without more knowledge of their mental states.

---

7   I'm indebted here to conversations with Eric Swanson.

But wait a minute! Without KAE, the last two paragraphs consist of one fallacious step after another. The player knows that the other player will not play an extreme option. Also, they know that if the extreme options are excluded, option 2 is strictly dominated. Without KAE, it doesn't follow that they can simply delete the extreme options. To delete an option just is to exclude it from the table. Without KAE, the fact that the player knows an option doesn't obtain isn't a sufficient reason to make this deletion. Since it is, in practice, a sufficient reason, it follows that KAE is true. Or, at least, that a restricted version of KAE applied to this case is true. Since the case seems arbitrary, it follows that KAE is true in general.

That's my primary argument for KAE. In general, it is reasonable to do as many rounds of deletion of dominated strategies as we have iterations of mutual knowledge of rationality and the structure of the game table. That is, it is reasonable for the theorist to do exactly as many rounds of deletion as there are iterations of mutual knowledge of rationality among the players. Without KAE, that match up isn't guaranteed, so KAE must be true.

4.3 Other Answers

If KAE is false, what should go in its place? What could be the state which does allow exclusion?

4.3.1 None of the Above

One might object to the presupposition of that question. Maybe exclusion is never allowed. Perhaps every table should partition the possibility space. In any table, the last state should be *None of the above*, so (assuming classical logic) it must always be true that some state in the table obtains.

If one is not completely convinced that classical logic is correct, this move won't seem particularly appealing. I suspect, however, that most readers are completely convinced that classical logic is correct, so I won't investigate that line. Instead, I'll look at two more pressing objections to the idea that decision tables should always have a *None of the above* option.

First, in many cases there is no sensible way to determine the probabilities or utilities that would go in this column. Imagine that I'm making a decision whose consequences are sensitive to which team wins the next Super Bowl. (Perhaps I'm planning a giant Super Bowl party, or I'm setting the odds for season-long bets at a sportsbook.) I work out the probabilities that each of the 32 teams in the National Football League (NFL) will win this year, and what the consequences of my various options would be in each case. If it's never permissible to exclude states from a decision table, if decision tables always have to be logically complete, I need a 33rd state: that none of these teams win. But how could that be? Maybe the League might be cancelled? Maybe a new team could be introduced mid-season and could win? There is not really a sensible way to even assign probabilities to these options. Worse still, there is no way to assign utilities to actions given that state. The expected return of an action given this state will depend on the probabilities of the different ways it could come about. The error bars on those probabilities are bigger than the probabilities themselves. There is simply no sensible value to put in the cell as the value of the pair *Schedule a large Super Bowl party in Las Vegas* and *None of these 32 teams win the league*. If that state comes about because the Super Bowl is cancelled, it's terrible. If it comes about because a new team gets added, that would create so much interest that it would be great. If I don't have any way of figuring out the relative probabilities of these events, I have no idea what the expected value is. So this approach makes decision tables useless.

Second, one should only be unwilling to exclude states from decision tables if one is so sceptical that one is unwilling to take any contingent proposition to be evidence. After all, taking something to be evidence involves excluding possibilities where it doesn't obtain from one's reasoning. If one doesn't take anything to be evidence, then it is unclear how one's probabilities can update. It can't be by regular conditionalisation. It could be by Jeffrey conditionalization (Hájek 2011: §7.2), if one thought that somehow it was impossible to ever learn that p, but sometimes possible to learn what p's probability is. Personally, I've never had a learning experience that told me the precise probability of some proposition without learning for sure some other proposition. I have never seen reason to think anyone else has either.

This is a quite general point about interest-relative epistemology, and one that will keep coming up in different ways throughout the book.

If one wants to do without knowledge, and just use probabilities (or credences), one owes us a story of how those probabilities change. The best stories about how probabilities change all involve some kind of interest-relativity.

4.3.2 Evidence

These considerations suggest a different answer to this exclusion problem; perhaps the decision maker can exclude p iff p is part of their evidence. Call this view EAE, for Evidence Allows Exclusion.

It isn't obvious that this is an alternative to KAE. If evidence and knowledge are co-extensive, as Timothy Williamson (2000) argued, it will not be. Since I'm going to argue in Chapter 9 that Williamson is wrong about this, I'm committed to EAE and KAE being distinct. So I need an argument against EAE.

My argument will be by cases. That p is part of one's evidence either entails that one knows p or does not. Either way, EAE doesn't pose a problem for my overall argument.

If it does, then whether EAE or KAE is true won't matter for the overall argument. I'm going to argue that some propositions that are known in typical situations might not be properly excluded if one's interests change. That will imply interest-relativity given KAE, but it will also imply interest-relativity given EAE plus the thesis that evidence entails knowledge.

If evidence doesn't entail knowledge, then EAE is implausible. If evidence isn't strong enough to let the decision maker know that propositions inconsistent with it are false, it surely isn't strong enough to let the decision maker know they can ignore propositions inconsistent with it.

The view I'll defend in Chapter 9 is that evidence does entail knowledge. There is a really simple argument for this view. One way to know that p is by properly deducing p from one's evidence. The deduction p, *therefore* p can be properly carried out. So one can know anything in one's evidence. I'm not relying on this argument here, and instead on the point that if evidence doesn't suffice for knowledge, it surely doesn't suffice for exclusion.

The same considerations show that CAE, the view that Certainty Allows Exclusion, doesn't threaten the larger argument for interest-relativity.

Either certainty entails knowledge or it doesn't. If it does, then CAE can be used in place of KAE below to derive interest-relativity. If it does not, and this might happen if certainty just is subjective certainty, then it is implausible that it suffices for proper exclusion.

4.3.3 Sufficiently High Probability

Perhaps one can exclude those propositions whose falsity is sufficiently high that treating them as definitely false doesn't make a difference to the decision one makes. Call this view PAE, for sufficiently high Probability Allows Exclusion.

The first thing to note is that if this is to be plausible, the notion of sufficiency here must be interest-relative. It's often fine to ignore propositions that have a 1 in 500 chance of being true. When planning what to do on a fine sunny day with a clear weather forecast, I simply ignore the chance that there will be a passing shower, even though that still has a 1 in 500 chance. On the other hand, it's absurd to ignore 1 in 500 chances when deciding what insurance to buy. About 1 house in 500 has a fire in a given year; that's not a conclusive reason to skip fire insurance for the year.

Second, as stated, this view has the odd consequence that decision makers can ignore situations that actually obtain. This doesn't seem very plausible. At least, it would be very odd to have a textbook representation of a decision problem where the actual world wasn't in one of the columns. So probably the best way to interpret PAE is as saying that falsehoods can be excluded iff they have sufficiently high probability.

Third, once one does that, PAE starts to look suspiciously like a form of KAE. In particular, it looks like the view I'll call IRT-CP in Chapter 6. That means (a) that it isn't obviously an alternative to KAE, and (b) the objections to IRT-CP are also objections to it. Since I'll go over those objections in detail in Section 8.2 and Section 8.3, I won't double them up here, but assume that they work against PAE.

4.3.4 Wrapping Up

I've argued that the states we can exclude from a decision table are the states that the agent knows not to obtain. The argument is largely by elimination. One might object that I haven't excluded *all* alternatives.

We could keep going asking whether one can exclude all and only those things that are justifiably believed to be false, or which are known to be known, or any number of other alternatives.

At this point, it is natural to object that some alternatives are too complicated to warrant much confidence. What we can properly take for granted in decision making is a very important fact about our doxastic states. If one is sympathetic to a broadly functionalist picture of mind, it might be the most important fact. If so, it isn't surprising that the most common form of appraisal of doxastic states, that they are knowledge, is the norm for appropriate exclusion. It would be very surprising if something considerably more complicated was the correct norm instead.

That's hardly a conclusive argument, but it seems like a good enough one to leave off the survey here, and return to the main narrative of asking what follows if Knowledge Allows Exclusion.

4.4 From KAE to Interest-Relativity

If KAE is true then there is a simple argument that Anisa loses knowledge when playing the Red-Blue game. Table 4.4 would be a bad table for Anisa to use when deciding what to do.

Table 4.4 What the Red-Blue game looks like if Anisa assumes that the Battle of Agincourt was in 1415.

	2+2=4	2+2 ≠ 4
Red-True	$50	0
Red-False	0	$50
Blue-True	$50	$50
Blue-False	0	0

If she used that table, then it would look like Blue-True is the weakly dominant option. That would mean that Blue-True is at least a rational choice, and perhaps the rational choice. Since Blue-True is not a rational choice, this table must be wrong. If Anisa knows that the Battle of Agincourt was in 1415, and knowledge structures decision tables, then everything on this table is correct. So Anisa does not know that the Battle of Agincourt was in 1415. Since she does know this when not playing the game, her knowledge is interest-relative.

4.5 Theoretical Knowledge

Knowledge structures proper practical deliberation. Because what can be taken as a structural assumption varies across different instances of practical reasoning, knowledge is sensitive to the interests of the inquirer. But this isn't the only way in which knowledge is sensitive to interests. It is also sensitive to which purely theoretical questions the inquirer is taking an interest in.

I've already mentioned one way in which this has to be true. One kind of theoretical question is *What should I do in this kind of situation?* If actually being in that kind of situation and having to decide what to do affects what one knows, then thinking abstractly about it should affect what one knows as well.

This kind of comparison, between practical deliberation about what to do and theoretical deliberation about what one should do in just that situation, suggests a few things. It suggests that if practical interests affect knowledge, then so do theoretical interests. It also suggests that they should do so in more or less the same way. So it would be good to have a story that assigns to knowledge the role of structuring theoretical deliberation, in just the way that it structures practical deliberation. That's more or less the story I'm going to tell, though there are some complications along the way.

The story I like starts with an observation by Pamela Hieronymi.

> A reason, I would insist, is an item in (actual or possible) reasoning. Reasoning is (actual or possible) thought directed at some question or conclusion. Thus, reasons must relate, in the first instance, not to states of mind but to questions or conclusions. (Hieronymi, 2013: 115–116)

So to a first approximation the inquirer knows that p only if they can properly use p as a reason in "thought directed at the question" they are considering. That is, they can use p as a step in this reasoning. This way of putting things connects Hieronymi's view of reasons to the idea present in both John Hawthorne and Jason Stanley (2008) and Jeremy Fantl and Matthew McGrath (2009) that things known are reasons. While I'm going to spend the rest of this section quibbling about whether this is quite right, it's a good first step.

It's enough to get us a fairly strong, but also fairly natural, kind of interest-relativity. In normal circumstances, Anisa knows that the Battle of Agincourt was in 1415. Now imagine not that she's playing the Red-Blue game, but thinking about how to play it. And she wonders what to do if the red sentence says that two plus two is four, and the blue sentence says that the Battle of Agincourt was in 1415. It would be a mistake for her to reason as follows: well, the Battle of Agincourt was in 1415, so playing Blue-True will get me $50, and nothing will get me more than $50, so I should play Blue-True. The mistake is the first step; she just can't take this for granted in this very context.

This is a very obscure kind of question to wonder about, but there are more natural questions that lead to the same kind of result. Imagine that the day after reading the book, but before playing any weird game, Anisa starts wondering how likely it is that the book was correct. History books do make mistakes, and she wants to estimate how likely it is that this was a mistake. Again, it would be an error to reason as follows: well, the Battle of Agincourt was in 1415, and that's what the book says, so the book is certainly correct. Again, the problem is the first step; she just can't take this for granted in this very context.

But it's not as if she can only take things for granted that are certain in that context. If that were true, she couldn't even start an inquiry into how likely it is the book got this wrong. She has to assume certain things are beyond the scope of present inquiry. She should not question that the book says that the battle occurred in 1415, or that there was a Battle of Agincourt, or that it is a widely written about (but also widely mythologised) battle, or that 1415 is before the invention of the moveable type printing press and so records from 1415 might be less reliable, and so on. None of these things are things that she knows with Cartesian certainty. Indeed, some of them are probably all-things-considered less likely than that the Battle of Agincourt was in 1415.[8] So it's not like there is some threshold of likelihood, or of evidential support, and inquiring into the likelihood of this statement implies that one can take for granted all and only things that clear this threshold. Rather, individual inquiries

---

8   When I was editing this book I realised I wasn't sure when the moveable type printing press was invented, and had to double check it was after 1415.

have their own logic, their own rules about what can and can't be taken for granted.

There is an interesting analogy here with the rules of evidence in criminal trials. Whether some facts can be admitted at a trial depends in part on what the trial is. For example, some jurisdictions allow evidence obtained in a search that illegally violated X's rights to be used in a trial of Y, though it could not be used when X was on trial. The picture I have of knowledge is similar; what one knows is what one can use in inquiry, and what one can use changes depending on the question under discussion. I'll have much more to say about this in Chapter 5.

So the starting point is that what's known is what can be used. What I'm going to ultimately defend is a much more restricted thesis. Using what is known provides immunity from a particular criticism: that your starting point might not be true. I'm going to say a little bit about why this immunity claim is correct, and then say much more about why I prefer this way of talking about the role of knowledge in reasoning.

When one says that it is good to use what one knows in reasoning, there are two natural ways to interpret this. One is that using what one knows is all-things-considered good unless there is some independent reason to the contrary. The other is to say that there is a kind of badness in reasoning one avoids if one uses what one knows. I'm going to be defending the second kind of reading. That's what I mean by saying that using what one knows provides immunity from a certain kind of criticism. The alternative requires that we can specify all the ways in which one might go wrong while using what one knows—those are the "independent reasons to the contrary". I don't think that's something we're now in a position to do.

The justification for the immunity claim is quite straightforward. It's incoherent to say of someone that they know that p, but they shouldn't have used p in reasoning because it might be false. That's Moore-paradoxical, if not outright contradictory. If it is incoherent to say *A, and X shouldn't have done B because C*, then *A* is a good reply to the criticism of *X* that she shouldn't have done *B* because *C*. So knowing that p is a good reply to the criticism that one shouldn't have used p in reasoning because it might be false.

Can we say something stronger? Can we say that knowing that p immunises the reasoner from all criticisms? Surely not; using irrelevant facts in inquiry is a legitimate criticism, even if the facts are known

(Ichikawa, 2012). Is there a true claim that's a bit more qualified, but still stronger than the immunity claim that I make?

One possibility would be to say that reasoning that starts with what is known is immune from all criticisms except those on a specified list. What might be on the list? I've already mentioned one thing—using irrelevant facts. Another thing might be that the reasoning itself is irrelevant to what one should be doing. If there is a drowning child in front of me, and I start idly musing about what the smallest prime greater than a million might be, I can be criticised for that reasoning. That criticism can be sustained even if my mathematical reasoning is impeccable, and I get the correct answer.[9]

Some facts are irrelevant to an inquiry. Others are relevant, but not part of the best path to resolving the inquiry. This can be grounds for criticism as well. It's in some cases a mild criticism. If one follows an obvious path to solving a problem, when there is an alternative quicker way to solving the problem using a clever trick, it isn't much of a complaint to say that the reasoning wasn't maximally efficient. There are many quicker proofs of a lot of things Euclid proved, but this hardly detracts from the greatness of Euclid's work. And, interestingly for what is to follow, using an inefficient means of inquiry does not prevent the inquiry ending in knowledge. After all, Euclid knew a lot of geometry, even though he rarely had maximally efficient proofs. There is a general lesson here—the fact that an inquirer was imperfect isn't in itself a reason to deny that they end up with knowledge.

Inefficiency in inquiry is often not a big deal; other mistakes in inquiry are more serious. Sometimes the premises do not support the conclusion. It's notoriously hard to say what is meant by support here. It seems to have some rough relationship to logical entailment, but it's hard to say more than that. Sometimes premises support a conclusion they do not entail—that's what happens in all inductive inquiry. Sometimes premises do not support a conclusion they do entail. If I reason, "3 is the first odd prime greater than 0, so 1,000,003 is the first odd prime greater than 1,000,000, and there are no even primes greater than 2, so 1,000,003 is the first prime greater than 1,000,000", I reason badly. I can't know on that basis that 1,000,003 is the first prime greater than 1,000,000. But the

---

9   As it turns out, that's 1,000,003.

premise, that 3 is the first odd prime greater than 0, entails the next step. It just fails to support it, in the relevant sense.

Maybe now we might suspect we've got enough criticisms on the table. Is there anything wrong about an inquiry where the following criteria are met?

- It is worthwhile to conduct the inquiry.
- It is sensible, and efficient enough, to choose these particular starting points.
- The starting points are all things that are known to be true.
- Every step after the starting point is supported by the steps immediately preceding it.

An inquiry with these features looks pretty good. If there is really nothing to complain about in such an inquiry, then the following is true. An inquirer who starts an inquiry with what they know is immune from all criticisms except perhaps (a) that they shouldn't be conducting this inquiry at all, (b) that their starting points are irrelevant (or perhaps inefficient) for reaching their conclusion, or (c) that their later steps are not supported by their earlier steps. While those are fairly non-trivial exception clauses, that's still a fairly strong claim about the role of knowledge in inquiry.

Unfortunately, there are puzzle cases that suggest that even an inquiry with those four features may be flawed. I'll just mention two such cases here. The point of these cases is that they suggest inquiry can be flawed in ever so many ways, and we should not be confident about putting together a complete list of the ways inquiry can go wrong.

First, there might be moral constraints on inquiry. Consider the following example, drawn from Rima Basu and Mark Schroeder (2019). Casey is at a fancy fundraising party, where the guests and the wait staff are all wearing suits. The person next to Casey is Black, and Casey reasons as follows.

1. Almost all the Black people here are on the wait staff.
2. The person next to me is Black.
3. So, the person next to me is on the wait staff.

That's not valid, but one might argue that it's a rational inductive inference. Alternatively, we can consider the case where Casey explicitly concludes that the person next to them is probably Black. We can imagine that all of the following things are true. It is reasonable for Casey to think about whether the person in question is on the wait staff; it matters for the reasonable practical purpose of getting a drink. The wait staff are not wearing distinctive clothes, so seeing what observational characteristics correlate with being on the wait staff is a reasonable approach to that inquiry. Casey knows that the premises of the inquiry are true, and the premises support the conclusion of the inquiry.

And yet, it seems something goes badly wrong if Casey reasons this way. If the conclusion is false, it doesn't seem like mere inductive bad luck. Arguably, there is a moral prohibition on reasoning in this way. Furthermore, this moral prohibition plausibly prevents Casey's reasoning from providing knowledge.

Now one might well question just about every step of the last two paragraphs. It's one thing to regret the lack of signals from attire as to who is on the wait staff; it's another thing to jump to using skin colour as the best proxy. Given how many other things Casey can see about this person (such as how they are moving, what they are carrying, how they are engaging with others), it isn't clear that the premises support the conclusion, even inductively.

Even if all those things are not true, it might be that Casey can get knowledge this way; the inquiry might be morally wrong without having any epistemic flaws that prevent it generating knowledge. Other examples of morally problematic inquiry suggest that there is no simple connection between an inquiry being morally bad, and it not generating knowledge. Many inquiries are morally problematic because they involve, or even constitute, privacy violations. But that doesn't mean the privacy violator doesn't come to know things about their victim. Indeed, part of the wrongness of the privacy violation is that they do come to know things about their victim.

Still, Casey can be criticised for inquiring in this way, even if the criticism does not imply that the inquiry produced no knowledge. That suggests that there are possible criticisms of inquiries that satisfy the four bullet points listed earlier.

Another source of trouble comes from holistic constraints on reasoning. What I have in mind here are rules that allow for a natural resolution of the puzzles of "transmission failure" that Crispin Wright (2002) discusses. Start with one of Wright's examples. Ada is walking by a park with a football pitch. It clearly isn't just a practice; the players are in uniforms and occupying familiar positions on the pitch, there is a referee and a crowd, and so on. One of the players kicks the ball into the net, the referee points to the centre of the ground, and half the players and crowd celebrate. After this happens, Ada reasons as follows.

1. The ball was kicked into the net, and no foul or violation was called.
2. So, a goal was scored.
3. So, a football match is being played, as opposed to, e.g., an ersatz match for the purposes of filming a movie.

As Wright points out, there is something wrong with the step from 2 to 3 here. As he also points out, it isn't trivial to say just what it is that's wrong. After all, 2 entails 3, and Ada knows that 2 entails 3. But it seems wrong to make just this *inference*.

Here's one natural suggestion about what's wrong.[10] It's too simple to be the full story, but it's a start. The transition Ada makes from 1 to 2 presupposes 3, and 1 is her only evidence for 2. When those two conditions are met, it is wrong to infer from 2 to 3. More generally, there is something wrong with inferring a conclusion from an intermediate step in reasoning if that conclusion must be presupposed in order to even reach that intermediate step.

This is too rough as it stands to be a full theory of what is going on in cases like Ada's, but the details aren't important at this point. What is important is that there might be some kind of holistic constraint on reasoning. In some sense, Ada goes wrong in taking 2 for granted when she infers 3. This doesn't intuitively undermine her claim to know both 2 and 3.

One important commonality between the last two cases, the moral encroachment and the transmission failure cases, is that the reasoning is not subject to the following kind of criticism. The speaker can't be criticised for taking as a premise something that might be false. Maybe there is something wrong with inferring something is probably true of an individual because it is true of most people in the group of which

---

10 This is far from an original suggestion. See Weisberg (2010) for discussion of it, and of related proposals, and for more discussion of the literature on Wright's examples.

the individual is part. But this restriction applies to the inference, not to the premises. We wouldn't say to the person who made this inference, "You shouldn't reason like that; it might not be true that most people in the group have this feature." If we did say that, they would have an easy reply. If Ada does do the problematic reasoning, it would be wrong to reply to her "You shouldn't reason like this; it might not have been a goal." She could simply, and correctly, say that it quite clearly was a goal.

This is the key to the correct rule linking knowledge and reasoning. If the inquirer uses as a step in reasoning something that she knows to be true, then she is immune to a certain kind of criticism. She is immune to the criticism that the premise she used might not be true.

I started this section by saying that such a reasoner is immune to all criticism, before trying to work out exceptions to that principle. So an exception needed to be included to allow that the reasoner might be criticised for using an irrelevant reason. The hope was that eventually a full list of such exceptions could be found. This project turned out to be wildly optimistic. I don't know that we need to include further exceptions to handle the moral encroachment or transmission failure cases. But I also don't know that we don't need to include extra exceptions. And I have no idea, and no idea how to find out, whether we need yet more exceptions.

Rather than say knowledge provides immunity to criticism except in these cases, and then try to fill out the list of cases, it's better to say that knowledge provides a particular kind of immunity. If the reasoner knows that the premise they use is true, they can't be criticised on the grounds that it might be false. This isn't a trivial claim. There were several examples involving Anisa where she could be criticised for using a premise that might be false. All of those seemed like legitimate criticisms even though the premise was one she knew before starting the inquiry. That criticism does not seem appropriate in the moral encroachment case, or the transmission failure case, or other cases like them that may be discovered.

I am assuming here that there is no trivial connection between *It might be that not-p*, and *The inquirer does not know that p*. If these claims express the same thing, at least in the particular context of evaluating the inquirer, then it would be trivial to say that knowledge provides immunity to criticism on the grounds that one's premises might not be true. The recent literature on epistemic modals, however, does not inspire confidence that any such trivial connection exists.[11] So this immunity seems like a non-trivial claim.

So the key principle I'll be working with is that one cannot be criticised for using what one knows in an inquiry on the grounds that one is using what might be false. That's a bit of a mouthful, so sometimes I'll simply say that one can rationally take for granted what one knows. I'll have a lot more to say about this principle in the rest of this book, especially in Chapter 9.

I'll spend the rest of this chapter talking about how this principle relates to the idea that knowledge is closed under competent deduction. There are interesting examples that seem to show that the principle leads to several distinct kinds of violations of that principle. I'll argue that this is not right, and for any plausible closure principle, adding the idea that one can take for granted what one knows does not yield a new objection to that principle.

The principle as stated is a little ambiguous, and to defend it I need to resolve that ambiguity. Surprisingly, I need to resolve it by taking the logically stronger disambiguation. Normally if a principle is ambiguous, and might lead to problems, the trick is to insist on the weaker reading. That's not what's about to happen.

When I say that an inquirer can rationally take for granted the things they know, this should be understood collectively. That's to say, I endorse the collective, and not (merely) the individual, version of the immunity to criticism principles stated here.

Take for Granted (Individual)
If an inquirer knows some things, then each of those things are such that they can take that thing for granted in conducting the inquiry.

Take for Granted (Collective)
If an inquirer knows some things, then they can take all of those things for granted in conducting the inquiry.

---

11 See Holliday and Mandelkern (2024) for a survey of how differently the two claims behave in embeddings and inferences, and a radical claim about how to best account for those differences.

I'll come back to the difference between these principles, and why I need to endorse the collective version, in Section 4.6.2. Until then I'll be talking about single pieces of knowledge at a time.

4.6 Knowledge and Closure

Here are two very plausible principles about knowledge, both taken from John Hawthorne (2005).

Single Premise Closure
If one knows p and competently deduces q from p, thereby coming to believe q, while retaining one's knowledge that p, one comes to know that q. (Hawthorne, 2005: 43)

Multiple Premise Closure
If one knows some premises and competently deduces q from those premises, thereby coming to believe q, while retaining one's knowledge of those premises throughout, one comes to know that q. (Hawthorne, 2005: 43)

Hawthorne endorses the first of these, but has reservations about the second for reasons related to the preface paradox. I'm similarly going to endorse the first and have reservations about the second. But my reasons don't have anything to do with the preface paradox. I argued in "Can We Do without Pragmatic Encroachment?" (Weatherson, 2005a) that concerns about the preface paradox are over-rated, and I think those arguments still hold up. But I have a slightly different qualification than Hawthorne does to Multiple Premise Closure, and I will discuss that more in Section 4.6.2.

It is not trivial to prove that my version of IRT satisfies these closure conditions. One reason for this is that I have not stated a sufficient condition for knowledge. All that I have said is that knowledge is incompatible with a certain kind of caution. So in principle I cannot show that if some conditions obtain then someone knows something. What I can show is that introducing new conditions linking knowledge with relevant questions does not introduce new violations of the closure conditions.

4.6.1 Single Premise Closure

But it turns out that even showing this is not completely trivial. Imagine yet another version of the Red-Blue game.[12] I'll call the player for this version of the game Margit, and I'll assume at various points that she acts rationally.

In this game, both of the sentences are claims about history that are well supported without being certain. And both of them are supported in the very same way. It turns out to be a little distracting to use concrete examples in this case, so just call the claims A and B. Imagine that Margit read both of these claims in the same reliable but not infallible history book, and she knows the book is reliable but not infallible, and she aims to maximise her expected returns. Then all four of the following things are true about the game.

1. Unconditionally, Margit is indifferent between playing Red-True and playing Blue-True.

2. Conditional on A, Margit prefers Red-True to Blue-True, because Red-True will certainly return $50 while Blue-True is not completely certain to win the money.

3. Conditional on B, Margit prefers Blue-True to Red-True, because Blue-True will certainly return $50 while Red-True is not completely certain to win the money.

4. Conditional on $A \wedge B$, Margit is back to being indifferent between playing Red-True and playing Blue-True.

From 1, 2, and 3, it follows in my version of IRT that Margit does not know either A or B. After all, conditionalising on either one of them changes her answer to a relevant question. The question being, *Which option maximises my expected returns?*, where this is understood as a mention-all question.

Now see what happens at point 4. Conditionalising on $A \wedge B$ does not change the answer to that question. So, assuming there is no other reason that Margit does not know $A \wedge B$, arguably she does know $A \wedge B$. That would be absurd; how could she know a conjunction without knowing either conjunct?

---

12 This game will resemble the examples that Zweber (2016) and Anderson and Hawthorne (2019b) use to raise doubts about whether pragmatic theories like mine really do endorse Single Premise Closure.

Here is how I used to answer this question. Define a technical notion of interest. Say that a person is interested in a conditional question *If p, Q?* if they are interested, in the ordinary sense, in both the true-false question *p?* and they are interested in the question *Q?*. If conditionalising on a proposition changes (or should change) their answer to any question in which they are interested in this technical sense, then they don't know that proposition. This solves the problem because conditionalising on $A \wedge B$ does change their answer to the question *If A, which option maximises expected returns?* on its mention-some reading. So even though 4 is correct, this does pose a problem for closure.

This was not a great solution for two reasons. One is that it seems extremely artificial to say that someone is interested in these conditional questions that they have never even formulated. Another is that it is hard to motivate why we should care that conditionalisation changes (or should change) one's answers to these artificial questions.

There was something right about the answer I used to give. It is that we should not just look at whether conditionalisation changes the answers a person gives to questions they are interested in. We should also look at whether it changes things 'under the hood'; whether it changes how they get to that answer. The idea of my old theory was that looking at these artificial questions was a way to indirectly look under the hood. What I got wrong was trying to find some other question whose answer changed when and only when what was under the hood changed. I should have just looked under the hood.

So let's look again at the two questions that are relevant. This time, don't think about what answer Margit gives, but about how she gets to that answer.

1. Which option maximises expected returns?
2. If $A \wedge B$, which option maximises expected returns?

In the most natural interpretation of what Margit does, there will be a step in her answer to 5 that has no parallel in her answer to 6.

She will note, and rely on, the fact that she has equally good evidence for A as for B. That is why each option is equally good by her lights. The equality of evidence really matters. If she had read that A in three books, but only one of those books added that B, then the two options would not have the same expected returns. She should check that nothing like this is going on; that the evidence really is equally balanced.

But nothing like this happens in answering 6. In that case, $A \wedge B$ is stipulated to be given. So there is no question about how good the evidence for either is. When answering a question about what to do if a condition obtains, we don't ask how good the evidence for the condition is. We just assume that it holds. So in answering 6, there is no step that acknowledges the equality of the evidence for both A and B.

So in fact Margit does not answer the two questions the same way. She ends up with the same conclusion, but she gets there by a different means. And that is enough, I say, to make it a different answer. If she knew $A \wedge B$ she could follow exactly the same steps in answering 5 and 6, but she cannot.

What should we say if she does follow the same steps? If this is irrational, nothing changes, since what matters for knowledge is which questions should be answered the same way, not which questions are answered the same way. (It does matter for belief, but that is not the current topic.) So I will assume that it is possible for Margit to rationally answer both questions the same way. (I will have much more to say about why this is a coherent assumption in Chapter 6.)

The way she should answer 6 is to take $A \wedge B$ as given. Hence she will take either option, Red-True or Blue-True, as being equivalent to just taking $50, which she knows is the best she can do in the game. So in answering question 6, she will take it as given that both of these options are maximally good.

By hypothesis, she is answering question 5 and question 6 the same way. So she will take it to be part of the setup of question 5 that both options return a sure $50. After all, that is part of the setup of question 6. But if she takes that as given, then conditionalising on either A or B does not change her expected returns. So now claims 2 and 3 are wrong; conditionalising on either conjunct won't make a difference because she treats each conjunct as given.

That is the totally general case. Assume that someone has competently deduced Y from X, and they know X. So they are entitled to answer the questions Q? and *If X, Q?* by the same method. Since the method for the latter takes X as given, so can the method for the former. So they can answer Q? taking X as given. What one can appropriately take as given is closed under competent deduction. (Why? Because in the answer to Q? that starts with X, you can just go on to derive Y, and then see that it is also a way to answer *If Y, Q?*.) So they can answer Q? taking Y as given. So they can answer Q? in the same way they answer *If Y, Q?*.

So assuming there is no other reason to deny Single Premise Closure, adding a clause about how one may answer questions does not give us a new reason to deny it.

4.6.2 Multiple Premise Closure

That shows that IRT satisfies Single Premise Closure. The argument that it satisfies Multiple Premise Closure starts with the observation that Multiple Premise Closure more or less follows from Single Premise Closure plus a principle I'll call And-Introduction Closure.

> **And-Introduction Closure**
> If one knows some propositions, and one competently infers their conjunction from those propositions, while retaining one's knowledge of all those propositions, then one knows the conjunction.

Start with the standard assumption that a conclusion is entailed by some premises iff it is entailed by their conjunction. (It would take us way too far afield to investigate what happens if we dropped that assumption.) Given that assumption, in principle the only inferential rule one needs with multiple premises is And-Introduction. In practice, people do not generally reason via conjunctions in this way. Someone who knows $A \vee B$, and who knows $\neg A$, does not first infer $(A \vee B) \wedge \neg A$, and then infer B from that. They just infer B. It's a harmless enough idealisation, however, to model them as first inferring the conjunction whenever they use multiple premises. So I will assume that if I can show that IRT does not cause problems for And-Introduction Closure, and I've already argued that it does not cause problems for Single Premise Closure, then it does not cause problems for Multiple Premise Closure.

Here is the quick argument that IRT does not cause problems for And-Introduction Closure.

1. The key feature of IRT, the one that potentially causes problems for And-Introduction closure, is that one knows

that *p* only if one can take *p* for granted in one's current inquiry.
2. If, in the course of an inquiry, one knows some premises, then one can take them for granted in that inquiry.
3. If one can take some premises for granted in an inquiry, then one can take their conjunction for granted in that inquiry.
4. So, there is no IRT-based reason that And-Introduction Closure fails.

Premise 1 is just a restatement of my version of IRT, and premise 3 should be uncontroversial. If one can take some premises for granted, then one (rationally) is ruling out possibilities where they are false. To rule out possibilities where they are false just is to take their conjunction for granted. So those premises should be fairly uncontroversial. What is controversial is that the argument is sound, and, in particular, that premise 2 is correct.

The conclusion is not that Multiple Premise Closure holds. Maybe you think it fails for some independent reason, distinct from IRT. I don't think the other reasons that have been offered in the literature are compelling, but I am not building the failure of these reasons into IRT. So the main assumption behind the argument is that if adding the 'take for granted' clause to our theory of knowledge does not lead to closure violations, then nothing else in the theory does. The argument for that is basically that there isn't much more to the theory. So I think the argument is sound.

Still, it might look like the argument must be wrong. After all, it is easy to cook up cases where it looks like IRT leads to a closure failure. Here is one such example. It is another version of the Red-Blue game. I'll call the player in this version Morten. In this version, the red sentence is, once again, *Two plus two equals four*. This time the blue sentence is a conjunction *A and B*, where both *A* and *B* express historical facts that Morten has excellent, but not perfect, evidence for.[13] Now the following four claims all seem true.

---

13 If you want to make this more concrete, pick a random history book off the shelf and choose two claims that are both reasonably specific—so there could easily be a mistake about the details—and not independently warranted.

1. Unconditionally, the only rational play is Red-True.
2. Conditional on A, the only rational play is Red-True. Even given A, playing Blue-True requires betting that B is true, and that's a pointless risk to run when playing Red-True only requires that two and two make four.
3. Conditional on B, the only rational play is Red-True. Even given B, playing Blue-True requires betting that A is true, and that's a pointless risk to run when playing Red-True only requires that two and two make four.
4. Conditional on $A \wedge B$, Blue-True is rationally permissible, and arguably rationally mandatory, since it weakly dominates Red-True.

So conditionalising on either one of A or B doesn't change anything, but conditionalising on $A \wedge B$ does change how Morten answers a question. So it looks like in this case Morten might know A, know B, and for all I've said be fully aware that these two things entail $A \wedge B$, but not know $A \wedge B$. So what's happened? How is this not a counterexample to premise 2?

The key thing to note is that when Morten is choosing what to do, the following things are all true about him.

- He can take A for granted. That is, he is rationally permitted to take A for granted in resolving his inquiry about what to do.
- Similarly, he can take B for granted.
- But he cannot both take A for granted and take B for granted. If both those things are taken for granted, then he can rationally infer that Blue-True will have a maximal payout, and hence that it is a rational play. And he cannot infer that.

It is cases like this one that required the clarification that I made at the end of Section 4.5. Morten here cannot take both of A and B for granted. So he doesn't know both those things. So this is not a case where he knows A, knows B, and doesn't know $A \wedge B$. Since he cannot take both A and B for granted, he does not know both of those things.

The picture I'm presenting here is similar to the picture Thomas Kroedel (2012) offers as a solution to the lottery paradox.[14] He argues that we can solve the lottery paradox if we take justification to be a kind of permissibility, not a kind of obligation. And just as we can have individual permissions that don't combine into a collective permission, we can have individually justified beliefs that are such that we can't justifiably believe each of them. This isn't exactly how I'd put it. For one thing, I'm talking about knowledge not justification. For another, it's not that knowledge is a species of permission, as much as it behaves like permission in certain contexts, and those are just the contexts where counterexamples to And-Introduction Closure arise. These are minor points of difference though; I'm still basically relying on Kroedel's ideas.

Thinking of things the way Kroedel suggests helps say something positive about what is going on in this game. So far, I've said something negative—Morten does not know both that A and that B. That's enough to show that the case is not a counterexample to And-Introduction Closure. A counterexample would, after all, have to be a case where Morten knows both A and B. But saying what's not the case is not a helpful way to say what is the case. To say something more positive, it helps to think about other cases where permissions do not agglomerate. To that end, I'll talk through one case involving professional norms.

Professor Paresseux is, like most academics, in a situation where professional morality requires he do his fair share, but is fairly open about what tasks he does that will constitute doing his fair share. Right now he has two requests for work, R1 and R2, and while he is not obliged to do both, he is obliged to do at least one. So he may turn down R1, and he may turn down R2, but he may not turn down both. So as not to keep the reader in suspense, let's say up front that he is going to turn down

---

14 Different writers take different things to be *the* lottery paradox. In all cases, they concern what kind of non-probabilistic attitude an ideal agent would take towards the proposition that a particular ticket in a large, fair lottery will lose. It seems unintuitive to say that they will not believe this, since the ticket might win. And this will lead to an inconsistency, since they will believe of every ticket that it will not win, but also believe that a ticket will win. But if you say it is not belief, you seem to either get scepticism, or the view that the ideal agent can believe p, and not believe q, even though they think q is more probable than p. Which of the four problems I just mentioned is most salient to a writer tends to depend on their background commitments, but most people defend views on which at least one of the problems is genuinely problematic.

both. Our question will be, what exactly does Professor Paresseux do that's wrong?

To make this a little more concrete, and a little more complicated, I want to add two features to the case. First, accepting R1 would be better than accepting R2. He is uniquely well placed to do R1, and it would create more work for others if he turns it down. (As, indeed, he will.) But the norms governing Professor Paresseux are not maximising norms, and he does not violate them if he accepts R2 and rejects R1. Second, Professor Paresseux first turns down R1, let's say in the morning, and then later that day, let's say after a hearty lunch, turns down R2. Given that, there are three models we can have for the case, all of which have some plausibility.

The first model says that he was wrong to turn down R1. Here's a little argument for that, using language that seems natural. He should have accepted one of the requests. Since he was well placed to perform R1, it's also true that if he did one of them, it should have been R1. So he should have accepted R1, and turning it down was the mistake. Oddly, it turns out to have been made true that he did the wrong thing in turning down R1 by his latter decision to turn down R2, but that's just an odd feature of the case.

The second model says that this odd feature is intolerably odd. It says he was wrong to turn down R2. Here's a little argument for that. At lunchtime, he hadn't done anything wrong. True, he had turned down R1, but he had moral permission to do that. It was only after lunch that he made it the case that he violated a norm. So the violation must have been after lunch. So the violation was in turning down R2.

A third model says that both of these arguments are inconclusive. What's really true is simply that Professor Paresseux should not have turned down both requests. Which one individually was wrong? That, says the third model, is indeterminate. One of them must be, since he could not permissibly turn down both. But there is no fact of the matter about which it is.

If I had to choose, I would say that the third is the most plausible model. The arguments for the first two models are not terrible—indeed I think both are plausible models—but the arguments are equally compelling, and incompatible. So I suspect neither is entirely right. The third model, which says both of them are partially right—there is something not quite ok about both refusals—seems to better fit the scenario. But what I more strongly think is that each of these models is more plausible than either of the following two.

The fourth model is that there is a strong kind of agglomeration failure. It is determinately true that Professor Paresseux acted permissibly in turning down R1, and it is determinately true that he acted permissibly in turning down R2, but overall he acted impermissibly. It's true that in the abstract Professor Paresseux could have turned down each one. But in the particular context he is in—where these are the options to fulfil his duty to do his share of the work, and he does neither—is not one where he can (determinately) avail himself of both of these permissions.

The fifth model says that since he had to do his share and did not, and both refusals are ways of not doing his share, both of them are impermissible. This seems like overkill. It is much more intuitive that Professor Paresseux has done one wrong thing than that he has done two wrong things.

I hope I haven't traumatised too many readers with tales of people shirking professional responsibilities, because having Professor Paresseux's example on the table helps us lay out the options for what to say about Morten, given a further assumption about how he acts.

Morten plays the version of the Red-Blue game I just described, where the blue sentence is the conjunction of two plausible (and true) claims from a well-regarded history book he just read, and the red sentence is that two plus two is four. Let's assume that Morten looks at the rules, infers via his historical knowledge that playing Blue-True will have a maximal return, and so plays Blue-True. I think that this play is irrational, and if Morten knew the conjunction it would be rational, so Morten does not know the conjunction. But what do we say about Morten's knowledge of each conjunct? It turns out that there are five somewhat natural options that correspond to the five models I offered about Professor Paresseux. I'll simply list them here.

1. Morten knows the conjunct for which he has better evidence, and does not know the conjunct for which he has less good evidence. It was impermissible to take for granted the thing that was less well supported. This parallels the idea that Professor Paresseux did something wrong in turning down the request he was better placed to fulfil.

2. Morten knows the conjunct that he first took for granted, and not the conjunct that he took for granted second. When he first took one of the conjuncts for granted, that was a permissible mental act, but given that he had done it, it was impermissible to take the second for granted. This parallels the idea that whichever request Professor Paresseux turns down second is the impermissible turn-down, because it's then he becomes in violation of his duty.

3. It is indeterminate which conjunct Morten knows. He doesn't know both, because if he did then he could take both for granted, and he cannot take both for granted. Given both conjuncts, Blue-True is a rational play. So he must not know one, but there is no reason to say it is this one rather than that one, so it is indeterminate which he doesn't know. This parallels the indeterminacy solution to Professor Paresseux's puzzle.

4. Morten does know both conjuncts, since knowledge requires permissible taking for granted, and each of his takings for granted are individually permissible. But he doesn't know the conjunction, and so And-Introduction Closure fails.

5. Morten does not know either conjunct.

The fifth model seems like the least plausible. Somewhat unfortunately, it is also the model I defended (or at least committed myself to) in "Can We Do without Pragmatic Encroachment?". There I stated that knowledge requires conditionalising on what is known not to change any answers to interesting questions, and any question taken conditionally on an interesting proposition is itself interesting. So each of the questions *What should I play given the first conjunct is true?* and *What should I play given the second conjunct is true?* are both interesting questions (in this technical sense of 'interesting'). Inquiring into the first question is incompatible with knowing the second conjunct, while inquiring into the second question is incompatible with knowing the first conjunct. This was a fun way out the problem, but it was also overkill. Morten loses one bit of knowledge, not two, so my earlier view must be wrong.

Which of the other four models is correct? I think the fourth, which violates And-Introduction Closure, is the least plausible. That's largely because it violates And-Introduction Closure. But the other three are all plausible, and are all consistent with And-Introduction Closure. (And note that all five are consistent with IRT. IRT itself says very little about this puzzle.) My preferred version of IRT says that typically the third option is correct—usually in cases like this it is indeterminate what is known.

There are mix-and-match options available. Perhaps if Morten's evidence for the first conjunct is (much) stronger than their evidence for the second conjunct, and it was the first one that they took for granted in reasoning, then they (determinately) know the first but not the second conjunct. I don't need to take a stance on whether cases like this ever arise to defend And-Introduction Closure. That's because all I need for any case like this is that one of the first three models be right. That can be true even if it is different models in different cases.

4.7 Summary

Putting all that together, IRT is consistent with Single Premise Closure and with And-Introduction Closure. Assuming that it is a harmless idealisation to treat anyone who uses multiple premises in reasoning as reasoning from the truth of all the conjunction of their premises, it follows that IRT is consistent with Multiple Premise Closure.

But this isn't quite the end of the story. Even if the arguments of the last two sections work, what they show is that there must be some way to explain away any apparent conflict between IRT and closure principles. The arguments do not, on their own, tell us what that explanation will look like, or whether it will have unacceptable consequences. Without such an explanation, we might be sceptical of the arguments of this chapter, and indeed of IRT itself. So I'll come back several times to issues about closure. In Chapter 6, I'll go over what IRT says about cases like Zweber's, and Anderson and Hawthorne's, more thoroughly.

Before I get to that though, it is time to say more about a notion that has done a lot of work so far but which has not been adequately investigated: inquiry.

5. Inquiry

The next three chapters are primarily defensive; they are responding to the three objections to IRT that seem to me most serious. But they aren't just defensive. I'm not just saying why the theory from the chapters to date is immune to these arguments. I'm also developing the theory. That's especially true in this chapter, which is why it is first. So what are these objections?

The first is what I'll call the *objection from double checking*. As Jessica Brown (2008) argued, there are plenty of cases where intuitively a person knows that p, but should check whether p is true. This seems to be a problem for IRT, since it is motivated by the thought that what's known is an appropriate starting point in inquiry. At first glance, it's very weird to have an inquiry into p, when the inquirer is in a position to simply say p, therefore p. I used to think that in these cases the defender of IRT would have to either say that they are not really cases of knowledge, or not really cases of appropriate inquiry. Unfortunately, neither of these options was particularly successful. I now think the objection should be addressed head on. It is possible to properly conduct an inquiry into p, even when one knows that p, and even when knowledge provides appropriate starting points for inquiry. That's because it is often appropriate to deliberately restrict oneself in inquiry, and use fewer resources than are otherwise available. The aim of this chapter is to defend the claims made in the last two sentences, and to show how they provide a response to the objection from double checking.

The second is what I'll call the *objection from close calls*. As Alex Zweber (2016) and, separately, Charity Anderson and John Hawthorne (2019a) showed, some simple versions of IRT say implausible things about cases where a person is choosing between very similar options. What I'm going to argue is that the problem their cases raise is not due to IRT, which is correct, but to the background assumption that choosers should maximise expected utility. My response is going to be that in the cases they describe, choosers should not maximise expected utility. That might sound like an absurdly radical view, since expected utility theory is at the heart of all contemporary decision theory. But expected utility theory has fairly implausible things to say about *close call* cases. A better theory, one that takes account of deliberation costs, is both more plausible, and consistent with IRT. I'll say much more about this in Chapter 6.

The third is what I'll call the *objection from abominable conjunctions*. This is the IRT-equivalent of the blank stare objection to modal realism. Many people find it simply implausible that knowledge could depend on something like interests, which are not relevant to the truth of what is purportedly known. The defender of IRT owes a reply to this widespread feeling. Part of my reply came back in Chapter 1. I think this feeling is a result of being in a very strange place in the history of epistemology, where the focus is on fallibilist, interest-invariant, concepts. But we can do better than that. It is hard to articulate the intuition behind the unhappiness with IRT without lapsing into the Justified True Belief (JTB) theory of knowledge. Most plausible solutions to the problems with the JTB theory end up introducing kinds of interest-relativity for independent reasons. I'll go over these responses in Chapter 7.

So those are the three objections I'm going to spend a lot of time on. There are three other classes of objection I'm not going to spend much time on.

The first class are objections to IRT that assume that knowledge changes when and only when one is in a 'high-stakes' situation. Since I don't assume that, those objections don't raise problems for my version of IRT.

The second class are objections to IRT that assume that some parts of epistemology are interest-invariant, while some are interest-relative. While I used to endorse such a theory, I no longer do. This book defends a global interest-relativism where knowledge, belief, rationality, and evidence are all interest-relative (in different ways). So these objections don't raise problems for my version of IRT either.

The third class are objections to IRT that only apply to versions of IRT that add on an opposition to contextualism or relativism. With this addition, IRT becomes what has been called *interest-relative invariantism*, or IRI. While I've defended that in the past, I'm not going to defend it here. The thesis of this book is that knowledge is interest-relative. If you want to understand the word 'knowledge' in the previous sentence in a contextualist or relativist way, go right ahead. Whatever metasemantic theory you have about the kind of words 'knows' and 'knowledge' are, I will be willing to defend the claim that knowledge is interest-relative.

5.1 Starting and Settling

At the heart of the influential picture of inquiry developed by Jane Friedman (2017, 2019b, 2019a, 2020, 2024b) is the view that humans are capable of a number of distinctive attitudes. To be inquiring into some question, she argues, is to have a *questioning attitude* towards that question. That's to say, she does not identify inquiry with particular actions, or at least with particular bodily movements. An actor might mimic the movements an inquirer makes without actually inquiring; a genuine inquirer might be sitting in an armchair quietly synthesising their evidence. So particular movements are neither sufficient nor necessary for real inquiry. Rather, inquiry is a state of mind, a questioning state of mind.

The contrast to having a questioning attitude is having a settled attitude.[1] Friedman holds that to believe something is to treat the question of whether it is true as being affirmatively settled, and I'm adopting the same position here. This attitude is deeply related to inquiry. Typically things are settled as the result of inquiry. Also typically, one does not inquire into something one has settled. Friedman makes a further claim: if one does inquire into something one has settled, this is a kind of mistake. It is incoherent to have both a questioning and a settled attitude towards the same question. I'm going to disagree with this further claim, while mostly adopting the broad picture she develops.

The main difference between her picture and the picture of inquiry I'm using concerns where beliefs go in inquiry. I think that treating something as settled is most fundamentally about willingness to use it

---

[1] These are contrasts, but they don't exhaust the space. One might not have an attitude to a question. I'd also say that one might not treat a question as settled while not inquiring into it, because one treats the question as unworthy of effort, or impossible to make progress on. As Friedman (2024a) notes, it gets complicated to say something coherent about these cases while allowing for the possibility of inquiry to be reopened.

as the beginning of a new inquiry. The essential feature of belief is that it starts inquiry, not that it ends inquiry. What makes an attitude a belief is not that inquiry into it is settled, it's that it can be used in the process of settling open questions. I used to think that whether one identified beliefs with settled states, or with the inputs to inquiry, was only a difference of emphasis, and a pretty minor one at that. After all, beliefs are typically the outputs of one inquiry and then serve as inputs to another; whether one takes one or other of these roles to be more fundamental seems like a pretty esoteric question. But I've come to think that actually quite a bit turns on it. If you think beliefs are fundamentally the things that inquiry starts with, then there is a little gap in the argument that one should not inquire into what one already believes.

That argument, the one to the conclusion that one should not inquire into what one already believes, seems pretty simple. Assume one believes that p and is inquiring into the question p?. Our theory is that beliefs are appropriate starting points for inquiry, so it looks like this one should end pretty quickly. One can just argue p, therefore p, and close the inquiry. If the inquiry stays open longer than that, one is doing it wrong.

This looks like a pretty strong argument for a conclusion that a number of people have reached via different routes.[2]

> If one knows the answer to some question at some time then one ought not to be investigating that question, or inquiring into it further ... at that time. (Friedman, 2017: 131)

> There is something to be said for the claim that the person who knows they have turned the coffee pot off should not be going back to check. (Hawthorne and Stanley, 2008: 587)

> Any such cases [of believing while inquiring] involve peculiarities (such as irrationality or fragmentation). (McGrath, 2021: 482n37)

So how could that argument fail? It could fail if there are reasons for adopting constraints on an inquiry. If there are reasons to not use all the tools at our disposal, there could be cases where an inquiry into p gets started, and we have reasons not to just say p, therefore p. At the highest possible level of abstraction, this doesn't sound very likely. It seems at

---

2   These quotes were compiled by Elise Woodard (2020).

first like there should be something like a principle of total evidence for inquiry, saying that you can use whatever tools, whatever evidence, you have to hand. Such a principle, however, turns out to be false.

To warm up to this, consider an analogy to legal inquiries. There we are all familiar with the idea that some evidence might be inadmissible in some inquiries. Now the reasons for this are typically not epistemic. It's rather that we think the system as a whole will be more just if some kinds of evidence are excluded from some inquiries. That looks a bit different to the situation where an individual inquirer is just trying to find what's true. But we'll see that the analogy here is not quite as bad as it first looks.

In the rest of this section, I'll go over six kinds of cases where one can sensibly inquire into what one already knows. I don't think any of these examples constitute knock-down proofs of the possibility of rational inquiry into what one knows, and for reasons I'll get to later in the chapter, I don't really need them to. It is helpful to see the range of cases where inquiry into what one knows is useful.

5.1.1 Sensitivity Chasing

Guido Melchior (2019) argues that the point of *checking* is to establish a sensitive belief in the checked proposition. To motivate this, think about the following case. Florian has just weighed out the coffee beans for his morning pot of coffee. Naturally he uses the best scales he has for this purpose; it's important to get the coffee right. He starts wondering whether his scales have recently stopped being reliable. What does he do next? Here's one thing he doesn't do. He doesn't look at the beans on the scale, note that the scale says 24g, note that he knows they are 24g (via that excellent scale), and conclude that the scale is still working. That's no good at all; he has to use some other scale to check this one.

This is like the Problem of Easy Knowledge (Cohen, 2002), but note that it doesn't rely on the scale being a source of basic knowledge. Florian might have lots of independent evidence that the scale is good; it's from a good manufacturer and has been producing plausible results for a while. Still, if he wants to check it, he has to use something else. Here's the part that seems most surprising to me. Add to the story that he has a backup scale, one that he thinks is pretty good but not as good as his best scale. It's fine to use the backup scale to check the main scale, and not fine to use the scale to check itself. The best explanation for this is that checking requires sensitivity. Using the scale to test itself is a method that isn't sensitive to whether the scale is working. Using some other scale, even a less reliable one, to check whether it is working, is at least somewhat sensitive. Checking is, at least in part, a matter of *sensitivity chasing*. One reason it is often good to check what one knows is that sensitivity chasing is often sensible.

Sensitivity chasing is a perfectly acceptable goal in inquiry. One might inquire into p for the purpose of making one's belief in p more sensitive. Now assume, as most epistemologists believe, that one can know p even if one's belief is insensitive in various ways. One can know p even if one would still believe p were p false.[3] If one has insensitive knowledge, it might be worthwhile to inquire into what one knows with the aim of generating sensitive knowledge. Indeed, this seems like a primary aim of what we call *checking*. Inquiring into p by saying p therefore p will not increase one's sensitivity to whether p is true. So it's worthwhile to not allow that move in the inquiry, if the aim is to increase sensitivity.

There are other examples that show the difference between knowing and checking. Slightly modifying an example from Frank Jackson (1987), imagine that someone wants to know what *The Age* said was the result of last night's game. One way to learn what *The Age* said would be to look up the result in *The Guardian*, and use one's background knowledge that they both report the same (correct) result. That's a way to come to know what *The Age* said. But it's not a way to check what *The Age* said. It's not a way to check because had *The Age* said anything different, you wouldn't have known. That's a kind of insensitivity. It's an insensitivity that's consistent with knowledge; one can know what a newspaper says by knowing the truth and that the newspaper reports the truth. This insensitivity is removed by proper checking. So checking aims for sensitivity that goes beyond belief, and beyond knowledge. Given that checking, i.e., chasing this kind of sensitivity, is rational, so is inquiring into what one knows.

---

3   One simple example from Saul Kripke (2011): I know that I do not falsely believe that I was born on the Galapagos Islands. But while this is knowledge, it is not a sensitive belief.

5.1.2 Rules

It's hard to always be perfectly rational. Sometimes it makes sense to not think too hard about things where getting the right answer would be quite literally more trouble than it's worth. I'll have much more to say about this point in Chapter 6, where I explore this insight from Frank Knight in greater depth:

> It is evident that the rational thing to do is to be irrational, where deliberation and estimation cost more than they are worth. (Knight, 1921: 67n1)

Knight is interested in the case where the rational thing to do is not inquire when inquiry would have minimal gains. There is another case that is more relevant here. Sometimes it is worth having a simple rule that says *Always inquire in these situations*, rather than having a meta-inquiry into whether inquiry is worthwhile right now. To make this a little less abstract, it might be worthwhile always checking that the door is locked when one closes it, even if one frequently knows that one has just locked the door. As Hawthorne and Amia Srinivasan (2013) point out, given the non-luminosity of evidence and knowledge, a simple rule like this might do better than any other realistic rule.

Often following rules about when to inquire will be part of one's professional responsibilities. I presented an example like this in chapter 7 of *Normative Externalism* (Weatherson, 2019): an inspector who is sent to do a random check of an establishment he had checked just a few days before. He knows everything is working well; he just checked it! But it's his job to check, and it's good to have random spot checks on top of regular checks, so it's good to run this inquiry. That's true even though the inspector knows how it will end.

5.1.3 Understanding

There is a famous puzzle about moral testimony. Something seems off about a person who simply believes moral principles on the basis of testimony, even from a trusted testifier. It's odd to convert to vegetarianism simply because someone you trust says that's what morality requires. There is also a famous answer to this puzzle, from Alison Hills (2009). (There are other answers too, including ones that deny the puzzle exists.

To avoid going down too many rabbit holes, I'm going to assume for now the answer Hills gives is correct.) Hills says that moral testimony can give us moral knowledge, like any kind of testimony can provide knowledge, but it can't provide understanding. What's weird about the person who becomes a vegetarian on testimonial grounds alone is that they can't explain their actions, since they don't know why they are acting this way.

Beyond moral testimony, there seem to be many everyday cases of knowledge without understanding. One can know that Franz Ferdinand was assassinated in Sarajevo on June 28, 1914, without knowing why that happened. Or, indeed, one can know why one part of that is true, e.g., why it was that *Franz Ferdinand* was assassinated in Sarajevo on June 28, 1914, without knowing why he was assassinated *in Sarajevo*; or why he was assassinated *on June 28, 1914*. Given those facts, it is possible to seek understanding of something that one already knows.

In many cases, but not all, the search for understanding will look like a somewhat different inquiry to the search for knowledge. If one wants to know why Franz Ferdinand was assassinated *in Sarajevo*, one will inquire into the role that city plays in the history of relations between Austria-Hungary and Serbia. That will be a different kind of inquiry to determining whether the assassination really happened. But in the moral case things aren't this clear. Imagine again our person who hears from a trusted source that eating meat is wrong, but doesn't understand why this is so. They should do some moral inquiry. The inquiry will look, as far as I can see, very similar to the inquiry they will do in case they are working out whether eating meat is wrong. That is, it will look just like an inquiry into whether eating meat is wrong.

I think the best way to systematise things here is to take appearances at face value. Even once one is convinced eating meat is in fact wrong, if one doesn't know why it is, one will continue to inquire into the morality of eating meat. This inquiry is justified by the aim of coming to understand the wrongness of eating meat.

5.1.4 Defragmentation

Recall Professor Paresseux from Section 4.6.2. He's told that the visiting speaker this week is his old graduate school colleague Professor

Assidue. But he puts no effort into remembering this fact, and it slips from the front of his mind. The talk is approaching, and Paresseux wonders to himself, who's talking to us this afternoon? So he Googles the department talk schedule, sees that it is Assidue, and then says to himself "Ah, I knew that, I saw the email the other day."

It is very hard to fit the category of information that has 'slipped one's mind' into familiar epistemological categories.[4] I think we should say that Paresseux is correct, and he did indeed know the answer to his inquiry before he started looking. After all, he could have retrieved the information by simply thinking hard about what had happened this week. The best explanation for why that's possible is that he did still know that Professor Assidue would be the speaker. But I also think it made sense for him to conduct an inquiry into this thing that he knew. It's much easier to Google something than to trawl one's memory for the answer, and more reliable too. So this looks like a sensible inquiry for him to have conducted.

Following Andy Egan (2008), I treat this as a case where Paresseux's mind is 'fragmented', in the sense of David Lewis (1982) and Robert Stalnaker (1984). There is a part that contains the information about who the speaker is. That part isn't at the front of his attention, so he doesn't act on it. Still, it is a part of him; he knows that stuff. Still, it is better to conduct an inquiry, i.e., a Google search, than to rely on this knowledge. So it is rational to inquire into something one knows.

5.1.5 Public Reason

One unfortunate position an inquirer can find themselves in is knowing something is true, even understanding why it is true, and being unable to convince anyone of their result. At this point one needs more reasons, but where to find them? Often, the way to find them will be to do what anyone else would do if they were trying to find out if the thing itself were true. Here are two such examples, drawn from rather different parts of philosophy.

Michael Strevens (2020) argues that the effectiveness of science in the last 350 years is partially due to the fact that scientists have adopted

---

4   The point here is related to the discussion in Section 2.7.1 about how sometimes *knows* seems to just mean *possesses the information*.

an "iron rule": *only empirical evidence counts*. There are any number of ways one might come to rationally believe a scientific theory other than evidence. It might follow from broadly metaphysical principles one holds (at least in the early modern sense of metaphysical), it might be more elegant than any other theory, it might promise to unify seemingly disparate phenomena. But if you want to convince the scientific community, which includes both the collective body and the majority of individual scientists, you need data. So you go looking for data, even for theories you know are true on non-empirical grounds. Strevens thinks this is individually irrational, but collectively for the best. It's irrational for any one person to have just one way to come to believe things. But by incentivising the search for data in this way, we've collectively created an institution that has taken the measure of the world in ways previously unimaginable. There is something else valuable about data—it's available, at least in principle, to everyone. So even if you can't recreate my metaphysical intuitions, you can rerun my experiments. The iron rule doesn't just lead to more measurements being taken, it imposes a kind of public reason constraint on science. Only evidence that everyone can accept as evidence, and indeed that they could (at least in theory) create for themselves, counts.

This way of putting the point should remind us of an important strand in contemporary political philosophy, namely that political rules should satisfy a *public reason* constraint. As Jonathan Quong puts it

> Public reason requires that the moral or political rules that regulate our common life be, in some sense, justifiable or acceptable to all those persons over whom the rules purport to have authority. (Quong, 2018)

Now as a matter of fact, we haven't had as much uptake of this meta-rule in politics as in science. But we can imagine a society where there is, in practice, a kind of public reason constraint. If you want your favourite rule to be part of the regulation of society, you have to come up with a justification of it that satisfies this constraint. In such a society, there will be people who have idiosyncratic ideas for rules that would be good rules for the community, ideas that they don't have public justifications for. In practice, the vast majority of these ideas will be bad ones. But some of them will not be. Indeed, a handful will even know that their ideas are good. Still, if this knowledge comes via idiosyncratic sources, they will need to come up with more public reasons if they want to see their rule implemented. As I suggested in the previous subsection, the way to find reasons for a moral claim is generally to inquire into whether that claim is true, or to at least act like that's what one is doing.

5.1.6 Evidence Gathering

In Section 9.6 I'm going to argue that having p as part of one's evidence might license inductive inferences that are not licensed by a smaller evidence set that doesn't include p, even if one knows p on the basis of that smaller set. If that's right, evidence gathering could be epistemically useful even if one already knows the evidence to be gathered.

5.1.7 Possible Responses

If this was a paper dedicated to proving that it is rational to inquire into what one knows, at this stage I'd have to show that a philosopher who denies that is ever rational has no good story to tell about these six cases. That would be a lot to show, since actually there is plenty that such a philosopher could say. They could deny that the inquiries are indeed rational. They could deny that the inquirers in question really do know the thing they are inquiring into, perhaps using IRT to back up that denial. They could deny that these are real inquiries, as opposed to some kind of ersatz inquiry. Or they could deny that this is really an inquiry into the very thing known, as opposed to an inquiry into some related proposition, like what the causal history of that thing was. They wouldn't even have to choose between these four; they could mix-and-match to deal with the putative counterexamples.

At the end of the day, I don't think these responses will cover all the cases. But it would be a massive digression to defend that claim, and it isn't necessary for what's going to happen in the rest of this chapter. All I need is that there are people who very much look like they are conducting rational, genuine inquiries into things they already know. If there is a subtle way of explaining away that appearance, that won't matter for the story that's to come, since such subtleties will end up being good news for my side of the debate about IRT. The worry we're building up to is that IRT has no good explanation of what's happening in cases where someone seems to rationally, genuinely inquire into something they already know. If there are in fact no such cases, that can't be a problem!

One reason for thinking that some of these cases will work is that there is a fairly general recipe for constructing the cases. It's due to Elise Woodard (2020) and (independently) Arienne Falbo (2021). Start with the following two assumptions. First, inquiry is not just about collecting knowledge, but generally about improving one's epistemic position.[5] Second, given fallibilism, one can know p but have a sub-optimal epistemic position. So one can know p, but (rationally) want to improve one's epistemic position with respect to p. If one acts to address that want, one will be inquiring into what one knows, and doing so rationally. Given IRT you should worry about whether every step in the last few sentences really does follow from the ones before it. But I suspect the general picture is right, especially, as Melchior (2019) stresses, in checks aimed at increasing sensitivity.

Looking ahead a little, the primary aim of the rest of the chapter will be to defuse some potential counterexamples to IRT that involve someone rationally inquiring, especially checking, what they know. My response will be disjunctive. Either inquiry solely aims at knowledge, or it does not. If inquiry does solely aim at knowledge, appearances in this case are deceiving, and the inquiry is not in fact rational. If, as I think, inquiry does not solely aim at knowledge, then the cases are not in fact counterexamples to IRT.

5.2 Using Knowledge in Inquiry

Sometimes an inquirer has reasons to deliberately hobble their own inquiry. They have reasons to conduct an inquiry with one hand tied behind their back. Perhaps those reasons come from the social norms of the enterprise they are engaged in, as Strevens suggests. Perhaps those reasons come from the fact that they are sensitivity chasing, as Melchior suggests, and only a restricted inquiry will increase sensitivity. Perhaps those reasons come from the fact that they are trying to follow rules, and the rules do not allow certain kinds of tools to be used. The unifying

---

5   When I say inquiry is about improving one's epistemic position, I don't mean that that's how inquirers represent what they are doing to themselves. That would be to over-intellectualise things. Rather, inquiry is about doing things that are, as a matter of fact, things that improve one's epistemic position. One can be improving one's epistemic position even if one self-represents one's actions in a more mundane way, e.g., as looking up when the coffee shop opens.

theme is that sometimes the inquirer wants not just to run an inquiry, but to run it in a particular way.

The core principle in my version of IRT is that someone who uses what they know in inquiry is immune to criticism on the grounds that what they are doing is epistemically risky. Equivalently, they are immune to criticism on the grounds that their premises might be false. That's compatible with saying that someone can know p, and be properly criticised for using p in inquiry. I motivated that restriction in Section 4.5 by looking at people whose use of p in inquiry can be criticised on relevance grounds. In this chapter we see several more reasons. Someone who has reasons to perform a restricted inquiry, especially someone whose aims can only be realised by conducting a properly restricted inquiry, can be criticised for overstepping those restrictions. That's fine, and totally consistent with IRT, as long as we pay attention not just to whether someone is being criticised, but why they are being criticised.

It isn't just my idiosyncratic version of IRT that escapes this criticism. Jeremy Fantl and Matthew McGrath defend a version of IRT that uses the following principle.

> When you know a proposition p, no weaknesses in your epistemic position with respect to p—no weaknesses, that is, in your standing on any truth-relevant dimension with respect to p—stand in the way of p justifying you in having further beliefs. (Fantl and McGrath, 2009: 64)

I'm going to come back in Section 9.9 to why I don't quite think that's right. But my disagreement turns on a fairly small technical point; I'm following Fantl and McGrath's lead much more than I'm diverging from them. These examples of properly restricted inquiry show how they too can accept rational inquiry into what one already knows.

Consider a person who is sensitivity chasing; they know p but want to have a more sensitive belief that p. So they conduct an inquiry into p, and reason to themselves p, therefore p. This closes the inquiry. Something has gone wrong. It isn't bad reasoning; one can't go wrong with identity. And it isn't that they use something they know as a premise; anything one knows can be used as a premise. It's that they had an aim that could only be met by a restricted inquiry, and they violated those restrictions. That's the incoherence here.

There is a way to read Fantl and McGrath's principle so that this case is a problem for them, but I don't think it's the right reading. The sensitivity of one's belief is, in their terms, part of the strength of one's epistemic position. So if one's belief was more sensitive, one wouldn't have a reason to be chasing sensitivity. So in this case, you might think it's weakness of epistemic position that's relevant; the weakness of epistemic position explains why the inquiry is being conducted in the first place. But I don't think that's fair. The principle only talks about how inquiry should be conducted, not about whether the inquiry should be conducted. So Fantl and McGrath could say, and I think this is the right way to interpret their position, that knowledge is compatible with the weakness in one's epistemic position being what explains why an inquiry is in order. It's just that knowledge is not compatible with that weakness preventing the application of the knowledge once the inquiry has begun.

5.3 Independence

These reflections on the nature of inquiry help tidy up a loose end from *Normative Externalism* (Weatherson, 2019). In that book I argued against David Christensen's Independence principle, but I didn't offer a fully satisfactory explanation for why the principle should seem plausible. Here's the principle in question.

Independence
In evaluating the epistemic credentials of another's expressed belief about P, in order to determine how (or whether) to modify my own belief about P, I should do so in a way that doesn't rely on the reasoning behind my initial belief about P. (Christensen, 2011: 1–2).

This is expressly stated as a principle about disagreement, but it is meant to apply to any kind of higher-order evidence. (This is made clear in "Formulating Independence" (Christensen, 2019), which also includes some new thoughts about how Christensen now thinks the principle should be stated.) I argued that this couldn't be right in general; it gives the wrong results in clear cases, and leads to regresses. Still, it seems plausible that something like this should be right. In *Normative Externalism* I hinted at an inquiry-theoretic proposal about what that similar truth might be. (See, for example, the response to Clayton

Littlejohn (2018), at the top of page 178.) But I never really spelled it out. Here's what I now think the right thing to say is.[6]

Peer disagreement, or really any other kind of higher-order evidence, gives a thinker a reason to conduct an inquiry into whether their earlier thinking was correct. Further, it gives them reason to conduct an inquiry that is restricted in a particular way. The restriction is that they should not rely on the reasoning from their earlier thinking. Putting those two things together, we get that disagreement about p gives someone who believes p reason to inquire into p using a different approach, any different approach, from what they previously used.

Once we've got a principle about reasons, we could try formulating this as a defeasible rule. It's plausible that one should adopt the defeasible rule of conducting such an inquiry whenever one sees a disagreement, or some other kind of potentially defeating higher-order evidence. As long as one builds enough into the defeasibility clause, such a rule won't be subject to the counterexamples I described, or the ones that have caused Christensen (2019) to have second thoughts about the right formulation of the rule. After all, every counterexample will naturally fall into the defeasibility clause.

Such a rule could be justified by the observation that it will probably be beneficial in the long run for people like us to adopt it. Double checking isn't that hard, and can be very useful. Getting stuck in a bad epistemic picture can have devastating consequences; it's good to step back from time to time to see if that's happening to us. Disagreements with peers are a natural trigger for that kind of inquiry. Those same benefits can explain why disagreement, or other kinds of higher-order evidence, give us reason to double check.

But why should one conduct a restricted inquiry here? Given the stakes, we're trying to work out whether we've got ourselves into a bad epistemic state, shouldn't we throw everything we have at the problem? That would be bad, since Independence expressly bars the thinker from using some of the tools at their disposal. It requires them to not do the same kind of inquiry they did before, which presumably was the

---

6 The picture I'm about to give is really similar to the one laid out by Andy Egan (2008). We're interested in different kinds of cases, but the idea that a cognitive system might work best by allowing one part to check on another using just the evidence the first part has endorsed is one I'm just taking from him. If I'd seen this connection when writing *Normative Externalism* I would have connected it to the discussion of Madisonian moral psychology in part I of that book.

one they thought best suited to the problem. That's a big restriction, and needs some justification. I can offer two kinds of justification, not entirely distinct.

The point of having a rule like this, a rule like *Double check your reasoning when a peer disagrees,* is to prevent us falling into epistemic states that are local but not global equilibria. The states we're worried about are ones where any small change will make the epistemic state worse, but large changes will make things better. Picturesquely, we've reached the top of a small hill when we want to climb a mountain. We should be somewhere higher, but any step will be downhill. It's good to not get stuck in places like this, and nudges from friends are a way out.

If we want to check whether we're in such a bad situation, we want a test that is sensitive to whether we are. That is, we want a test that would say something different if we were in that situation to what it would say if we were doing well. (This is Melchior's point about the aim of tests.) Just conducting the same inquiry we previously conducted will typically not be sensitive in this way. Or, more precisely, it will be sensitive to something like performance errors, but not competence errors. We need something more sensitive if the aim is to avoid getting stuck in local equilibria, and that requires setting aside the work we've previously done.

One of the reasons that local equilibria can be sticky is that we know our way around them well. We know all the ways in which one part of the picture we have supports the other parts. We typically don't know how to think about other pictures so clearly. We don't know, don't see, the ways in which other pictures might 'hang together' as well as ours does. We are inevitably going to be biased towards our own ways of thinking. So it's worthwhile to try to level the playing field, by looking at how things would seem if we didn't have our own distinctive way of thinking.

None of this is to take back anything I said in *Normative Externalism*. Disagreement with a peer known to have the same evidence does not give someone a reason to reject a well-formed belief. It gives them a reason to double check that belief. As I've been stressing all chapter, one can double check one's beliefs, and even one's knowledge. That is what should happen here.

Finally, thinking of disagreement as providing a reason to double check provides a nice explanation of one of the harder examples in *Normative Externalism,* the case of Efrosyni (see Weatherson, 2019: 222).

She does a calculation, then double checks it by a different technique, then hears that a peer disagrees. What should she do now? I think typically she should do nothing. The disagreement gives her a reason to double check each calculation she did, but she's already carried out that double check. This is, I think, the intuitively right result. If someone has already double checked their work, they typically do not need to check again. Perhaps in some rare case they could get reason to double check the 'combined' inquiry, consisting of the initial inquiry plus the double check. But that's rare; usually they should respond to the disagreement by showing their work.

With this picture of the relationship between knowledge, inquiry, and checking in place, it's time (at last) to return to potential counterexamples to IRT.

5.4 Double Checking

In her 2008 paper "Subject-Sensitive Invariantism and the Knowledge Norm for Practical Reasoning", Jessica Brown (2008) runs through a bunch of cases where, she says, intuitively someone knows a proposition but they cannot use it in practical deliberation. The first of these cases has been frequently cited as a problem for the kind of view I'm defending.

> A student is spending the day shadowing a surgeon. In the morning he observes her in clinic examining patient A who has a diseased left kidney. The decision is taken to remove it that afternoon. Later, the student observes the surgeon in theatre where patient A is lying anaesthetised on the operating table. The operation hasn't started as the surgeon is consulting the patient's notes. The student is puzzled and asks one of the nurses what's going on:
>
> *Student*: I don't understand. Why is she looking at the patient's records? She was in clinic with the patient this morning. Doesn't she even know which kidney it is?
> *Nurse*: Of course, she knows which kidney it is. But, imagine what it would be like if she removed the wrong kidney. She shouldn't operate before checking the patient's records.

I think there are pretty good arguments that checking the chart is the right thing to do even if the surgeon knows which kidney is diseased, so this case isn't a problem for the views about knowledge and action that I'm defending.

In medical contexts, intuitions about appropriate action very rarely track expected utility maximisation.⁷ This is one reason why it is so easy to come up with medical counterexamples to act utilitarianism for introductory ethics classes. Instead, intuitions about appropriate actions here are more likely to align with rule utilitarianism. The rule *Double check the notes before removing an organ* seems like it will on average maximise utility, even if it would not help in this case.

To connect this to the discussion in Section 5.1, the surgeon here is doing a bit of mostly harmless sensitivity chasing. Before checking the notes, their belief that the left kidney was diseased was not sensitive to the possibility that they'd misremembered the morning meeting; after checking the notes it is. Since busy surgeons do sometimes misremember meetings some hours earlier, this is a reasonable bit of sensitivity for the surgeon to chase, and for the rule-makers to require be chased.

All that can be true even if the surgeon knows which kidney is diseased. If they inquired into which kidney should be removed, and used their knowledge about which kidney was diseased, they would get the right answer. In some sense this would be a perfectly conducted inquiry. But it would not be an inquiry that delivered what the surgeon was looking for, and what the regulators require them to look for: a belief that was sensitive to the possibility of an error in memory.

These considerations don't just defend IRT against the example, they show how IRT can be used to resolve a puzzle about a related case. Continue Brown's story by imagining that every time the surgeon raises the scalpel to make the first incision, they instead go back to look at the notes to check they are removing the correct kidney. Now we have the following conversation.

> *Student*: I don't understand. Why is she looking at the patient's records for the seventeenth time? She just looked at the notes each minute for the last sixteen minutes; she knows which kidney it is.
> *Nurse*: Of course, she knows which kidney it is. But, imagine what it would be like if she removed the wrong kidney. She shouldn't operate before checking the patient's records. (Brown, 2008: 176)

This is a really bad defence of the surgeon's actions. We are owed a story about why it is a bad defence. My story starts with the point that Student

---

7   Jonathan Ichikawa (2017: 152ff) makes this point well in responding to Brown.

is right to ask why she is inquiring into something she knows. While as we've seen there are cases where that is appropriate, these cases are somewhat unusual. It's a reasonable default assumption that inquiry into something one knows is mistaken. That assumption is only defeated if there is some other worthwhile epistemic good that can be attained. In this case, there isn't, since sensitivity to whether one misread the chart the last sixteen times isn't a worthwhile kind of sensitivity to get.

In general, anyone who wants to separate out knowledge from action, and do so on account of the fact that sometimes we double check things we know, owes a story about why we don't also triple-check, quadruple-check, and so on. I suspect such a story won't be easy to tell.

Brown has another example that hasn't attracted nearly as much attention in the literature. This is unfortunate since I think it's a more pressing problem for the view Brown is attacking.

> A husband is berating his friend for not telling him that his wife has been having an affair even though the friend has known of the affair for weeks.
>
> *Husband*: Why didn't you say she was having an affair? You've known for weeks.
> *Friend*: Ok, I admit I knew, but it wouldn't have been right for me to say anything before I was absolutely sure. I knew the damage it would cause to your marriage. (Brown, 2008: 176–177)

In this case, the tricks I was deploying in Section 5.1 don't seem to help. There is no further epistemic good that Friend obtains by waiting further.

That said, my intuition here is that Friend's speech is just incoherent. Or, at least, it is incoherent if we take the final statement at face value. I think we shouldn't do that; Friend didn't really know about the affair.[8]

There are two things that might be going on in this case. My best guess is that the explanation for why Friend's statement seems so natural relies on both of them.

---

8   The particular versions of IRT Brown was responding to in the 2008 paper were heavily motivated by intuitions about cases. Brown argues, quite correctly I think, that those theories aren't entitled to appeal to arguments that the intuitions which go against them are mistaken. After all, if IRT is just motivated by intuitions, the argument that knowledge is not sensitive to interests is just as good an argument against those intuitions as the arguments that IRT defenders can make about this example. Happily, my version of IRT is not motivated just by intuitions about cases, so I don't have to worry about this dialectical point.

First, we do sometimes use 'know' in a purely informational sense. We saw this in Section 5.1.4 with Paresseux's claim that he *knew* Assidue was visiting. He possessed the information, though little more than that. Still, in context this can be enough to ascribe knowledge.

Second, we can be very flexible about past-tense knowledge claims when we, the current speakers, know how things turned out. After our sports team loses a game they should have won, we might say "I had a bad feeling about today, I knew we were going to mess it up". In most cases it would be weird to say the speaker even thought their team would mess up, let alone believed it. (Why didn't they bet on the opposition if they thought the result was a foregone conclusion?) But even if they did believe it, we really don't think *bad feelings* are appropriate grounds for knowledge. And yet, the speakers claim that they knew the team would mess up sounds fine.

Is Friend's statement like Paresseux's knowing (i.e., possessing the information) that Assidue would be visiting, or the sports fan's knowing (i.e., having an accurate premonition) that their team would mess up? My guess is that it's a bit of both. Either way, the Friend didn't know, in the sense of *know* relevant to epistemology, about the affair.

The general methodological point is that these last two senses of knowledge do seem different to what we typically talk about in epistemology. It's possible, as I noted in Section 2.7.1, that considering the information-possession sense of knowledge is important for thinking through whether any kind of contextualism is true. I don't think the 'bad feeling' cases are relevant to anything in epistemology, save for cases where we might need to explain away intuitions that they are involved in. Maybe that's what's happening in Brown's second case.

5.5 The Need to Inquire

So far I've mostly talked about inquiries that a person is actually conducting. But we should also think about the inquiries that they should conduct. Consider the following two abstractly described possibilities.

A person believes p for good reasons, and it is true, and there are no weird things happening that characterise typical gaps between rational true belief and knowledge. There is some action φ they are considering that will have mildly good consequences if p, and absolutely catastrophic consequences if $\neg p$. One of the alternatives to φ is first checking whether p, which would be trivial, and then doing φ iff p. We've seen lots of these cases before, but here's the new twist. The person absolutely does not care about the catastrophic consequences. They will all fall on people the person could not care less about. So they are planning to simply do φ, for the good consequences. Since p is true, nothing bad will happen. Still, it seems something has gone wrong. We want to say that they've been reckless, that they've taken an immoral risk. But it isn't risky to do something that you know won't have bad consequences. So they do not know that p, and for similar reasons to why Anisa doesn't know that p. Yet the version of IRT that I've given so far doesn't say that they don't know that p.

The second case has the same initial structure as the first. The person believes p for good reasons, it's true, and there is no funny business going on—no fake barns or the like blocking knowledge. They are thinking about doing φ. They know that if p is true, φ will have a small benefit. They also know that it would be completely trivial to verify whether p is true. They also in some sense know that if they do φ, and p is false, it will be absolutely catastrophic. And they care about the catastrophe. But they've sort of forgotten this fact about φ. It's not that it has totally vanished from their mind. But they aren't attending to it, and it doesn't form any part of their deliberation when thinking about φ. So they do φ, nothing bad happens, and later when someone asks them whether they were worried about the possible catastrophe, they are shocked that they would do something so reckless. They are shocked, that is, that they forgot that it was important to confirm whether p was true before doing φ. It feels, from the inside, like they got away with taking a terrible risk. But if they knew p, it should not seem like a risk, it should seem like rational action. (Just like they would think doing φ after checking whether p was rational action.) So this too should be a case where we say knowledge fails for practical reasons. (I'm going to come back to a version of this case in Section 8.1, where it will be useful for highlighting one of the few points where I disagree with the theory that Jeremy Fantl and Matthew McGrath (2002, 2009) endorse.)

The natural thing to say here is that in each case, the person should conduct an inquiry. They should check whether p is true. In that inquiry, they shouldn't take p for granted. They shouldn't take it for granted for a very particular reason, because it might be false. If they knew p, they could take it for granted, or, at least, if they couldn't, it would be for some reason other than that p might be false. So they don't know that p.

What these two types of case show is that knowledge is not just sensitive to what one is actually inquiring into, it is also sensitive to what one should be inquiring into. If one should inquire into Q, and were one to inquire into Q, one shouldn't take p for granted because it might be false—one doesn't know p.

This is a kind of moral encroachment in the sense of Rima Basu and Mark Schroeder (2019). What one knows might be sensitive to one's moral obligations in inquiry. Imagine two people both take p for granted in making a decision that affects other people. This is mostly fine because p is true, and they had good reasons to take it for granted. Still, there was some risk to others, and they could have checked whether p was actually true before acting, but in each case they had other things they would rather be doing than checking p. What differs between the two people is what they would rather be doing. The first could have checked, but it would have taken them away from a rescue operation in progress; the second could have checked, but it would have taken them away from their social media feed. If the theory I've developed so far is correct, then the first knows that p, and the second does not, and the difference comes down to the differing moral importance of contributing to rescue operations and social media.

It's worth recalling here that the methodology I'm using in this book is perhaps a little different to a common methodology in this area. I don't think that if you fill out the two cases from the last paragraph in full detail, it will be intuitively obvious that one person knows and the other doesn't, and that's evidence for IRT. Rather, I think that it's plausible that one isn't being reckless by acting on what one knows, and this principle, combined with anti-sceptical principles and judgments about which acts are indeed reckless, leads to IRT. As always, these cases allow for four broad classes of response: the sceptic who denies there is knowledge even in the low-stakes case; the epistemicist who denies the intuitions about which actions are reckless; the orthodox theorist who says that acting on what one knows can be reckless; and the pragmatist, who accepts both the intuitions about which acts are reckless and how knowledge connects to recklessness, and infers that knowledge is sensitive to pragmatic, and in this case moral, factors.

5.6 Multiple Inquiries

IRT says that what one knows depends on what one is inquiring into. It would be very convenient if there was a position in the logical form of knowledge ascriptions for inquiries. That is, it would be very convenient if the logical form of *S knows that p* was something like $Ktspi$, where t is the time, s is the knower, p is what's known, and i is the inquiry it is known in. Then we could say that one condition on such a knowledge claim being true is that at t, s can properly use p as a starting point in inquiry i.[9] Unfortunately for IRT, that's not the logical form of knowledge ascriptions. The t, s, and p are there all right, but not the i. Fortunately for IRT, the logical form does have reference to a knower, that s. Since knowers undertake inquiries, we can bring in the inquiries via the knower. All knowledge is inquiry-relative, we say, and it is relative to the inquiries of the person to whom knowledge is being ascribed.

If every person was, at each time, undertaking precisely one inquiry, everything would fall into place very nicely. Given t and s, we could guarantee the unique existence of an i, and it would be as if there was an i in the logical form, as IRT would like. Unfortunately, that's not close to being true. Some people at some times are making no inquiries, e.g., when they are asleep. And some people at some times are making many inquiries. The former case is no problem for IRT. If the person is making no inquiries, then what they know is determined by 'traditional' factors, such as what they believe, whether those beliefs are true, grounded in the evidence, safe, and so on. The case where someone is engaged in multiple inquiries is a little harder.

The view I'll defend is that the person knows p only if p can properly be used as a starting point in all the inquiries the person is engaged in. This has a surprising, and not entirely welcome, side effect. It means that some people don't know p, and hence can't use p in an inquiry i, even though they could use p as a starting point to i if i were the only inquiry

---

9   More precisely, as I said in Section 4.5, if they use p in i, that won't be subject to criticism on the grounds that p might be false. I'll use the more informal version in the text in what follows to increase readability.

they were engaged in. This is a somewhat more sceptical result than I like, but I suspect it's the best choice out of a bad lot. The only other options I can see are to either try to find ways to get *i* back into the logical form of knowledge ascriptions, or to adopt a novel form of relativism that says knowledge claims are true or false relative to inquiries, or to say that the person conducting multiple inquiries is fragmented, and each of the fragments has their own knowledge. None of these moves strikes me as remotely plausible, and so we're forced to have some kind of view where we quantify over the inquiries a person is engaged in.

In the rest of this section, I have three aims. First, to make what I've said so far less abstract, by describing a case where someone has multiple inquiries, and this matters in surprising ways. Second, to say why it isn't great that IRT is forced to say that someone doesn't know something that is otherwise usable in an inquiry they are engaged in. Third, to say why this isn't a devastating result, even though it's not exactly a happy one.

Our example of someone with multiple inquiries will be a historian called Tori. She has been taught, like everyone else, that the Battle of Hastings was in 1066. For most purposes she takes that to be one of the fixed points in the historical record. But she's noticed some anomalies in some of the documents from around that time, anomalies that would be explained by the battle being in 1067. She's seen enough documents to know that the overwhelming likelihood is that these anomalies have some simple explanation, like a transcription error. But in her spare time over the last few years, she has been investigating off and on whether the best explanation might be that everyone else has the date of the battle wrong, and in fact it was in 1067.

If it is worth inquiring into the date of the Battle of Hastings, it is not sensible to take the date of the battle as fixed. That would make the inquiry very short. So if it's reasonable for Tori to conduct this inquiry, then while she is conducting it, she does not know when the Battle of Hastings took place.

If this inquiry into the date is something she has been working on in her spare time for years, she has presumably had other jobs that did not involve trying to overturn the historical record about one of the central events in British history. In some of those jobs, it will have been sensible to take as given when the Battle of Hastings, and hence the beginning of Norman rule over Britain, took place. So there will be contexts, ones where her primary focus is on an everyday question where one takes for granted the common assumptions about British history, but she still has as a background project this idea that maybe the Battle of Hastings took place a year later, where IRT seems to get into trouble. It wants to say that for the purposes of her everyday inquiries, Tori knows the Battle of Hastings took place in 1066. After all, this is a true, rational belief, that is based in the right way in the facts, and which is reasonably taken as a starting point for this very inquiry. That looks like, relative to that inquiry, it is knowledge. But for the purposes of finding out the best explanation of the anomalies, she does not know when the battle took place, on pain of not being able to rationally investigate one possible explanation.

My version of IRT says that knowledge is relative to inquirers, not to inquiries, so I can't say that she knows the date relative to one inquiry but not another. That's not great. In the everyday inquiry Tori is exactly like someone who knows when the Battle of Hastings was in what look like all the relevant features, and yet she doesn't know. How can we explain away this anomaly?

The first thing to note is that even if Tori loses the knowledge that the Battle of Hastings was in 1066, she keeps her voluminous evidence that the Battle happened then. In most inquiries, anything she might infer from a claim about the Battle's date, she can infer from that evidence. So she'll still, on the whole, be able to draw the same conclusions in other inquiries as if she kept that knowledge.

Usually there are two reasons for keeping the conclusions of one's inquiries and not one's evidence. First, it helps with clutter avoidance (Harman, 1986: 12). If a knowledge of history required knowing not just a bunch of things about what happened, when it happened, and ideally why it happened, but also knowing how and where one learned these facts, then even the most basic knowledge of history would be beyond most of us. Second, it makes certain kind of inferences much smoother to go through various steps rather than applying something like cut-elimination and getting rid of the middle steps. That is, it's easier for Tori to infer from some evidence that the Battle of Hastings was in 1066, and then from that and some other evidence to draw further conclusions, than it is to draw inferences directly from the underlying evidence. But while both of these considerations are very powerful ones in general, one would definitely not like to never store or rely on intermediate conclusions in inquiry, they aren't nearly as powerful in any specific case. If there's one step in an inquiry that one is unsure of on other grounds, it's not a huge effort to retain one's evidence for *that step*, and replace inferences that rely on it with inferences that rely on the underlying evidence.

The other thing to note is that we can explain Tori's behaviour in inquiries without positing more knowledge to her than IRT allows. The key thing is to replace the familiar Knowledge Norm of Assertion with the slightly more complicated Sufficient Evidence Norm of Assertion.

Knowledge Norm of Assertion
One must: Assert p only if one knows that p.

Sufficient Evidence Norm of Assertion
One must: Assert p only if one's evidence is sufficient for one's audience to know that p.

If one identifies evidence with knowledge, then it's hard to see any space between these two. I don't quite endorse that identification for reasons that I'll go over more in Chapter 9, but I mention it here just to note that this need not be a radical revision.

If the norms do come apart, then the latter seems to play better with IRT. Imagine that S is talking to some people who are facing a long-shot bet on whether p. These people would not be best off, in expectation, taking p for granted. Unfortunately, S doesn't care about the welfare of these people, though for some reason they do care about being a good informant and testifier. Further imagine that S's evidence for p, while strong, isn't quite strong enough to justify the audience in taking this long-shot bet. Then it is wrong for S to simply say that p.

The picture behind the Sufficient Evidence Norm of Assertion is that one should say p only if one's audience can take p as a starting point in inquiry. Sometimes one might violate this norm without being subject to blame, as when it turns out one's audience has an unexpectedly long-odds bet on p. In normal cases, however, where one knows at least something about one's audience, one should calibrate one's assertions to the projects of one's audience.

This picture seems to get two possible cases where Tori is involved in a group inquiry just right.

In the first (more normal) case, Tori is working with a group of people who do not share her worry about the anomalies in the dating of the Battle of Hastings. They think the date is a settled fact. In their presence Tori can speak as if it is settled. After all, her evidence suffices for her audience to know when the Battle was, given their lack of interest in odd anomalies.

In the second (somewhat odder) case, Tori is working with a group of people, one of whom shares her concerns about these anomalies. In the context of the other inquiry (i.e., not the inquiry into the date of the Battle), Tori says, "The Battle of Hastings was in 1066." It would be reasonable for the other person who shares her concerns about the anomalies to conclude that Tori had satisfied herself that the anomalies were just mistakes, and the Battle really was in 1066. That's because, I say, the unqualified assertion would be improper unless Tori had resolved these concerns to a standard that would be satisfying to the two of them. This case is a bit odd, as it does require the coincidental presence of two people with unusual interests, but I think the Sufficient Evidence Norm plus IRT gets them right.

Two final notes about this case.

First, I've crafted the Sufficient Evidence Norm to be the variation on the Knowledge Norm that a defender of IRT should like. But one might suspect the Knowledge Norm on independent grounds, e.g., because it gets the cases in Maitra and Weatherson (2010) wrong. I think the Sufficient Evidence Norm should be tinkered with to handle those cases, but I'm not exactly sure how this should go. Still, the tinkering shouldn't undermine the way IRT handles these cases.

Second, there is a really interesting historical question around here. Imagine you have a community that governs itself by the Sufficient Evidence Norm. And then someone comes along and invents the scientific journal, and all of a sudden it's possible to assert things with no knowledge of what is at stake for one's audience. How should one react, especially given the usefulness of the scientific journal for conducting inquiries that are widely distributed over space and time?

A natural move would be to develop some new interest-invariant standards for printed assertion, and hopefully make it clear to both writers and readers what these standards are.

Once upon a time I had hoped this book would include an argument that the development of interest-invariant epistemology was just such a reaction to the invention of the printing press and, somewhat later, to the adoption of scientific journals as important conduits for sharing information in distributed inquiries. I still think something like this is arguably true, at least if we mean the development of interest-invariant norms for what I called in Chapter 1 'sub-optimal' epistemology. But defending this claim would require a different book, and a writer with very different skills, to this one.

So I'll just leave this as a conjecture for future research. What most philosophers call 'traditional' epistemological views, i.e., fallibilism plus interest-invariance, might just be a response to a relatively recent technological innovation.

6. Ties

I have mentioned a couple of times that a natural version of IRT leads to unpleasant closure failures. Adam Zweber (2016) and, separately, Charity Anderson and John Hawthorne (2019a), showed that the following principle cannot be the only way interests enter into our theory of knowledge.

Conditional Preferences
If S knows that p, and is trying to decide between X and Y, then her preferences over X and Y are the same unconditionally as they are conditional on p.

They show if you add this principle and nothing else to a natural interest-relative theory of knowledge, you get a theory where a person can know $p \wedge q$ but not know p. Further, they argue that the natural ways to modify IRT to avoid this result make the theory implausibly sceptical. The various ways I've defended IRT over the years are not vulnerable to the first objection, since I was always careful to avoid this kind of closure failure. But they were vulnerable to the second objection, since they did lead to some very sceptical results in the cases that Zweber, and Anderson and Hawthorne, discuss. So the point of this chapter is to describe a version of IRT that avoids their challenge.

Surprisingly, the response will not involve making any particularly dramatic changes to the theory of knowledge. What it will involve is making a fairly dramatic change to the underlying decision theory. That's one reason I'm spending a whole chapter on this objection; the changes you need to make to respond to it run fairly deep. In particular, they involve breaking the tight connection that most theorists assume between rational action and expected utility maximisation. The other reason for spending so much time on these examples is that thinking through them reveals a lot about the relationship between reasons, rational action, and knowledge.

6.1 An Example

Let's start with an example from a great thinker. It will require a little exegesis, but that's not unusual when using classic texts.

> Well Frankie Lee and Judas Priest
> They were the best of friends
> So when Frankie Lee needed money one day
> Judas quickly pulled out a roll of tens
> And placed them on the footstool
> Just above the potted plain
> Saying "Take your pick, Frankie boy,
> My loss will be your gain."
>
> "The Ballad of Frankie Lee and Judas Priest", 1968.
> Lyrics from Dylan (2016: 225)

On a common reading of this, Judas Priest isn't just asking Frankie Lee how much money he wants to take, but which individual notes. Let's simplify, and say that it is common ground that Frankie Lee should only take $10, so his choice is which note to take. This will be enough to set up the puzzle.

Assume something else that isn't in the text, but which isn't an implausible addition to the story. The world Frankie Lee and Judas Priest live in is not completely free of counterfeit notes. It would be bad for Frankie Lee to take a counterfeit note. It won't matter just how common these notes are, or how bad it would be. The puzzle will be most vivid if each of these are relatively small quantities. So there aren't that many counterfeit notes in circulation, and the (expected) disutility to Frankie Lee of having one of them is not great. There is some chance that he will get in trouble, but the chance isn't high, and the trouble isn't any worse than he's suffered before. Still, other things exactly equal, Frankie Lee would prefer a genuine note to a counterfeit one.

Now for some terminology to help us state the problem Frankie Lee is in. Assume there are k notes on the footstool. Call them $n_1, ..., n_k$. Let c_i be the proposition that note n_i is counterfeit, and its negation g_i be that it is genuine. Let g, without a subscript, be the conjunction

$g_1 \wedge ... \wedge g_n$; i.e., the proposition that all the notes are genuine. Let t_i be the act of taking note n_i. Let U be Frankie Lee's utility function, and Cr his credence function.

In our first version of the example, we'll make two more assumptions. Apart from the issue of whether the note is real or counterfeit, Frankie Lee is indifferent between the notes, so for some h, l, $U(t_i | g_i) = h$ and $U(t_i | c_i) = l$ for all i, with of course $h > l$. Frankie Lee thinks each of the banknotes is equally likely to be genuine, so for some p, $Cr(g_i) = p$ for all i. (The probability of any of them being counterfeit is independent of the probability of any of the others being counterfeit.)

That's enough to get us three puzzles for the form of IRT that just uses Conditional Preferences. I'm going to refer to this form of IRT a lot, so let's give it the memorable moniker IRT-CP. That is, IRT-CP is what you get by taking a standard theory of knowledge, adding Conditional Preferences as a further constraint on knowledge, and stopping there. I don't know that anyone endorses IRT-CP, but it's a good theory to have on the table. It says a number of implausible things about Frankie Lee, and the big challenge, as I see it, is to craft a version of IRT that doesn't fall into the same traps.

First, Frankie Lee doesn't know of any note that it is genuine. As things stand, Frankie is indifferent between t_i and t_j for any i, j. But conditional on g_i, Frankie prefers t_i to t_j. Right now, the expected utility of taking either i or j is $ph + (1-p)l$. If Frankie Lee conditionalises on g_i, then the utility of t_j doesn't change, but the utility of t_i now becomes h, and that's higher than $ph + (1-p)l$. Since IRT-CP says that one doesn't know p if conditionalising on p changes one's preferences over pragmatically salient options, and t_i and t_j are really salient to Frankie Lee, it follows that he doesn't know g_i. Since i was arbitrary in this proof, he doesn't know of any of the notes that they are genuine. That's not very intuitive, but worse is to follow.

Second, Frankie Lee does know that all the notes are genuine, although he doesn't know of any note that it is genuine. Conditional on g, Frankie Lee's preferences are the same as they are unconditionally. He used to be indifferent between the notes; after conditionalising he is still indifferent. So the one principle that IRT-CP adds to a standard theory of knowledge does not rule out that Frankie Lee knows g. So he knows g; but doesn't know any of its constituent conjuncts. This is a very unappealing result.

To generate the third problem, we need to change the example a bit. Keep that the probabilities of each note being genuine are equal and independent. But this time assume that the notes are laid out in a line, and Frankie Lee is at one end of that line. So to get a note that is further away from him, he has to reach further. And this has an ever so small disutility. Let r_i be the disutility of reaching for note i. And assume this value increases as i increases, but is always smaller than $(1-p)(h-l)$. That last quantity is important, because it is the difference between the utility of taking an arbitrary note (with no penalty for the cost of reaching for it), and the utility of taking a genuine banknote.

If all these assumptions are added, Frankie Lee knows one more thing: g_1. That's because as things stand, he prefers t_1 to the other options. Conditional on g_i for any $i \geq 2$, he prefers t_i to t_1. So if $i \geq 2$, conditionalising on g_i changes Frankie's preferences, so he doesn't know g_i.

This third puzzle is striking for two reasons. One is that it involves a change of strict preferences. Unconditionally, Frankie strictly prefers t_1 to t_i; conditional on gi he strictly prefers t_i to t_1. When I first saw these puzzles, I thought we could possibly get around them by restricting attention to cases where conditionalisation changes a strict preference. This example shows that way of rescuing IRT-CP won't work. The other reason is that it heightens the implausibility of the sceptical result that Frankie doesn't know g_i. It's one thing to say that the weird situation that Judas Priest puts Frankie Lee makes Frankie Lee lose a lot of knowledge he ordinarily has. That's just IRT in action; change the practical situation and someone might lose knowledge. It's another to say that within this very situation, Frankie Lee knows of some notes that they are genuine but does not know that others are genuine, even though his evidence for the genuineness of each note is the same.

So we have three puzzles to try to solve, if we want to defend anything like IRT-CP.

1. In the case where Frankie Lee has no reason to choose one note rather than another, he doesn't know of any note that it is genuine. This is surprisingly sceptical.

2. In the case where he has a weak reason to choose one note, he knows that note is genuine, but not the others. This retains the surprisingly sceptical consequence of the first puzzle, and adds a surprising asymmetry.
3. In both cases, there seems to be a really bad closure failure, with Frankie Lee knowing that all the notes are genuine, but not knowing of all or most individual notes that they are genuine.

Before we leave Frankie Lee for a while, let's note one variation on the case that somewhat helps IRT. Imagine that the country they are in has just reached the level of technological sophistication where it can mass produce plastic banknotes. Further, no one in the country has yet figured out how to produce plausible forgeries of plastic banknotes, and Frankie Lee knows this. Finally, assume that one of the notes, lucky n_8, is one of the new plastic notes, while the others are the old paper notes. If Frankie Lee cares about counterfeit avoidance at all, he should take n_8. He should do so because it definitely isn't a counterfeit, while each of the others might be. So in that case, Frankie Lee doesn't know that the notes other than n_8 are genuine, at least if whatever might be false isn't known.

Now we have a case where IRT-CP gives the right answers for the right reasons. A theory that disagrees with IRT-CP about this case has to either (a) deny this intuition that the uniquely rational choice for Frankie Lee is n_8, or (b) say that Frankie Lee should choose n_8 because the other choices are too risky, even though he knows the risk in question will not eventuate. Neither option is particularly appealing, at least if one is unhappy with making Moore-paradoxical assertions, so this is a good case for IRT-CP. Or, more carefully, it's good news for some version of IRT. This case is some evidence that the problem is not with the very idea of interest-relativity, but with the implementation of it. We'll see more such evidence as the chapter goes along.

6.2 Responding to the Challenge, Quickly

The second half of this chapter is going to get into the weeds a bit about how choices do and should get made in cases like Frankie Lee's. Before we do that, I am going to outline how my version of IRT, which differs from IRT-CP, handles these cases.

Let's start with closure, and assume that Frankie Lee doesn't know of any note that it is genuine. And assume that's because the conditional utility of a salient act differs significantly, based on that note being genuine, compared to its unconditional utility. Now we can avoid the closure problem by stressing that what matters is not that the conditional and unconditional questions end up with the same verdict, but that the process of getting to that verdict is the same. This is why if Frankie Lee doesn't know of any note that it's genuine, he also doesn't know g. Right now, when choosing a note (and trying to maximise expected utility), he should be indifferent because the risk that any note is counterfeit, given his evidence, is more or less the same as the risk that any other note is counterfeit. When he is choosing conditional on g, he doesn't have to attend to risks, or his evidence, or anything that might be more or less equal to anything else. He just takes it as fixed, for purposes of answering the question of what to choose conditional on g, that the notes are genuine. He ends up in the same place both times, indifference between the notes, but he gets there via different pathways. That's enough to defeat knowledge that g.

I'm appealing again here to a point I first made back in Section 3.5. In English, saying that two questions are answered the same way is ambiguous. It might mean that we end up in the same place when answering the two questions. Or it might mean that we get to that place the same way. There are any number of examples of this. The questions *What is three plus two*, and *How many Platonic solids are there*, get answered the same way in the first sense, but not the second sense. Conditional Preference stresses that certain conditional and unconditional questions get answered the same way in this first sense. My version of IRT says that what matters is that these conditional and unconditional questions get answered the same way in the second sense.

That deals with the closure problem satisfactorily, but it does not help with the sceptical problem. To solve that problem we need to rethink our theory of decision. I added, almost as an aside, an assumption in the earlier discussion that Frankie Lee was trying to maximise expected utility. That's a mistake; he shouldn't do that. In a lot of cases like Frankie Lee's, the rational thing to do is to simply ignore the possibility that the notes are counterfeit. This will sometimes lead to taking a choice that doesn't maximise either actual or expected utility. But choice-making procedures can be costly. Difficult choice-making procedures involve computational, hedonic, and investigative costs. It is worth giving up some expected utility in the outcome to use a cheaper decision procedure. One way to do that is to simply ignore some risks.

If Frankie Lee ignores the risk that the notes are counterfeit, then the argument that he doesn't know g_1, g_2, etc., doesn't get off the ground. Given that he's ignoring the risk that the notes are counterfeit, conditionalising on them not being counterfeit changes precisely nothing. So there is no pragmatic argument that he does not know they are genuine. This approach will avoid the sceptical problems if, but only if, this kind of 'ignoring' is rational and widespread. I aim to make a case that it is. But first I want to make things, if anything, worse for IRT, by stressing how quotidian examples with the structure of Frankie Lee's are. This will prevent me from being able to dismiss the example as a theorist's fantasy, but will ultimately help see why ignoring the downside risks is so natural, and so rational.

6.3 Back to Earth

The Frankie Lee and Judas Priest case is weird. Who offers someone money, then asks them to pick which note to take? Intuitions about such weird cases are sometimes deprecated. Perhaps the contrivance doesn't reveal deep problems with a philosophical theory, but merely a quirk of our intuitions. I am not going to take a stand on any big questions about the epistemic significance of intuitions about weird cases here. Rather, I'm going to note that cases with the same structure as the story of Frankie Lee and Judas Priest are incredibly common in the real world. Thinking about the real-world examples can show us how pressing are the problems these cases raise. It also helps us see the way out of these problems.

So let's leave Frankie Lee for now, just above the potted plain, and think about a new character. We will call this one David, and he is buying a few groceries on the way home from work. In particular, he has to buy a can of chickpeas, a bottle of milk, and a carton of eggs. To make life easy, we'll assume each of these costs the same amount: $5.[1] None of these purchases is entirely risk free. Canned goods are pretty safe, but sometimes they go bad. Milk is normally removed from sale when it goes bad, but not always. And eggs can crack, either in transit or just on the shelf. In David's world, just like ours, each of these risks is greater than the one that came before.

David has a favourite brand of chickpeas, of milk, and of eggs, and he knows where in the store they are located. So his shopping is pretty easy. But it isn't completely straightforward.

First, he gets the chickpeas. That's simple; he grabs the nearest can, and unless it is badly dented, or leaking, he puts it in his basket.

Next, he goes onto the milk. The milk bottles have sell-by dates printed in big letters on the front.[2] David checks that he isn't picking up one that is about to expire. His store has been known to have adjacent bottles of milk with sell-by dates ten days apart, so it's worth checking. But as long as the date is far enough in the future, he takes it and moves on.

Finally, he comes to the eggs. (Nothing so alike as eggs, he always thinks to himself, a little anachronistically.) Here he has to do a little more work. He takes the first carton, opens it to see there are no cracks on the top of the eggs, and, finding none, puts that in his basket too. He knows some of his friends do more than this—flipping the carton over to check for cracks underneath. But the one time he tried that, the eggs ended up on the floor. And he knows some of his friends do less—just picking up the carton by the underside, and only checking for cracks if the underside is sticky where the eggs have leaked. He thinks that makes sense too, but he is a little paranoid, and likes visual confirmation of what he's getting. All done, he heads to the checkout, pays his $15, and goes home.

The choice David faces when getting the chickpeas is like the choice Frankie Lee faces. In a normal store, it will be more like the version where Frankie Lee has to reach further for some notes than others, but

---

1 If that sounds implausible to you, make the can/bottle/carton a different size, or change the currency to some other dollars than the one you're instinctively using. I think this example works tolerably well when understand as involving, for example, East Caribbean dollars.

2 This kind of labeling is common for milk in Australian supermarkets, but not, typically, in American supermarkets.

sometimes there will be multiple cans equidistant from David. More normally though, some of the cans will be towards the front, and others towards the back, and it will be easier to grab one of the ones from the front. That's why it is weird to get one from the back; reaching incurs costs without any particular payoff.

Ignore this complication for now and focus on the ways in which David's options in the supermarket are like Frankie Lee's. He has to choose from among a bunch of very similar seeming options. In at least the chickpeas example, there is something you'd want to say that he knows: canned goods sold at reputable stores are safe. But the arguments above seem to show that David does not know this, at least if IRT-CP is true. Indeed, it seems to show this as long as Conditional Preferences is true, even if it isn't the full story of how interests matter to knowledge. Assuming there is some positive probability of the chickpeas not being safe, and the costs of reaching for some other can are low enough, David is in exactly the same situation as Frankie Lee. Right now, he maximises utility by taking the front-most can. But conditional on one of the other cans being safe, he maximises utility by taking it. So he does not know of any of the other cans that they are safe.

Frankie Lee's situation is weird. Who lays out some ten dollar bills and asks you to pick one? (Judas Priest, I guess.) But David's situation is not weird. Looking at a fully stocked shelf of industrially produced food, and needing to pick one can out of an array of similar items, is a very common experience. If a theory of knowledge yields bizarre verdicts about a case like this, it is no defence at all to say the situation is too obscure. In this modern world, it's an everyday occurrence.

6.4 I Have Questions

So far in this chapter I've mostly assumed that these two questions are equivalent:

1. Which option has highest expected utility?
2. What to do?

In doing this, I've faithfully reproduced the arguments of some critics of IRT. Those critics were hardly being unfair to proponents of IRT in treating these questions as being alike. They are explicitly treated as being interchangeable in, for example, my "Can We Do without Pragmatic Encroachment?". But this was a mistake I made in defending IRT, and the beginning of a solution to the problems raised by Frankie Lee is to separate the questions out. I already mentioned one respect in which these questions differ back in Section 3.6. I'll rehearse that difference, briefly mention a second difference, then spend some time on a third difference.

The point I made much of back in Section 3.6 was that someone might know the utility facts, but not know what to do. When Frankie sits down, with his fingers to his chin, and tries to decide which of the tens to take, it's possible he knows that they each have the same utility. But he still has to pick one, and with his head spinning he can't decide which one to take. In cases like these answering questions about utility comparisons won't settle questions about what to do.[3]

A second reason for not treating the questions alike is that to treat them alike assumes away something that should not be assumed away. It simply assumes that risk-sensitive theories of choice, as defended by John Quiggin (1982) and Lara Buchak (2013), are mistaken. We probably shouldn't simply assume that. It turns out the difference between expected utility theory and these heterodox alternatives isn't particularly relevant to Frankie's or David's choices, so I'll leave this aside for the rest of the chapter.

The third way in which treating the questions as equivalent is wrong takes a little longer to explain. The short version is that rational people are satisficers, and for a satisficer you can answer the question *What to do* without taking a stand on questions about relative utility. The longer version is set out in the next section.

6.5 You'll Never Be Satisfied (If You Try to Maximise)

The standard model of practical rationality that we use in philosophy is that of expected utility maximisation. But there are both theoretical and experimental reasons to think that this is not the right model for choices

---

3 James M. Joyce (2018) suggests the following terminology. If Frankie is rational, then utility considerations settle questions about what to *choose*, but not questions about what to *pick* in the case of a tie. I haven't quite followed that terminology; I've let Frankie pick and choose more freely than that. But I'm following Joyce in stressing this conceptual distinction.

such as that faced by Frankie or David. Maximising expected utility is resource intensive, especially in contexts like a modern supermarket, and the returns on this resource expenditure are unimpressive. What people mostly do, and what they should do, is choose in a way that is sensitive to the costs of adopting one or other way.

There are two annoying terminological issues around here that I mostly want to set aside, but need to briefly address in order to forestall confusion.

I'm going to assume maximising expected utility means taking the option with the highest expected utility given facts that are readily available. So if one simply doesn't process a relevant but observationally obvious fact, that can lead to an irrational choice. I might alternatively have said that the choice was rational (given the facts the chooser was aware of), but the observational process was irrational. But I suspect that terminology would just add needless complication.

I'm going to come back to another point that is partially terminological, and partially substantive. That's whether we should identify the choice consequentialists recommend in virtue of the fact that it maximises expected utility with one of the options (in the ordinary sense of option), or something antecedent.

I'm going to call any search procedure that is sensitive to resource considerations a satisficing procedure. This isn't an uncommon usage. Charles Manski (2017) uses the term this way, and notes that it has rarely been defined more precisely than that. But it isn't the only way that it is used. Mauro Papi (2013) uses the term to exclusively mean that the chooser has a 'reservation level', and they choose the first option that crosses it. This kind of meaning will be something that becomes important again in a bit. And Chris Tucker (2016), following a long tradition in philosophy of religion, uses it to mean any choice procedure that does not optimise. Elena Reutskaja and colleagues (2011) contrast a "hybrid" model that is sensitive to resource constraints with a "satisficing" model that has a fixed reservation level. They end up offering reasons to think ordinary people do (and perhaps should) adopt this hybrid model. So though they don't call this a satisficing approach, it just is a version of what Manski calls satisficing. Andrew Caplin and colleagues (2011), on the other hand, describe a very similar model to Reutskaja and colleagues' hybrid model—one where agents try to find something above a reservation level but the reservation level is sensitive to search costs—as a form of satisficing. So the terminology around here is a mess. I propose to use Manski's terminology: agents satisfice if they choose in a way that is sensitive to resource constraints. Ideally they would maximise, subject to constraints, but saying just what this comes to runs into obvious regress problems (Savage, 1967). Let's set aside this theoretical point for a little, and go back to David and the chickpeas.

When David is facing the shelf of (roughly equidistant) chickpeas, he can rationally take any one of them—apart perhaps from ones that are seriously damaged. How can expected utility theory capture that fact? It says that more than one choice is permissible only if the choices are equal in expected utility. So the different cans are equal in expected utility. But on reflection, this is an implausible claim. Some of the cans are ever so slightly easier to reach. Some of the cans will have ever so slight damage—a tiny dint here, a small tear in the label there—that just might indicate a more serious flaw. Of course, these small damages are almost always irrelevant, but as long as the probability that they indicate damage is positive, it breaks the equality of the expected utility of the cans. Even if there is no visible damage, some of the labels will be ever so slightly more faded, which indicates that the cans are older, which ever so slightly increases the probability that the goods will go bad before David gets to use them. Of course, in reality this won't matter more than one time in a million, but one in a million chances matter if you are asking whether two expected utilities are strictly equal.

The common thread to the last paragraph is that these objects on the shelves are almost duplicates, but the most careful quality control doesn't produce consumer goods that are actual duplicates. This is particularly true in Frankie Lee's choice situation. If all the notes he looks at are really duplicates, down to the serial numbers, he should run away. There are always some differences. It is unlikely that these differences make precisely zero difference to the expected utility of each choice. Even if they do, discovering that is hard work.

So it seems likely that, according to the expected utility model, it isn't true that David could permissibly take any can of chickpeas that is easily reachable and not obviously flawed. Even if that is true, it is extremely unlikely that David could know it to be true. But one thing we know about situations like David's is that any one of the (easily reached, not clearly flawed) cans can be permissibly chosen, and David can easily know that. So the expected utility model, as I've so far described it, is false.

I'll return in the next section to the question of whether this is a problem for theories of decision based around expected utility maximisation broadly, or whether it is just a problem for the particular way I've spelled out the expected utility theory. But for now I want to run through two more arguments against the idea that supermarket shoppers like David should be maximising expected utility (so understood).

In all but a vanishingly small class of cases, the different cans will not have the same expected utility. Indeed, that they have the same expected utility is a measure zero event. One way to note that expected utility maximisation can't be the right theory of choice-worthiness is that cases where multiple cans are equally choice-worthy is not a measure zero event; it's the standard case. And figuring out which can has the highest expected utility is a going to be work. It's possible in principle, I suppose, that someone could be skilled at it, in the sense that they could instinctively pick out the can whose shape, label fading, etc. reveal it to have the highest expected utility. Such a skill seems likely to be rare—though I'll come back to this point below when considering some other skills that are probably less rare. For most people, maximising expected utility will not be something that can be done through effortless skill alone; it will take effort. This effort will be costly, and almost certainly not worth it. Although one of the cans will be ever so fractionally higher in expected utility than the others, the cost of finding out which can this is will be greater than the difference in expected utility of the cans. So aiming to maximise expected utility will have the perverse effect of reducing one's overall utility, in a predictable way.

The costs of trying to maximise expected utility go beyond the costs of engaging in search and computation. There is evidence that people who employ maximising strategies in consumer search end up worse off than those who don't. Schwartz et al. (2002) reported that consumers could be divided in "satisficers" and "maximisers". And once this division is made, it turns out that the maximisers are less happy with individual choices, and with their life in general. This finding has been extended to work on career choice (Iyengar, Wells, and Schwartz, 2006) where the maximisers end up with higher salaries but less job satisfaction, and to friend choice (Newman, Schug, Yuki, Yamada, and Nezlek, 2018), where again the maximisers seem to end up less satisfied.

There is evidence in those works I just cited that maximising is bad at what it sets out to achieve. But there are both empirical and theoretical reasons to be cautious about accepting these results at face value.

Whether maximisers are worse off seems to be tied up to the "paradox of choice" (Schwartz, 2004), the idea that sometimes giving people even more choices makes them less happy with their outcome, because they are more prone to regret. But it is unclear whether such a paradox exists. One meta-analysis (Scheibehenne, Greifeneder, and Todd, 2010) did not show the effect existing at all, though a later meta-analysis finds a significant mediated effect (Chernev, Böckenholt, and Goodman, 2015). But it could also be that the result is a feature of an idiosyncratic way of carving up the maximisers from the satisficers. Another way of dividing them up produces no effect at all (Diab, Gillespie, and Highhouse, 2008).

The theoretical reasons relate to Newcomb's problem. Even if we knew that maximisers were less satisfied with how things are going than satisficers, it isn't obvious that any one person would be better off switching. They might be like a two-boxer who would get nothing if they took one-box. There is a little evidence in Sheena Iyengar and colleagues (2006) that tells against this explanation of what is happening, but not nearly enough to rule it out conclusively.

The upshot of all this is that there are potentially two kinds of cost of engaging in certain kinds of search and choice procedures. Some procedures are more costly to implement than others: they take more time, or more energy, or even more money. But further, some procedures might have a hedonic cost that extends beyond the time that the procedure is implemented. There is no theoretical or empirical guarantee that choosing widget W by procedure P1 will produce the same amount of happiness as choosing widget W by procedure P2. And especially for choices that are intended to produce happiness, this kind of factor should matter to us. In short, there are many more ways to assess a consumer choice procedure than the quality of the products it ends up choosing. This will be the key to our resolution of the puzzles about closure.

6.6 Deliberation Costs and Infinite Regresses

The idea that people should reason by choosing arbitrarily between choices that are close enough is not a new one. Experimental work by Reutskaja and colleagues (2011) suggests this is how people do reason. But the idea that people should reason this way goes back much further. It is often traced back to a footnote in Frank Knight (1921). Here is the text that provides the context for the note.

> Let us take Marshall's example of a boy gathering and eating berries ... We can hardly suppose that the boy goes through such mental operations as drawing curves or making estimates of utility and disutility scales. What he does, in so far as he deliberates between the alternatives at all*, is to consider together with reference to successive amounts of his "commodity," the utility of each increment against its "cost in effort," and evaluate the net result as either positive or negative. (Knight, 1921: 66–67)

The footnote attached to "at all" says this:

> Which, to be sure, is not very far. Nor is this any criticism of the boy. Quite the contrary! It is evident that the rational thing to do is to be irrational, where deliberation and estimation cost more than they are worth. That this is very often true, and that men still oftener (perhaps) behave as if it were, does not vitiate economic reasoning to the extent that might be supposed. For these irrationalities (whether rational or irrational!) tend to offset each other. (Knight, 1921: 67n1)

Knight doesn't really give an argument for the claim that these effects will offset. As John Conlisk (1996) shows in his fantastic survey of the late 20th-century literature on bounded rationality, it very often isn't true. Especially in game theoretic contexts, the thought that other players might think that "deliberation and estimation cost more than they are worth" can have striking consequences. That's not relevant to us though; we're just interested in the claim about rationality.

There is something paradoxical, almost incoherent, about Knight's formulation. If it is "rational to be irrational", then being "irrational" can't really be irrational. There are two natural ways to get out of this paradox. One, loosely following David Christensen (2007) would be to say that "Murphy's Law" applies here. Whatever one does will be irrational in some sense. Still, some actions are less irrational than others, and the least irrational will be to decline to engage in deliberation that costs more than it is worth. I suspect what Knight had in mind though was something different (if not obviously better). He is using "rational" as more or less a rigid designator of the property of choosing as a Marshallian maximiser does. What he means here is that the disposition to not choose in that way will be, in the long run, the disposition with maximal returns.

This latter idea is what motivates the thought that rational agents will take what Conlisk calls "deliberation costs" into account. Conlisk thinks that this is what rational agents will do, but he notes that there is a problem with it.

> However, we quickly collide with a perplexing obstacle. Suppose that we first formulate a decision problem as a conventional optimization based on the assumption of unbounded rationality and thus on the assumption of zero deliberation cost. Suppose we then recognize that deliberation cost is positive; so we fold this further cost into the original problem. The difficulty is that the augmented optimization problem will itself be costly to analyze; and this new deliberation cost will be neglected. We can then formulate a third problem which includes the cost of solving the second, and then a fourth problem, and so on. We quickly find ourselves in an infinite and seemingly intractable regress. In rough notation, let P denote the initial problem, and let F(.) denote the operation of folding deliberation cost into a problem. Then the regress of problems is P, F(P), $F^2(P)$, ... (Conlisk, 1996: 687)

Conlisk's own solution to this problem is not particularly satisfying. He notes that once we get to F^3 and F^4, the problems are "overly convoluted" and seem to be safely ignored. This isn't enough for two reasons. First, even a problem that is convoluted to state can have serious consequences when we think about solving it. (What would *Econometrica* publish if this weren't true?) Second, as is often noted, $F^2(P)$ might be a harder problem to solve than P, so simply stopping the regress there and treating the rational agent as solving this problem seems to be an unmotivated choice.

As Conlisk notes, this problem has a long history, and is often used to dismiss the idea that folding deliberation costs into our model of the optimising agent is a good idea. I use 'dismiss' advisedly. Conlisk points out that there is very little *discussion* of the infinite regress problem in the literature before his paper in 1996. The same remains true after 1996.

Instead, people appeal to the regress in a sentence or two to set aside approaches that incorporate deliberation cost in the way that Conlisk suggests.

Up to around the time of Conlisk's article, the infinite regress problem was often appealed to by people arguing that we should, in effect, ignore deliberation costs. After his article, the appeals to the regress come from a different direction. The appeals now typically come from theorists arguing that deliberation costs are real, but the regress means it will be impossible to consistently incorporate them into a model of an optimising agent. So we should instead rely on experimental techniques to see how people actually handle deliberation costs; the theory of optimisation has reached its limit. This kind of move is found in writers as diverse as Gigerenzer and Selten (2001), Odell (2002), Pingle (2006), Mangan, Hughes, and Slack (2010), Ogaki and Tanaka (2017), and Chakravarti (2017). Proponents of taking deliberation costs seriously within broadly optimising approaches, like Miles Kimball (2015), say that solving the regress problem is the biggest barrier to having such an approach taken seriously by economists.

It really matters for the story of this book that there is a solution to the infinite regress problem within a broadly optimising framework. More precisely, IRT needs there to be a solution to the regress problem that does not defeat knowledge. At least some of the time, the fact that a belief was formed by a rationally problematic procedure means that the belief is not a piece of knowledge. As we might say, the irrationality of the procedure is a defeater of the claim to knowledge. But perhaps if the procedure is optimal (even if not rational) that defeats the defeater. 'Optimal' here need not mean rationally optimal; it means optimal given the computational limitations on the agent. But now I've said enough to suggest that the regress problem will arise.

Here's how I plan to solve the regress problem. What matters for optimality is that the thinker is following the procedure that is the optimal solution to $F(P)$. It doesn't matter that they compute that it is the optimal solution, or even that they are following it because it is the optimal solution. It is an external, success-oriented condition, that does not require that it be followed in the right way, e.g., by computing the optimal answer. The thinker just has to do the right thing. This kind of externalism solves the regress problem by denying it gets started. There is no higher-order problem to solve, because the thinker doesn't have to solve that problem in order to act rationally. They just have to have dispositions that mean they mimic the correct solution.

This solution to the regress problem is easy to state, but a little harder to motivate. There are two big questions to answer before we can say it is really motivated.

1. Why should we allow this kind of unreflective rule-following in our solution to the regress?
2. Why should we think that F(P) is the point where this consideration kicks in, as opposed to P, or anything else?

There are a few ways to answer 1. One motivation traces back to the work by the artificial intelligence researcher Stuart Russell (1997). (Although really it starts with the philosophers Russell cites as inspiration, such as Christopher Cherniak (1986) and Gilbert Harman (1973).) He stresses that we should think about the problem from the outside, as it were, not from inside the agent's perspective. How would we program a machine that we knew would have to face the world with various limitations? We will give it rules to follow, but we won't necessarily give it the desire (or even the capacity) to follow those rules self-consciously. What's more useful is giving it knowledge of the limitations of the rules. That can be done without following the rules as such. It just requires having good dispositions to complicate the rules one is following in cases where such complication will be justified.

Another motivation is right there in the quote from Knight that set this literature going. Most writers quote the footnote, where Knight suggests it might be rational to be irrational. But look back at what he's saying in the text. The point is that it can be perfectly rational to use considerations other than drawing curves and making utility scales. What one has to do is follow internal rules that (non-accidentally) track what one would do if one was a self-consciously perfect Marshallian agent. That's what I'm saying too.

Finally, there is the simple point that on pain of regress any set of rules whatsoever must say that there are some rules that are simply followed. This is one of the less controversial conclusions of the debates about rule-following that were started by Wittgenstein (1953). That we must at some stage simply follow rules, not follow them in virtue of following another rule, say the rule to compute how to follow the first rule and act accordingly, is an inevitable consequence of thinking that finite creatures can be rule followers.

So question 1 is not really a big problem. But question 2 is more serious. Why F(P), and why not something else? The short answer will be that any reason to think that rational actors maximize *expected* utility, as opposed to actual utility, will also be a reason to think that they solve F(P) and not P. The longer answer is a bit more roundabout, but it helps us to see what a solution to F(P) will look like.

Start by stepping back and thinking about why we cared about *expected* utility in the first place. Why not just say that the best thing to do is to produce the best outcome, and be done with it? Well, we don't say that because we take it as a fixed point of our inquiry that agents are informationally limited, and that the best thing to do is what is best given that limitation. Given some plausible assumptions, the best thing for the informationally limited agent to do would be to maximise expected utility. This is a second-best option, but the best is unavailable given the limitations that we are treating as unavoidable.

Agents are not just informationally limited: they are computationally limited too. We could treat computational limits as the core limitation to be modelled. As Conlisk says, it is "entertaining to imagine" theorists who worked in just this way (Conlisk, 1996: 691). So let's imagine we meet some Martian economists, and they take computational, and not informational, limitations as the core constraint on rational choosers. So in their models, every agent has all the information relevant to their choice, but can't always compute what to do with that information.

Conlisk doesn't spell out the details of this thought experiment, and it's a little tricky to say exactly how it should work. (I'm indebted here to Harvey Lederman.) After all, you might think that 'information' should include things like information about the results of various computations, or about what would be best to do given their information. So how can we make sense of a being that is computationally but not informationally limited?

Here's one way to make sense of what Conlisk's Martians might be like. Assume that the Martians are very strict positivists. (This isn't going to make them optimal social scientists, but presumably we never thought they were.) So the truths can be divided up into observation sentences, and things derived from observation sentences by definition and deduction. In their preferred models, every agent knows every true observation sentence—including those about observations that have not yet been made. But they don't know all the results of deriving further truths from the observation sentences by definition and deduction. So such an agent might know precisely all the points she has to drive to today, and know the cost of traveling between any two points, but not know the optimal route to take on her travels. That last claim won't be 'information' in the relevant sense since it is not an observation sentence.

The point is not that the Martian economists think that every agent knows every observation sentence, any more than human economists think that every agent has a solution to every traveling salesman problem in their back pocket. Rather, it's that they think that this is a good modelling assumption. Conlisk has some fun imagining what Martian economists who make this modelling assumption might say in defence of their practice. They might disparage their colleagues who take informational limitations seriously as introducing ad hoc stipulations into theory. They might argue that informational limitations are bound to cancel out, or be eliminated by competition. They might argue that apparent informational limitations are really just computational ones, or at least can be modelled as computational ones. (Here it might be helpful to think of the Martian economists as positivists, and in particular as positivists who think that the notion of observation sentence is flexible enough to behave differently in different theoretical contexts.) And so on, replicating almost every complaint that human economists have ever made about theorists who want to take computational limitations seriously.

What Conlisk doesn't add is that they might suggest that there is a regress worry for any attempt to add informational constraints. Imagine that inside one of these models, an agent is deciding what to have for dinner. Let Q be the initial optimisation problem as the Martians see it. That is, Q is the problem of finding the best outcome, the best dinner, given full knowledge of the situation, but the actual computational limitations of the agent. Then we suggest that we should also account for the informational limitations. Let's see if this will work, they say. Let I be the function that transforms a problem into one that is sensitive to the informational limitations of the agent. But if we're really sensitive to informational limitations, we should note that I(Q) is also a problem the agent has to solve under conditions of less than full information.[4] So the informationally challenged agent will have to solve not just I(Q), but $I^2(Q)$, and $I^3(Q)$ and so on.[5]

Orthodox defenders of (human versions of) rational choice theory have to think this is a bad argument. I think most of them will agree with roughly the solution I'm adopting. The right problem to solve is I(Q), on a model where Q is in fact the problem of choosing the objectively best option. Put in philosophers' terms, we should think of Q as rigidly, and transparently, designating the problem the agent is facing. So I(Q) is not the problem of doing what's best given how little one knows about both the world and one's place in it. Rather, it's the problem of how to do the best one can in this very situation, given one's ignorance about the world. Even if one doesn't know precisely the situation one is in, and one doesn't know what utility function one has, or for that matter what knowledge one has, one should maximise expected utility given actual expectations and actual utility. The problem to solve is I(Q), not $I^2(Q)$.

But the bigger thing to say is that neither we nor the Martians really started with the right original problem. The original problem, O, is the problem of choosing the objectively best option; i.e., choosing what to have for dinner. The humans start by considering the problem I(O), i.e., P, and then debate whether we should stick with that problem, or move to F(I(O)). The Martians start by considering the problem F(O), i.e., Q, then debate whether we should stick with that or move to I(F(O)). And the answer in both cases is that we should move.

Given the plausible commutativity principle that introducing two limitations to theorising has the same effect whichever order we introduce them, I(F(O)) = F(I(O)). That is, F(P) = I(Q). And that's the problem that we should think the rational agent is solving.

But why solve that, rather than something more or less close to O? Well, think about what we say about an agent in a Jackson case who tries to solve O not I(O). (A Jackson case, in this sense, is a case where

---

4   At this point the Martians might note that all they are relying on here is that agents in their model violate negative introspection: sometimes they don't know something without knowing that they don't know it. They could cite Humberstone (2016: 380–402) for why this is a sensible modelling assumption.

5   At this point, some of the Martians note that the existence of Elster (1979) restored their faith in humanity.

the choice with highest expected value is known to not have the highest objective value. So trying to get the highest objective value will mean definitely not maximising expected value.) We think it will be sheer luck if they succeed. We think in the long run they will almost certainly do worse than if they tried to solve I(O). And in the rare case where they do better, we think it isn't a credit to them, but to their luck. In cases where the well-being of others is involved, we think aiming for the solution to O involves needless, and often immoral, risk-taking.

The Martians can quite rightly say the same things about why F(O) is a more theoretically interesting problem than O. Assume we are in a situation where F(O) is known to differ from O. For example, imagine the decision maker will get a reward if they announce the correct answer to whether a particular sentence is a truth-functional tautology, and they are allowed to pay a small fee to use a computer that can decide whether any given sentence is a tautology. The solution to O is to announce the correct answer, whatever it is. The solution to F(O) is to pay to use the computer. The Martians might point out that in the long run, solving F(O) will yield better results. That if the agent does solve problems like O correctly, even in the long run, this will just mean they were lucky, not rational. That if the reward is that a third party does not suffer, then it is immorally reckless to not solve F(O), i.e., to not consult the computer. In general, whatever we can say that motivated "Rational Choice Theory", as opposed to "Choose the Best Choice Theory", they can say too.

Both the human and the Martian arguments look good to me. We should add in both computational and informational limitations into our model of the ideal agent. But note something else that comes from thinking about these Jackson cases. In solving a limitation sensitive problem, we aren't trying to approximate a solution to the limitation insensitive problem. This is part of why the regress can stop here. To solve F(X), we don't have to solve X, and then see how close the various computationally feasible solutions get to this solution. That's true in general because of Jackson cases, but it's especially true when X is itself a complex problem. In trying to solve F(I(O)), i.e., I(F(O)), we aren't trying to maximise expected value, and then approximate that solution given computational limitations. Nor are we trying to be optimal by Martian standards (i.e., solve F(O)), then approximate that given informational limitations. We're just trying to get as good an outcome as we can, given our limitations.

Doing that does not require solving any iterated problem about how well we can solve F(I(O)) given various limitations, any more than rationally picking berries requires drawing Marshallian curves.

So that's the solution to the regress. It is legitimate to think that there is a rule that rational creatures follow immediately, on pain of thinking that all theories of rationality imply regresses. And thinking about the contingency of how Rational Choice Theory got to be the way it is suggests that the solution to what Conlisk calls F(P), or what I've called F(I(O)), will be that point.

What might that stopping point look like in practice? In his discussion of the regress, Miles Kimball (2015) suggests a few options. I want to focus on two of them.

> Least transgressive are models in which an agent sits down once in a long while to think very carefully about how carefully to think about decisions of a frequently encountered type. For example, it is not impossible that someone might spend one afternoon considering how much time to spend on each of many grocery-shopping trips in comparison shopping. In this type of modelling, the infrequent computations of how carefully to think about repeated types of decisions could be approximated as if there were no computational cost, even though the context of the problem implies that those computational costs are strictly positive. (Kimball, 2015: 174)

That's obviously relevant to David in the supermarket. He could, in principle, spend one Saturday afternoon thinking about how carefully to check each of the items in the supermarket before putting it in his shopping cart. Then in future trips, he could just carry out this plan. This isn't terrible, but I don't think it's optimal. For one thing, there are much better things to do with Saturday afternoons. For another, it suggests we are back in the business of equating solving F(P) with approximately solving P. And that's a mistake. Better to just say that David is rational if he just does the things that he would do were he to waste a Saturday afternoon this way, and then plan it out. That thought leads to Kimball's more radical suggestion for how to avoid the regress,

> [M]odelling economic actors as doing constrained optimization in relation to a simpler economic model than the model treated as true in the analysis. This simpler economic model treated as true by the agent can be called a "folk theory". (Kimball, 2015: 175)

It's this last idea I plan to explore in more detail. (It has some similarities to the discussion of small worlds in (Joyce, 1999: 70–77).) The short version is that David can, and should, have a little toy model of the supermarket in his head, and should optimize relative to that model. The model will be false, and David will know it is false. And that won't matter, as long as David treats the model the right way.

6.7 Ignorance is Bliss

There are a lot of things that could have gone wrong with a can of chickpeas. They could have gone bad inside the can. They could have been contaminated, either deliberately or through carelessness. They could have been sitting around so long they have expired. All these things are, at least logically, possible.

These possibilities, while serious, are rare and hard to detect. It is unheard of for someone to deliberately contaminate canned chickpeas, even though other grocery products like strawberries have been targeted. To check for expiry dates, one must scan each can, which is time-consuming due to the small type. A badly dented can may increase the risk of unintentional contamination, but most cans have no dents or only minor ones.

Given the rarity of these problems and the difficulty in obtaining evidence that significantly increases the probability of them occurring, the rational choice is to act in a way that is not affected by whether these problems actually occur. It is best to be vigilant, in the sense of Dan Sperber and colleagues (2010). In this context, that means considering only those problems for which there is evidence that they are worth considering, and ignoring the rest. To ignore a potential problem is to choose in a way that is insensitive to the evidence for that problem. That makes sense for both the banknotes and the chickpeas, because engaging in a choice procedure that is sensitive to the probability of the problem will, in the long run, make you worse off.

In Kimball's terms, the rational shopper will have a toy model of the supermarket in which the contents of undamaged cans are safe to eat. This model is defeasible, but typically not defeated. (In Joyce's terms, the small worlds are all ones in which the undamaged cans are safe.) A thinker who uses that toy model won't change their view by conditionalising on the fact that a particular can is safe. So it is consistent with IRT that they know the can is safe. That gets us out of the worst of the sceptical challenges. By similar reasoning, Frankie Lee knows all of the banknotes are genuine.

This chapter started with the problem that cases like Frankie Lee's seemed to lead to rampant scepticism given pragmatic theories like IRT. The solution to this problem was more pragmatism. Rational choosers typically do not use a model where the probability of a forgery or contamination is 0.99999. This model is more trouble than it's worth, since there is no actionable difference between it and one where the probability is 1. In cases where one can do something about the risk, like taking the plastic banknote, or checking inside the egg carton, it is often worthwhile to do something. In those cases, but only those cases, IRT does have sceptical consequences. In general, the simpler model is the better choice, and when it is, IRT is consistent with the chooser having a lot of knowledge.

So David does know that the chickpeas are safe. He believes this on the basis of evidence that is connected in the right way to the truth of the proposition that the chickpeas are safe. There is a potential pragmatic defeater from the fact that Conditional Preference seems to rule out this knowledge. But there is a pragmatic defeater of that pragmatic defeater. Conditional Preferences only implies scepticism in David's case if David is insensitive to deliberation costs when choosing. He shouldn't be, on practical grounds. He should use a toy model that says all safe-looking cans are safe. Once he uses that toy model, there is no pragmatic defeat of his well-supported, well-grounded true belief. He knows the chickpeas are safe.

On the other hand, David doesn't know the eggs aren't cracked. The toy model that says all available eggs are uncracked is bad. It isn't bad because it's wrong. It's bad because there is a model that will yield better long run results even once we account for its complexity. That's the model that says that only eggs that have been visually inspected are certain to be uncracked; all other eggs are at best probably uncracked. So David doesn't know the eggs aren't cracked. Note this would be true even if improvements in the supply chain made the probability of cracked eggs much lower than it is today. What matters in the canned goods case is not just that the risk of contamination is low, it's also that there isn't anything to do about it. As long as it remains easy to flip the lid of egg cartons to check whether they are cracked, it will be hard to know without flipping that they aren't cracked.

This is another illustration of how the form of IRT I endorse really doesn't care about stakes. The stakes in this case are not zero—buying cracked eggs wastes money and that's why David should check. But it isn't 'high stakes' in anything like the sense that phrase is used. The stakes are exactly the same as in the chickpeas case. What matters is not the cost of being wrong about an assumption, but rather the relative cost of being wrong compared to the probability that one is wrong and the cost of checking.

The milk case is only slightly more complicated. At least in some places, the expiry date for milk is written in very large print on the front of the bottle. In those cases, it is worth checking that you aren't buying milk that expires tomorrow. So before you check, you don't know that the milk you pick up doesn't expire tomorrow. (And, like in the eggs case, that's true even if the shop very rarely sells milk that close to the expiry date.) But there is no way to check whether a particular container of milk, far from its expiration date, has gone bad. You can't easily open a milk bottle in the supermarket and smell it, for example. So that's the kind of rare and uncheckable problem that the sensible chooser will ignore. Their toy model will include that in a well-functioning store, all milk that is well away from the expiry date is safe. So once they've checked the expiry date, they know it is safe (assuming it is safe).

And in the normal case, Frankie Lee knows that the notes aren't forgeries. His toy model of the currency, like ours, should be that all bank notes are genuine unless there is a clear sign that they are not.[6] So we have a solution from within IRT to both the closure problems and the sceptical problems.

In the next chapter, I'll look at problems that can be addressed without taking this many detours into decision theory.

---

6 Or at least some clear enough sign. Arguably, the fact that a note is a high value one that someone is trying to use in the betting ring half an hour before the Melbourne Cup is in itself a sign that it is not genuine. A sceptical theory that says no one in that betting ring knows whether they are passing on forged bank notes is not a problematic sceptical theory.

7. Changes

My version of IRT version shares defects with more familiar versions of IRT. For instance, it is subject to the criticism that Crispin Wright makes here.

> [A] situation may arise ... when we can truly affirm an 'ugly conjunction' like:
>
>> X didn't (have enough evidence to) know P at t but does at t*
>> and has exactly the same body of P-relevant evidence at t* as at t.
>
> Such a remark seems drastically foreign to the concept of knowledge we actually have. It seems absurd to suppose that a thinker can acquire knowledge without further investigation simply because his practical interests happen so to change as to reduce the importance of the matter at hand. Another potential kind of ugly conjunction is the synchronic case for different subjects:
>
>> X knows that P but Y does not, and X and Y have exactly the same body of P-relevant evidence.
>
> when affirmed purely because X and Y have sufficiently different practical interests. IRI, as we noted earlier, must seemingly allow that instances of such a conjunction can be true. (Wright, 2018: 368)

That's right; I do allow that instances of such a conjunction can be true. A similar objection has been made by Gillian Russell and John Doris (2009), by Michael Blome-Tillmann (2009), and by Daniel Eaton and Timothy Pickavance (2015). My main reply to these objections is that they over-generate and would be successful objections to any theory that separates knowledge from rational true belief. Since knowledge does not equal rational true belief, no such objection can work.[1]

---

[1] This reply was first made in my (2016b), and earlier replies to Russell and Doris, as well as Blome-Tillman, were made in my (2011), although I now believe that

7.1 Overview of Replies

I'm going to quickly go over five responses to this objection. I think at some level all five are correct. The first two, however, would probably do little to persuade anyone not already committed to IRT. The last three are more persuasive, and I'll develop each of them in a subsequent section.

The first thing one could say about these objections is that they simply highlight a prominent feature of the view—namely, that it allows knowledge to turn on non-alethic features—and then object to that very feature. As a result, the objections are blatantly question-begging. It doesn't accomplish much more than pointing out the obvious. The opponents think that this view is radical. And of course the objections to radical views will end up being question-begging (Lewis, 1982). Saying that one's opponents are begging the question might make you feel better—you don't have to be persuaded by their arguments—but doesn't actually move the debate forward. We can, and must, do better.

A second thing to say is that on some versions of IRT, it will be very hard to state the objection. Consider a version of IRT that also accepts E=K, the thesis that one's evidence is all and only what one knows. This is hardly an obscure version of the view; it's what is defended by Jason Stanley (2005). Now it will not be true, according to such a view, that there are, as Wright suggests, two people who have the same evidence but different knowledge. That's impossible, since having different knowledge literally entails, in this view, that they have different evidence. But does this make the objection go away, or does it just make it harder to state? I'm mostly inclined to think it's the latter. There is still something weird about people who have the same input from the world, and the same reactions to that input, but who differ in what they know about the world. So this response, while more useful than the last one, i.e., not totally useless, won't quite work either.

A third response challenges head on the intuition about 'weirdness' mentioned in the previous paragraph. One of the consequences of the vast Gettier literature is that there are any number of cases where people have the same inputs, the same true beliefs based on those inputs, but different knowledge. It's trivial to get these inter-world versions of a case

---

those replies did not quite get to the heart of the matter.

like this, and maybe that's enough to undermine the intuition. More generally, it's hard to state, and endorse, the intuition that the interest-relative theory is flawed without implicitly committing oneself to something closely resembling the JTB theory of knowledge. And since that theory is false, that's kind of bad news for that intuition. Or, perhaps more carefully, either that theory is false, or justification is understood in terms of knowledge, as on the E=K picture. And appealing to E=K might be an independent way to respond to the challenge. I'll spell out this response more fully in Section 7.2.

A fourth response aims to undermine the intuition in a different way. There is something fundamentally right about the JTB theory of knowledge, at least if we don't presuppose that the justification, the J, gets an internalist spin. But it can't be that the theory is extensionally correct. What is it? My conjecture is that knowledge is *built*, in the sense described by Karen Bennett (2017), out of those three components—justification, truth, and belief. Now this needs a notion of building that doesn't involve necessitation, and spelling that out would be a task for a different (and longer!) book. I'll try and say enough in Section 7.3 to make it at least minimally plausible that this conjecture is true, and that it is consistent with IRT.

The fifth response, and the one I want to lean on the most, comes from Nilanjan Das (2016). On the most plausible ways of articulating what the differences are between JTB and knowledge, it's not just that the differences will depend on 'non-standard' factors, it's that they will often depend on interests. Whether a belief is safe, or sensitive, or produced by a reliable method, or apt, or virtuous, or any other plausible criteria you might want, depends in part on the interests of the believer. More carefully, whether a belief satisfies any one of those properties can be counterfactually dependent on the interests of the believer. So I conclude these objections massively over-generate. If they are right, they show that practically every theory of knowledge produced in the last several decades is false. But it's really implausible that these kinds of considerations could show that. So the objection fails. I'll end in Section 7.4 by spelling out this response.

7.2 So Long JTB

The story of investigations into knowledge over the last sixty years is the story of making the list of things knowledge is sensitive to ever longer. The thesis of this book is that human interests, in particular the interests of the would-be knower, should be added to that list. But to defend that thesis, and especially to defend it from the kind of blank stare objection that I'm worrying about in this chapter, it helps to have the list in front of us. So I'm going to describe a mundane case of knowledge, then discuss various ways in which that knowledge could be lost if the world were different.

Our protagonist, Charlotte, is reading a book about the build up to World War One. In the base case, the book is Christopher Clark's *The Sleepwalkers* (Clark, 2012), though in some of the variants we'll discuss she reads a less impressive book. In it she reads the remarkable story of Henriette Caillaux, the second wife of anti-war French politician Joseph Caillaux. As you may already know, Henriette Caillaux shot and killed Gaston Calmette, the editor of *Le Figaro*, after *Le Figaro* published a string of damaging articles about Joseph Caillaux. The killing took place on March 16, 1914, and the trial was that July. It ended on July 28 with her acquittal.

Charlotte reads all of this and believes it. And indeed it is true. And the book is reliable. Although Charlotte does believe what the book says about Henriette Caillaux, she is not credulous. She is an attentive enough, and skilled enough, reader of contemporary history to know when historians are likely to be going out on a limb, and when they are not being as clear as one might like in reflecting how equivocal the evidence is. But Clark is a good historian, and Charlotte is a good reader, and the beliefs she takes from the book are both true and supported by the underlying evidence.

Focus for now on this proposition.

> Henriette Caillaux's trial for the murder of Gaston Calmette ended in her acquittal in late July 1914.

Call this proposition p. In this base case, Charlotte knows that p. But there are ever so many ways in which Charlotte could fail to have known it. The following three are particularly important.

Variant J
Charlotte didn't finish the book. She only got as far as the start of Caillaux's trial, but lost interest in the machinations of the diplomats in the late stages of the July crisis. Still, she had a strong hunch that Caillaux would be acquitted and, on just this basis, firmly believed that she would be.

Variant T
Charlotte is in a world where things went just as in the actual world up to the trial, but then Caillaux was found guilty. Despite this, Charlotte reads a book that is word-for-word identical to Clark's book. That is, it falsely says that Caillaux was acquitted, before quickly moving back to talking about the war. Charlotte believes, falsely, that p.

Variant B
Charlotte reads the book to the end, but she can't believe that Caillaux would be acquitted. The evidence was conclusive, she thought. She is torn because she also can't really believe a historian would get such a clear fact wrong. But she also can't believe anyone would be acquitted in such a trial. So she withholds judgment on the matter, not sure what actually happened in Caillaux's trial.

Charlotte does not know that p in all three scenarios. These cases are good evidence that knowledge requires justification, truth, and belief. In Variant J, Charlotte's belief in p is not justified, but rather a mere hunch, so she doesn't know. In Variant T, Charlotte's belief is incorrect, making it an honest mistake and hence not knowledge. In Variant B, Charlotte lacks knowledge because she doesn't even believe p; she has the evidence, but does not accept it.

There are philosophers who argue that the conditions in all three cases are not strictly necessary. However, I won't be discussing these points as it would take us too far afield. Instead, I'll assume that Variant J demonstrates the need for justification or some form of rationality for knowledge. Variant T shows that knowledge requires truth, and Variant B shows that belief or strong acceptance is necessary for knowledge.

For a short while in the mid-20th century, some philosophers thought these conditions were not merely necessary for knowledge, but jointly sufficient. To know that p just is to have a justified, true belief that p. This became known, largely in retrospect, as the JTB theory of knowledge. It fell out of fashion dramatically after a short but decisive criticism was published by Edmund Gettier (1963). But Gettier's criticism was not original; he had independently rediscovered a point made by the 8th-century philosopher Dharmottara (Nagel, 2014). Here is a version of the kind of case Dharmottara discovered.

> *Variant D*
> Charlotte stops reading before the denouement. She thinks Caillaux was acquitted, not on a hunch, but because she read in another book that official France was too disorganized in July 1914 to convict any murderers. This is untrue, but Charlotte used it to arrive at the correct conclusion that p.

In Variant D, Charlotte lacks knowledge of p because basing one's reasoning on a falsehood typically does not establish knowledge. So whether one knows is influenced by the accuracy of the grounds for one's belief. The subsequent variations may not be as straightforward, as determining whether Charlotte knows p will be more controversial. They are all instances where it is plausible that knowledge is sensitive to more factors than we've seen so far. The first case is a version of an example from Gilbert Harman (1973: 143ff).

> *Variant H*
> Charlotte's unfamiliarity with Henriette Caillaux is surprising, because in her world Caillaux is as infamous as killers like Ned Kelly, Jack the Ripper, and Lee Harvey Oswald. Her killing of Calmette has been the subject of numerous novels, plays, and movies. But all these renditions have a fictionalised ending: Caillaux is convicted and executed. The authorities were so embarrassed by the actual ending of the trial, where Caillaux was acquitted, that they successfully conspired to convince the public that this never happened. Charlotte, coincidentally, is the only person who hasn't heard of Caillaux's story. When she reads a word-for-word copy of Clark's book, she doesn't realize it's controversial and believes that p. If she had encountered any of these older books or plays, she would have assumed her book was mistaken since it's 'common knowledge' that Caillaux was convicted.

Intuitions may vary on this, but in Variant H, I don't think Charlotte knows that p. If that's right, then whether Charlotte knows that p is sensitive not just to the evidence she has, but to the evidence that is all around her. If she's swimming in a sea of evidence against p, and by the sheerest luck has not run into it, the evidence she does not have can block knowledge that p.

The previous example relied on the possibility of counter-evidence being everywhere. Possibly all that matters is that the counter-evidence is in just the right *somewhere*.

> *Variant S*
> In this world, an over-zealous copy-editor makes a last minute change to the very first printing of Clark's text. Not able to believe that Caillaux was acquitted—the evidence was so conclusive—they change the word 'acquittal' to 'conviction' in the sentence describing the end of the trial. Happily, this error is quickly caught, and only the first printing of the book contains the mistake. Charlotte discovered the book in a second-hand shop, which had two copies—one from the flawed first printing and one from a later printing. She bought the later one simply because it was the first one she saw. If she had entered the history section from the other direction, she would have bought the first printing and believed that p was false.

Plausibly, Charlotte doesn't know that p because it was a matter of luck that she purchased the later printing instead of the earlier one. Her method of forming beliefs, which involves buying a seemingly authoritative history book and accepting its plausible and well-supported claims, fails in this particular instance in a nearby possible world where she obtains the other copy. This type of luck is not compatible with knowledge. In contemporary terminology, a belief forming method yields knowledge only if it is *safe*. A method is safe only if it doesn't go wrong in nearby, realistic, scenarios (Williamson, 2000). So whether one knows is sensitive to not just the evidence one has, but the evidence one could easily have had.

Safety in this sense is a tricky notion. In Variant K, it seems to me that Charlotte does know that p.

> *Variant K*
> Charlotte detests reading books on paper, and only ever reads on her Kindle (an electronic book-reading device). Just like in Variant S, there was an error in the first printing of Clark's book. But the Kindle version never contained this error, and in any case, Kindle versions are updated frequently so even if it had, the error would have been quickly corrected. Charlotte reads the book on her Kindle, and comes to believe that p.

In this case, Charlotte believes p on good evidence from a trustworthy source, and there is no realistic possibility where she goes wrong on this question by trusting this source. That seems to me like enough for knowledge. I'll return to the difference between Variants S and K in Section 7.4, but first I want to look at two more cases.

> *Variant C*
> Charlotte reads Clark's book and believes p. But like in Variant B, she was sure that Caillaux would be convicted. And she still thinks it is absurd that someone would be acquitted given this evidence. Rather than responding to these conflicting pressures by withholding judgment, she responds by both believing that p is true, and believing it is false. She is just inconsistent, like so many of us are in so many ways.

It seems to me that in this case, Charlotte does not know that p. The incoherence in her beliefs on this very point undermines her claim to knowledge. With one more change, we get to the case that motivates this book.

> *Variant I*
> Charlotte reads the book, and believes that p. She is then offered a bet by a curiously benevolent deity. If she takes the bet, and p is true, she wins a dinner at her favourite bistro, Le Temps des Cerises. If she takes the bet, and p is false, she is cast into The Bad Place for eternity. If she declines the bet, life goes on as normal. Now she's deciding what to do.

By this stage you won't be surprised to hear that I think Variant I is just like Variant C in being a case in which Charlotte lacks knowledge. What I want to defend is something even stronger than that. In Variants C and I Charlotte lacks knowledge for just the same reason; it would be incoherent to believe p. Knowledge requires coherence and rationality, and in Variant I, if Charlotte believes p, she is either irrational or incoherent. I'll come back to this point about the relationship between Variants C and I in Section 7.3. First I want to reflect a bit on what we've seen in the earlier cases.

Most of the people who think that it is implausible that interests matter to knowledge are happy acknowledging the varieties of sensitivity that are revealed by Variants J, T, B, D, H, S, K, and C. (Or at least they acknowledge most of these; maybe they have idiosyncratic objections to including one or other kind of sensitivity.) They just think this one new kind of sensitivity is a bridge too far. It is a bit of a puzzle to me why we should think sensitivity to interests is more philosophically problematic than the other kinds of sensitivity we've seen so far. It might help to get you to share my puzzlement by starting with what looks like a simple question. What should we call the class of factors knowledge is sensitive to which is revealed by these variants, but which does not include interests?

One option is to call them the 'traditional' factors. Now since discussion of, say, safety only really became widespread in the 1990s, the tradition of including it in one's theory of knowledge is quite a new one. But I don't mind calling new things traditional. I'm Australian, and we have great traditions like the traditional Essendon-Collingwood Anzac Day match, which also dates to the 1990s. This terminology is a bit unstable though. After all, we've been discussing the role of interests in epistemology since at least 2002 (Fantl and McGrath, 2002), so that's almost long enough to be traditional as well.

Another option is to say that they are the factors that are truth-connected, or truth-relevant. But there's no way to make sense of this notion in a way that gets at what is wanted. For one thing, it's really not obvious that coherence constraints (like we need for Variant C) are connected to truth. For another, all Variant I suggests is that we need a principle like the following in our theory of knowledge.

> Someone knows something only if their evidence is strong enough for them to rationally treat the thing as a fixed starting point in their inquiries.

On the face of it, that's at least as truth-connected as the relatively uncontroversial requirement that knowledge be based on evidence. It just says knowledge requires strong evidence. Now, of course, it also says just how strong the evidence must be depends on what their inquiries are. Is that problematic? It might be if you think that every aspect of a requirement on knowledge is truth-relevant.

That last claim really can't be right. Or, at least, it can't be right unless you believe the JTB theory of knowledge. If the JTB theory is false, then any premise one might use in a Wright-style argument against IRT is bound to have counterexamples. Recall the particular way Wright argued against IRT

> X didn't (have enough evidence to) know P at t but does at t* and has exactly the same body of P-relevant evidence at t* as at t. (Wright, 2018: 368)

If evidence primarily affects justification, then similarity of evidence at t and t* should just tell us that X is rational in believing P at both times or neither. Let's say that it's both times. Then as long as one could be in a JTB-but-not-knowledge-situation at t and a knowledge-with-the-same-evidence-situation at t*, Wright's conjunction should be possible. Here's one way that could happen.

> *Variant S**
> Charlotte reads the book on her Kindle, and believes that p at t_0. The next day, at t, she can't believe she read that p and reads the book again. It still says that p, but this is bizarre because a new version of the book that says $\neg p$ was pushed out to all Kindles. Due to a network failure, Charlotte's Kindle was the only one not to get the push. She now doesn't know that p; this case is just like the safety cases and the Harman cases. The next day at t* a corrected version of the book that says p is pushed out to all Kindles, including Charlotte's. Again perplexed, she triple checks, and comes to believe, and know, that p.

The ugly conjunction that IRT endorses is something that theories that are sensitive to safety considerations, or evidential availability considerations, also endorse. And the true theory is sensitive to one or other kind of these considerations.

7.3 Making Up Knowledge

All that said, I've come to think there is something right about the JTB theory. Or, as I'd prefer, the RTB theory; as in Rational True Belief.[2] It isn't extensional adequacy; Dharmottara refuted that 1300 years ago. But it can be expressed using the modern[3] notion of grounding. Or, as I'd prefer, using the notion of a *building relation* that Bennett (2017) describes.

Consider a very abstractly described case where all of 1–4 are true.

1. S knows that p.
2. p.

---

2 I think it's strange to apply the notion of justification to beliefs, and much more natural to talk about rational beliefs.
3 Well, modern if you think it's not the same notion as Meister Eckhart's notion of grounding. I'm a little agnostic on that.

3. S's attitude to p is rational.

4. S believes that p.

I think that when 1 is true, it is made true by 2–4. Following Bennett, we might say that the fact expressed in 1 is built from the facts expressed in 2–4. Now to make this work, we need a notion of building (or grounding) that's contingent, since 2–4 do not collectively entail 1. Defending the coherence of such a notion in detail would make for a very different book to this one. But I'll say a few words about why I think such a notion is going to be needed.

When I say that 1 is made true by 2-4, I mean that it is metaphysically explained by 2–4. They provide a complete explanation of 1's truth. Now here's the key step. A complete explanation need not be an entailing explanation. I'll give a relatively uncontroversial example of this involving causal explanation, then suggest a different philosophical example.

It is, famously, hard to explain the origins of World War One. But without settling all the causal and explanatory issues about the war's origins, we can confidently make the following two claims.

C
Had a giant asteroid struck Sarajevo on June 27, 1914, the war would not have started when it did.

NE
It is no part of the explanation of the start of the war that no such giant asteroid struck Sarajevo on June 27, 1914.

The counterfactual claim, C, can easily be verified by thinking about the consequences of giant asteroid strikes. (See, for example, the extinction of the dinosaurs.)

The claim about explanation, NE, can be verified by thinking about how absurd the task of explanation would be if it were false. For every possible event that could have changed history, but didn't, we'd have to include its non-happening in our explanation of the war. The non-occurrence of every possible alien invasion, mass pandemic, or tulip mania that could have happened, and would have made a difference, would be part of our explanation.

So the origins of the war are sensitive to whether there was a giant asteroid strike, but the lack of a giant asteroid strike is no part of the complete explanation for why the war took place. Complete causal explanations can leave out things that are counterfactually relevant to whether the event took place. That means that they aren't entailing explanations, since if everything in the complete explanation happened, but so did an asteroid strike, the war wouldn't have taken place.

We see the same thing in commonsense morality. This is one of the key points behind Bernard Williams's "One Thought Too Many" argument (Williams, 1976). If one's child is drowning in a pool, one has a reason to dive in and rescue them. Moreover, it's a complete reason. When someone asks, "Why did you do that?", you've given them a complete reason if you say, "My child was drowning". And you should accept that answer even if you think there are cases where that would be the wrong thing to do. Set up your preferred horror story moral example where diving in to rescue the child would lead to the destruction of the world. Had that horror story been actual, it perhaps would not have been morally required to dive into the pool. But in reality, a complete explanation of why it was required was that one's child was drowning.

The same thing is true about the relationship between knowledge and interests. What one knows is always (in principle) sensitive to what one's interests are. But in cases where one knows, one's knowledge is not explained by what one's interests are. Rather, it is explained just by the factors that go into RTB, and perhaps the interplay between them.

Some of the objections to IRT might rely on conflating the concepts of building and of counterfactual dependence. In their critique of IRT, Gillian Russell and John Doris (2009) repeatedly talk about how implausible it is that a change in interests can "make" one have knowledge. Strictly speaking, I don't think a change in interests does make one have knowledge. It's true that one might have knowledge, and not have had that knowledge had one's interests been different. But it doesn't follow that facts about interests stand in a making, or building, relationship to facts about knowledge. They could be, and should be, treated as things relevant to whether facts about truth, belief and rationality suffice in the circumstances for knowledge. Those factors, and only those factors, make for knowledge. That's true whether we're talking about familiar counterexamples to the JTB (or RTB) theories, or whether we're talking about interest-relativity.

The distinction between building and counterfactual sensitivity explains part of why the verdicts of IRT can sound implausible, but it doesn't explain all of it. To defend IRT from the claim that it renders implausible verdicts, we need something more. So I'll end this chapter with an argument by Nilanjan Das that responds to this kind of objection. The argument is going to be that every plausible theory of knowledge is committed to some kind of interest-relativity, and so the intuitions that my version of IRT violates are violated by every plausible theory of knowledge. Such intuitions must be wrong, and therefore can't form the basis of a good objection.

7.4 Every Theory is Interest-Relative

Think about the difference between Variant S and Variant K.[4] Variant S was meant to be a simple case where Charlotte does not know something because of a safety violation. Knowledge is incompatible with a certain kind of luck. To know something is to do better than make a lucky guess. Charlotte isn't guessing, but she seems to be lucky in a similar kind of way to the guesser, so she doesn't know. But in Variant K, she isn't lucky. It's no coincidence that her book said the correct thing. There is no serious possibility of her being misled on this point.

Since Charlotte knows that p in Variant K, but not in Variant S, knowledge is sensitive to one's preferred format for reading books. This is hardly a 'truth-relevant' feature, so knowledge isn't only relevant to truth-relevant features. Knowledge generally depends on whether one was lucky, and the factors that determine whether one was lucky on an occasion need not be truth-relevant.

The same pattern recurs in other cases. In Variant H, Charlotte lacked knowledge because of evidence around her. But imagine a variant of that variant where Charlotte recently emigrated to a country where no one ever talks about Henriette Caillaux. In the variant, Charlotte knows that p. So her knowledge of French history is sensitive to her emigration status. And emigration status isn't truth-relevant or truth-connected.

If knowledge is sensitive to external factors, and it isn't required that knowledge be infallible, then knowledge will be sensitive to things that

---

4   Though they are making somewhat different points, there is a resemblance between these cases and the cases that Gendler and Hawthorne (2005) use to raise trouble for fake barn intuitions.

are not particularly truth-relevant. Any fallibilist, externalist theory of knowledge will have to face a version of a reference class problem, in order to say whether a particular true belief was a matter of luck. In general, the factors that place one in this reference class rather than another are not truth-relevant, but they are relevant to whether one can be said to know something.

That's enough to argue against sweeping generalisations about what knowledge could or could not be sensitive to. Knowledge could be sensitive to anything, because anything could matter to which reference class one is in. Das (2016: 116) shows that we can say something stronger. Cases like these can be used to directly argue for interest-relativity, even if one rejects all the other arguments in the existing literature on IRT.

Knowledge requires not getting it right just by luck. Making that intuition precise is a lot of work, but it means at least that the following is true. If the method the person used to form their belief frequently goes wrong in their actual environment, then even on occasions that the method gets the right answer, it isn't knowledge. But what's their environment? It's not just spaces within a fixed distance from them. Rather, it's spaces that in which they could easily have ended up being. It's spaces where it's a matter of luck that they are or aren't in them. So my environment, in the relevant sense, consists of a network of college towns and universities throughout the globe, and excludes any number of places a short drive away. But should I become more interested in nearby suburbs than far away colleges, my environment would change. That is to say, environment is an interest-relative notion.

If knowledge is sensitive to what one's environment is like, and one's environment in the relevant sense is interest-relative, then knowledge is going to be interest-relative. That's what is going on with Charlotte and the Kindle. Two people can be alike in what signals they receive from the world, and alike in their immediate surroundings, but be in different environments because of their different interests. If the method they use to form beliefs on the basis of that signal has differing levels of success in different environments, then whether they have knowledge will be sensitive to which environment they are in. That will depend on any number of 'non-traditional' factors, including their interests.

Now this isn't the only way, or even the main way, that interests matter to knowledge. But it is a way. And it shows that objections that rely on the very idea of knowledge being interest-relative must overgenerate. Unless such objections are tied to a rejection of the idea that safety or reliability or any other external factor matters to knowledge, they rule out too much.

That concludes the defence of IRT over the last three chapters. The final two chapters of the book return to setting out the view, going over two important, but technical, points. First, I argue that rational belief is not sensitive to interests in quite the same way that knowledge is. And second, I argue that evidence is interest-relative, but also in not quite the same way that knowledge is.

8. Rationality

This chapter is about rational belief. My version of IRT allows a new kind of gap between rational true belief and knowledge, and I'll argue we should treat this as a philosophical discovery, not a refutation of the view. Then I'll present two arguments for the possibility of rationally having credence 1 in a proposition without believing it. The first is due to Timothy Williamson; the second is new. These arguments refute two claims about the relationship between belief and credence. One is a descriptive claim: to believe p just is to have credence in p at or above some threshold. The other is a normative claim: one rationally believes p just in case one rationally has credence in it at or above some threshold. Even if those two arguments concerning belief and credence 1 don't work, and rational credence 1 does entail rational belief, there are independent arguments against the descriptive and normative claims if the 'threshold' in them is non-maximal. I'll end the chapter by noting how the view of rational belief that comes out of IRT is immune to the problems associated with understanding belief in terms of a credal threshold.

8.1 Atomism about Rational Belief

In Chapter 3 I suggested that the following two conditions were individually necessary for belief that p, and suggested they might be jointly sufficient.[1]

1. In some possible decision problem, p is taken for granted.
2. For every question the agent is interested in, the agent answers the question the same way (i.e., giving the same

---

[1] This section is based on Weatherson (2012).

answer for the same reasons) whether the question is asked unconditionally or conditional on p.

At this point one might think that offering a theory of rational belief would be easy. It is rational to believe p just in case it is rational to satisfy these conditions. Unfortunately, this nice thought can't be right. It can be irrational to satisfy these conditions while rationally believing p.

Coraline is like Anisa and Chamari, in that she has read a reliable book saying that the Battle of Agincourt was in 1415. And she now believes that the Battle of Agincourt was indeed in 1415, for the very good reason that she read it in a reliable book.

In front of her is a sealed envelope, and inside the envelope a number is written on a slip of paper. Let X denote that number, non-rigidly. (So when I say Coraline believes $X = x$, it means she believes that the number written on the slip of paper is x, where x rigidly denotes some number.) Coraline is offered the following bet:

- If she declines the bet, nothing happens.
- If she accepts the bet, and the Battle of Agincourt was in 1415, she wins $1.
- If she accepts the bet, and the Battle of Agincourt was not in 1415, she loses X dollars.

For some reason, Coraline is convinced that $X = 10$. This is very strange, since she was shown the slip of paper just a few minutes ago, and it clearly showed that $X = 10^9$. Coraline wouldn't bet on when the Battle of Agincourt was at odds of a billion to one. But she would take that bet at ten to one, which is what she thinks she is faced with. Indeed, she doesn't even conceptualise it as a bet; it's a free dollar she thinks. Right now, she is disposed to treat the date of the battle as a given. She is disposed to lose this disposition should a very long-odds bet appear to depend on it. But she doesn't believe she is facing such a bet.

So Coraline accepts the bet; she thinks it is a free dollar. Since that's when the battle took place, she wins the dollar. All's well that ends well. But it really was a wildly irrational bet to take. You shouldn't bet at those odds on something you remember from a history book. Neither memory nor history books are that reliable. Coraline was not rational to treat the questions *Should I take this bet?*, and *Conditional on the Battle of Agincourt being in 1415, should I take this bet?* the same way. Her treating them the same way was fortunate—she won a dollar—but irrational.

Yet it seems odd to say that Coraline's belief about the Battle of Agincourt was irrational. What was irrational was her belief about the envelope, not her belief about the battle. To say that a particular disposition was irrational is to make a holistic assessment of the person with the disposition. But whether a belief is rational or not is, relatively speaking, atomistic.

That suggests the following condition on rational belief: S's belief that p is irrational if

1. S irrationally has one of the dispositions that is characteristic of belief that p; and
2. What explains S having a disposition that is irrational in that way is her attitudes towards p, not (solely) her attitudes towards other propositions, or her skills in practical reasoning.

Intuitively, Coraline's irrational acceptance of the belief is explained by her (irrational) belief about what's in the envelope, not her (rational) belief about the Battle of Agincourt. We can take the relevant notion of explanation as a primitive if we like; it's in no worse philosophical shape than other notions we take as a primitive. But it is possible to spell it out a little more.

Coraline has a pattern of irrational dispositions related to the envelope. If you offer her $50 or X dollars, she'll take the $50. Alternatively, if you change the bet so it isn't about Agincourt, but is instead about any other thing for which she has excellent but not quite conclusive evidence, she'll still take the bet. On the other hand, she does not have a pattern of irrational dispositions related to the Battle of Agincourt. She has this one, but if you change the payouts so they are not related to this particular envelope, then for all we have said so far, she won't do anything irrational.

That difference in patterns matters. We know that it's the beliefs about the envelope, and not the beliefs about the battle, that are explanatory because of this pattern. We could try and create a reductive analysis of explanation in clause 2 using facts about patterns, like the way David Lewis tries to create a reductive analysis of causation using similar facts about patterns in "Causation as Influence" (Lewis, 2004). But doing so would invariably run up against edge cases that would be more trouble to resolve than they are worth. There are ever so many ways in which someone could have an irrational disposition about any particular case. We can imagine Coraline having a rational belief about the envelope, but still taking the bet because of any of the following reasons:

- It has been her life goal to lose a billion dollars in a day, so taking the bet strictly dominates not taking it.
- She believes (irrationally) that anyone who loses a billion dollars in a day goes to heaven, and she (rationally) values heaven above any monetary amount.
- She consistently makes reasoning errors about billions, so the prospect of losing a billion dollars rarely triggers an awareness that she should reconsider things she normally takes for granted.

The last one of these is especially interesting. The picture of rational agency I'm working with here owes a lot to the notion of epistemic vigilance, as developed by Dan Sperber and colleagues (Sperber et al., 2010). The rational agent will have all these beliefs in their head that they will drop when the costs of being wrong about them are too high, or the costs of re-opening inquiry into them are too low. They can't reason, at least in any conscious way, about whether to drop these beliefs, because to do that is, in some sense, to call the belief into doubt. And what's at issue is whether they should call the belief into doubt. So what they need is some kind of disposition to replace a belief that p with an attitude that p is highly probable, and this disposition should correlate with the cases where taking p for granted will not maximise expected utility. This disposition will be a kind of vigilance. As Sperber and his collaborators show, we need some notion of vigilance to explain a lot of different aspects of epistemic evaluation. I think that notion can be usefully pressed into service here.[2]

If you need something like vigilance in your theory of belief, then you have to allow that vigilance might fail. Maybe some irrational

---

[2] Kenneth Boyd (2016) suggests a somewhat similar role for vigilance in the course of defending an interest-invariant epistemic theory. Obviously I don't agree with his conclusions, but my use of Sperber's work does echo his.

dispositions can be traced to that failure, and not to any propositional attitude the decider has. For example, if Coraline systematically fails to be vigilant when exactly one billion dollars is at stake, then we might want to say that her belief in p is still rational, and she is practically, rather than theoretically, irrational. (Why could this happen? Perhaps she thinks of Dr Evil every time she hears the phrase "One billion dollars", and this distractor prevents her normally reliable skill of being vigilant from kicking in.)

If one tries to turn the vague talk of patterns of bets involving one proposition or another into a reductive analysis of when one particular belief is irrational, one will inevitably run into hard cases where a decider has multiple failures. We can't say that what makes Coraline's belief about the envelope, and not her belief about the battle, irrational is that if you replaced the envelope, she would invariably have a rational disposition. After all, she might have some other irrational belief about whatever we replace the envelope with. Or she might have some failure of practical reasoning, like a vigilance failure. Any kind of universal claim, like that it is only bets about the envelope that she gets wrong, won't do the job we need.

In "Knowledge, Bets and Interests", I tried to use the machinery of credences to make something like this point (Weatherson, 2012). The idea was that Coraline's belief in p was rational because her belief just was her high credence in p, and that credence was rational. I still think that's approximately right, but it can't be the full story. For one thing, beliefs and credences aren't as closely connected metaphysically as this suggests. To have a belief in p isn't just to have a high credence, it's to be disposed to let p play a certain role. (This will become important in the next two sections.) For another thing, it is hard to identify precisely what a credence is in the case of an irrational agent. The usual ways we identify credences, via betting dispositions or representation theorems, assume away all irrationality. But an irrational person might still have some rational beliefs.

Attempts to generalise accounts of credences so that they cover the irrational person will end up saying something like what I've said about patterns. What it is to have credence 0.6 in p isn't to have a set of preferences that satisfies all the presuppositions of such and such a representation theorem, which in turn maps one's preferences onto a probability function and a family of utility functions such that

$Pr(p) = 0.6$. That can't be right because some people have credence about 0.6 in p while not uniformly conforming to these constraints. But what makes them intuitive cases of credence roughly 0.6 in p is that generally they behave like the perfectly rational person with credence 0.6 in p, and most of the exceptions are explained by other features of their cognitive system other than their attitude to p.

In other words, we don't have a full theory of credences for irrational beings right now, and when we get one, it won't be much simpler than the theory in terms of patterns and explanations I've offered here. So it's best for now to just understand belief in terms of a pattern of dispositions, and say that the belief is rational just in case that pattern is rational. And that might mean that on some occasions p-related activity is irrational even though the pattern of p-related activity is a rational pattern. Any given action, like any thing whatsoever, can be classified in any number of ways. What matters here is what explains the irrationality of a particular irrational act, and that will be a matter of which patterns of irrational dispositions the actor has.

However we explain Coraline's belief, the upshot is that she has a rational, true belief that is not knowledge. This is a novel kind of Dharmottara case (or Gettier case for folks who prefer that nomenclature). It's not the exact kind of case that Dharmottara originally described. Coraline doesn't infer anything about the Battle of Agincourt from a false belief. But it's a mistake to think that the class of rational, true beliefs that are not knowledge form a natural kind. In general, negatively defined classes are disjunctive; there are ever so many ways to not have a property. An upshot of this discussion of Coraline is that there is one more kind of Dharmottara case than was previously recognised. But as, for example, Williamson (2013) and Jennifer Nagel (2013) have shown, we already knew that this is a very disjunctive class. So the fact that it doesn't look anything like Dharmottara's example shouldn't make us doubt it is a rational, true belief that is not knowledge.

8.2 Coin Puzzles

So rational belief is not identical to rationally having the dispositions that constitute belief. But nor is rational belief a matter of rational high credence. In this section and the next I'll argue that even rational credence 1 does not suffice for rational belief. Then in the next section I'll run through some relatively familiar arguments that no threshold short of 1 could suffice for belief. If the argument of this section or the next is successful, those 'familiar arguments' will be unnecessary. But the two arguments I'm about to give are controversial even by the standards of a book arguing for IRT, so I'm including them as backups.

The point of these sections is primarily normative, but it should have metaphysical consequences. I'm interested in arguing against the 'Lockean' thesis that to believe p just is to have a high credence in p. Normally, this threshold of high enough belief for credence is taken to be interest-invariant, so this is a rival to IRT. But there is some variation in the literature about whether the phrase *the Lockean thesis* refers to a metaphysical claim, i.e., belief is high credence, or a normative claim, i.e., rational belief is rational high credence. Since everyone who accepts the metaphysical claim also accepts the normative claim, and usually takes it to be a consequence of the metaphysical claim, arguing against the normative claim is a way of arguing against the metaphysical claim. This section and the next argue that no matter how high the Lockean sets the threshold, their theory fails, since rational credence 1 does not entail rational belief. In Section 8.4, I'll go over puzzles that arise for Lockean theories that set the threshold below one.

The first puzzle for Lockeans comes from an argument that Williamson (2007) made about certain kinds of infinitary events. A fair coin is about to be tossed. It will be tossed repeatedly until it lands heads twice. The coin tosses will get faster and faster, so even if there is an infinite sequence of tosses, it will finish in a finite time. (This isn't physically realistic, but this need not detain us. All that will really matter for the example is that someone could believe this will happen, and it's physically possible that someone has that belief.)

Consider the following three propositions

A. At least one of the coin tosses will land either heads or tails.

B. At least one of the coin tosses will land heads.

C. At least one of the coin tosses after the first toss will land heads.

So if the first coin toss lands heads, and the rest land tails, B is true and C is false.

Now consider a few versions of the Red-Blue game (perhaps played by someone who takes this to be a realistic scenario). In the first instance, the red sentence says that B is true, and the blue sentence says that C is true. In the second instance, the red sentence says that A is true, and the blue sentence says that B is true. In both cases, it seems that the unique rational play is Red-True. But it's really hard to explain this in a way consistent with the Lockean view.

Williamson argues that we have good reason to believe that the probability of all three sentences is 1. For B to be false requires C to be false, and for one more coin toss to land tails. So the probability that B is false is one-half the probability that C is false. But we also have good reason to believe that the probabilities of B and C are the same. In both cases, they are false if a countable infinity of coin tosses land tails. Assuming that the probability of some sequence having a property supervenes on the probabilities of individual events in that sequence (conditional, perhaps, on other events in the sequence), it follows that the probabilities of B and C are identical. The only way for the probability that B is false to be half the probability that C is false, while B and C have the same probability, is for both of them to have probability 1. Since the probability of A is at least as high as the probability of B (since it is true whenever B is true, but not conversely), it follows that the probability of all three is 1.

Since betting on A weakly dominates betting on B, and betting on B weakly dominates betting on C, we shouldn't have the same attitudes towards bets on these three propositions. Given a choice between betting on B and betting on C, we should prefer to bet on B since there is no way that could make us worse off, and some way it could make us better off. Given that choice, we should prefer to bet on B (i.e., play Red-True when B and C are expressed by the red and blue sentences), because it might be that B is true and C false.

Assume (something the Lockean may not wish to acknowledge) that to say something might be the case is to reject believing its negation. Then a rational person faced with these choices will not believe *Either B is false or C is true*; they will take its negation to be possible. But that proposition is at least as probable as C, so it too has probability 1. So probability 1 does not suffice for belief. This is a real problem for the Lockean—no probability suffices for belief, not even probability 1.

8.3 Playing Games

Some people might be nervous about resting too much weight on infinitary examples like the coin sequence. So I'll show how the same puzzle arises in a simple, and finite, game.[3] The game itself is a nice illustration of how a number of distinct solution concepts in game theory come apart. (Indeed, the use I'll make of it isn't a million miles from the use that Kohlberg and Mertens (1986) make of it.) To set the problem up, I need to say a few words about how I think of game theory. This won't be at all original—most of what I say is taken from important works by Robert Stalnaker (1994, 1996, 1998, 1999). But the underlying philosophical points are important, and it is easy to get confused about them.[4] So I'll set the basic points slowly, and then circle back to the puzzle for the Lockeans.[5]

Start with a simple decision problem, where the agent has a choice between two acts A_1 and A_2, and there are two possible states of the world, S_1 and S_2, and the agent knows the payouts for each act-state pair are given by Table 8.1.

Table 8.1 An underspecified decision problem.

	S_1	S_2
A_1	4	0
A_2	1	1

What to do? I hope you share the intuition that it is radically underdetermined by the information I've given you so far. If S_2 is much more probable than S_1, then A_2 should be chosen; otherwise A_1 should be chosen. But I haven't said anything about the relative probability of those two states.

---

3   This section is based on material from Weatherson (2016a: §1).
4   At least, I used to get these points all wrong, and that's got to be evidence they are easy to get confused about, right?
5   I'm grateful to the participants in a game theory seminar at Arché in 2011, especially Josh Dever and Levi Spectre, for very helpful discussions that helped me see through my previous confusions.

Now compare that to a simple game. The players are Row and Column; Row will choose a row, Column will choose a column, and then the payouts will be given by the cell at the row and column's intersection. Row has two choices, which I'll call A_1 and A_2. Column also has two choices, which I'll call S_1 and S_2. It is common knowledge that each player is rational, and that the payouts for the pairs of choices are given in Table 8.2. (As always, Row's payouts are given first.)

Table 8.2 A simple game.

	S_1	S_2
A_1	4, 0	0, 1
A_2	1, 0	1, 1

What should Row do? This one is easy. Column gets 1 for sure if she plays S_2, and 0 for sure if she plays S_1. So she'll play S_2. And given that she's playing S_2, it is best for Row to play A_2.

The game in Table 8.2 is just a variant of the decision problem in Table 8.1. The relevant states of the world are choices of Column. Unlike the decision problem, there is a determinate answer to what Row should do in the game. More importantly for present purposes, the game can be solved without explicitly saying anything about probabilities. This is because we deduce all we need to know about probabilities from the assumption that Column is rational. Since Column is rational, they will play S_2. Since Column will play S_2, Row should play A_2.

Looking at games this way helps us understand why theorists sometimes think of game theory as "interactive epistemology" (Aumann, 1999). The theorist's work is to solve for what a rational agent should think other rational agents in the game should do. This is why game theory makes heavy use of equilibrium concepts. As theorists, we adopt a theory of rational choice, and see what happens if that theory is common ground amongst the players. In effect, we treat *rationality* as an unknown variable that we solve for given premises about which choices are rational in which games.[6] Not surprisingly, there are going to be multiple solutions to the puzzles we face.

---

6   If we're solving for a variable, what are the equations we're using as input. The standard methodology is to say they are intuitions. Game theorists make as much

This way of thinking naturally leads to the epistemological interpretation of mixed strategies. The most important solution concept in modern game theory is the Nash equilibrium. A set of moves is a Nash equilibrium if no player can improve their outcome by deviating from the equilibrium, conditional on no other player deviating. In many simple games, the only Nash equilibria involve mixed strategies. Table 8.3 is one simple example.

Table 8.3 Death in Damascus as a game.

	S_1	S_2
A_1	0, 1	10, 0
A_2	9, 0	-1, 1

The only Nash equilibrium for this game is that Row plays a mixed strategy playing both A_1 and A_2 with probability ½, while Column plays the mixed strategy that gives S_1 probability 0.55, and S_2 with probability 0.45.

Now what is a mixed strategy? The *metaphysical* interpretation of mixed strategies is that players use some randomising device to pick what to do. This interpretation is often implicit in the way many textbooks introduce mixed strategies.

But the understanding of game theory as interactive epistemology naturally suggests an *epistemological* interpretation of mixed strategies, as Stalnaker argues.

> One could easily ... [model players] ... turning the choice over to a randomizing device, but while it might be harmless to permit this, players satisfying the cognitive idealizations that game theory and decision theory make could have no motive for playing a mixed strategy. So how are we to understand Nash equilibrium in model theoretic terms as a solution concept? We should follow the suggestion of Bayesian game theorists, interpreting mixed strategy profiles as representations, not of players' choices, but of their beliefs. (Stalnaker, 1994: 57–58)

---

use of intuitions analytic philosophers. See, for example, Cho and Kreps (1987).

For our purposes, the important thing about the epistemological interpretation of mixed strategies is that it allows us to make sense of the difference between playing a pure strategy and playing a mixed strategy where one of the 'parts' of the mixture is played with probability one.

With that in mind, consider the game I'll call Up-Down.[7] Informally, in this game A and B must each play a card with an arrow pointing up, or a card with an arrow pointing down. I will capitalise A's moves, i.e., A can play UP or DOWN, and italicise B's moves, i.e., B can play *up* or *down*. If at least one player plays a card with an arrow facing up, each player gets $1. If two cards with arrows facing down are played, each gets nothing. Each cares just about their own wealth, so getting $1 is worth 1 util. All of this is common knowledge. More formally, the payouts are given in Table 8.4, with A on the row and B on the column.

Table 8.4 The Up-Down game.

	up	*down*
UP	1, 1	1, 1
DOWN	1, 1	0, 0

I'll first work through Up-Down assuming Uniqueness: the epistemological theory that there is precisely one rational credence to have in any salient proposition about how the game will play. Some philosophers think that Uniqueness always holds (White, 2005). I align with those, such as Jill North (2010) and Miriam Schoenfield (2013), who reject this view. For now, I'll assume Uniqueness holds because it simplifies the analysis I'm about to offer; later, we'll relax the assumption.

Up-Down is symmetric. So given Uniqueness, A and B should have the same probability of playing UP/*up*. Call this common probability x. It cannot be that $x < 1$. A's expected return from UP is 1, while the expected return from DOWN is x. If $x^* < 1$ and A is rational, they'll definitely play UP. If A will definitely play UP, the probability they'll play UP is 1, contradicting the assumption that $x < 1$.

---

7   In earlier work I'd called it Red-Green, but this is too easily confused with the Red-Blue game that plays such an important role in *Chapter 2*.

So we know $x = 1$. Arguably, we don't know that A will play UP. Assume we could know this. Whatever reason we would have for concluding that would be a reason for any rational person to conclude that B will play *up*. A is rational, so A will conclude this. So A's expected return from either strategy is 1. So A should be indifferent between UP and DOWN. Since all we know about A is that they are rational, and we know they are indifferent between UP and DOWN, we can't conclude, i.e., can't know, they will play UP.

There is an obvious objection to this argument. At one point I moved from the claim that A's expected return from UP and DOWN is the same, to the conclusion that A has just as much reason to play UP and DOWN. That looks like it is assuming that expected utility maximisation is the full theory of rationality. That, in turn, is something we might want to question.

In Chapter 6 I said that expected utility maximisation can't be the right theory of decision for agents who face non-trivial comptutational costs. This shouldn't be relevant here. A and B face pretty simple computations, and we can assume that the cost of those computations is negligible for each of them.

A more serious objection is that A has a reason beyond utility maximisation to play UP, namely that UP weakly dominates DOWN. After all, there's one possibility on the table where UP does better than DOWN, and none where DOWN does better. So perhaps even if UP and DOWN have the same expected utility, there is a reason to play UP.

As I've set up this game, this isn't actually an extra reason A has. To see this, it helps to compare the case to the kinds of games where Stalnaker (in the papers cited above) thinks that weak dominance does provide a distinct reason to make a choice. He is talking about games where the agents' attitude towards the possible payouts is different to their attitude towards each other. For example, the players may have common knowledge of the payouts, but only common belief in the rationality of each other. Or perhaps they even have rational, true belief in the rationality of each other, but crucially not knowledge. If that's right, but only if that's right, then it makes sense to use weak dominance reasoning.

The key motivation behind weak dominance reasoning is that taking a weakly dominated option is a needless risk. If UP will definitely return

1, while DOWN may return 0, then DOWN is risky in a way that UP is not. The notion of *risk* here need not be understood probabilistically. Even if it the probability that DOWN will return 1 is 1, there is still that payout of 0 sitting on the table, and so there is a risk.

Here we need to slow down. There is no outcome on the table where UP returns 1. But if the table is wrong, then UP might return 0. It might return anything at all. The only way that DOWN is risky while UP is not is if there is no risk that the table is mistaken.

Now one might object by pointing out that we stipulated A knows the table is correct and cannot be mistaken. We also stipulated that A knows that B is rational. So if rationality implies playing UP/*up*, there is no way that DOWN can return 0.

This is why Stalnaker's assumption that there is an asymmetry between the players' attitude towards the table and towards each other matters. If the players have a stronger attitude towards the rationality of each other than towards the correctness of the table, there is a sense in which irrational outcomes on the table are more of a risk than outcomes that are not on the table.

However, if the players think the players being irrational is exactly as live a possibility as the table being mistaken, then it is unreasonable to treat outcomes on the table which are only reached when the players are irrational as more relevant to decisions than outcomes not on the table at all.

That's why weak dominance reasoning is inappropriate in the Up-Down game. In some sense there is a risk DOWN could lead to a payout of 0. B might make an irrational move, even though, by stipulation, A knows that they will not. In the very same sense, there is a risk UP could lead to a payout of 0. The table could be wrong, even though A knows that it is not.

That's why the possibility of weak dominance reasoning doesn't undermine the reductio argument I've offered against UP/*up* being the uniquely rational play. It also helps us see why we ultimately don't need the assumption of Uniqueness to generate the objection.

Let's state the argument more carefully without Uniqueness. Assume, again for reductio, that some rational person C has credence $\varepsilon > 0$ that A will play DOWN. (It could be that C is a theorist, like us, or they could be one of the players.) We will now try to build a full model of C's attitudes towards the game.

Since it is common ground that A is an expected utility maximiser, C must have at least credence ε that A has credence 1 that B will play *up*. Is this coherent?

One reason to think not is that even without Uniqueness, it is strange to think that one rational agent could regard a possibility as infinitely less likely than another, given the exact same evidence.

Another reason to think this combination of views is incoherent is that without Uniqueness, the possibility of weak dominance reasoning comes back. If C has credence ε that A will play DOWN, then it is consistent with B's rationality that B has credence ε that A will play DOWN. Somehow C must have credence 1 that B does not have the same credences they do about what A will do, even though they and B have exactly the same evidence.

Uniqueness implies that C should have credence 1 that B will have the same credences as they do. I think Uniqueness is wrong, so I don't think that's a plausible constraint. But it's another thing to say that C should have credence 0 that someone in the same evidential situation as them has the same credences.

So even without Uniqueness, there are two reasons to think that it is wrong to have credence $\varepsilon > 0$ that A will play DOWN. Further, the argument that we can't know A will play UP did not rely on Uniqueness. So this is a case where credence 1 doesn't imply knowledge, and since the proof is known to us, and full belief is incompatible with knowing that you can't know, this is a case where credence 1 doesn't imply full belief. So whether A plays UP, like whether the coin will ever land tails, is a case where belief comes apart from high credence, even if by high credence we literally mean credence 1. This is a problem for the Lockean, and, like Williamson's coin, it is also a problem for the view that belief is credence 1.

8.4 Puzzles for Lockeans

I've already mentioned two classes of puzzles, those to do with infinite sequences of coin tosses and those to do with weak dominance in games. But there are other puzzles that apply especially to the kind of Lockean who identifies belief with credence above some non-maximal, interest-invariant, threshold.

8.4.1 Arbitrariness

The first problem for the Lockeans, and in a way the deepest, is that it makes the boundary between belief and non-belief arbitrary. This is a point that was well made some years ago now by Stalnaker (1984: 91). Unless these numbers are made salient by the environment, there is no special difference between believing p to degree 0.9876 and believing it to degree 0.9875. But if the belief threshold is 0.98755, this will be the difference between believing p and not believing it, which is an important difference.

The usual response to this is to say that the boundary is vague.[8] This won't help at all on theories of vagueness which endorse classical logic, like epistemicism (Williamson, 1994), or supervaluationism, or my preferred comparative truth theory (Weatherson, 2005b). In any of those theories there will still be a true existential claim that the threshold exists and is unimportant.

Even without settling what the right theory of vagueness is, we can see why this can't be right by thinking about what it means to say that a boundary is a vague point on a scale. Most comparative adjectives are vague, and the vagueness consists in which vague point on a scale is the boundary for their application. For example, whether a day is hot depends on whether it is above some vague point on a temperature scale. Vague comparative adjectives like 'hot' don't enter into non-trivial lawlike generalisations. There are laws involving the underlying scale, i.e., temperature, but no laws that are distinctively about the days that are hot. The most you can do is give some kind of generic claim. For instance, you can say that hot days are exhausting, or that electricity use is higher on hot days. But these are generics, and the interesting law-like claims will involve degrees of heat, not the hot/non-hot binary.

It's a fairly central presupposition of this book that belief is more connected to lawlike psychological generalisations than these mere generics. Folk psychology is full of lawlike generalisations that are essentially about belief. These are social science laws, not laws of fundamental physics, so the laws in question with be exception-ridden,

---

8   Versions of this response are made by Richard Foley (1993: Ch. 4), Daniel Hunter (1996), and Matthew Lee (2017b).

ceteris paribus laws. But they are laws nonetheless; they are explanatory and counterfactually resilient.

The Lockean fundamentally doesn't believe that these generalisations of folk psychology are anything more than generics, so this is a somewhat question-begging argument. The Lockean thinks the real laws are about credences, just like the real laws about hot days concern the underlying temperature scale. So my assumption that there are folk psychological laws about belief is strictly speaking question-begging. Nonetheless, it is true. I suspect any argument I could give for it would be less plausible than simply stating the claim, so I won't really try to argue for it. What I will do is illustrate why I believe it, and hopefully remind you why you believe it too.

Start by considering this generalisation.

- If someone wants an outcome O, and they believe that doing X is the only way to get O, and they believe that doing X will neither incur any costs that are large in comparison to how good O is, nor prevent them being able to do something that brings about some other outcome that is comparatively good, then they will do X.

This isn't a universal—some people are just practically irrational. But it's stronger than just a generic claim about high temperatures. It would still be true if the world were different in ever so many ways, and in cases where the person does X, this generalisation is part of the explanation for why they do X.

The Lockean denies almost all of that. They say this principle has widespread counterexamples, even among rational agents. Even when it is true, it isn't explanatory. Rather, it is a summary of some genuinely explanatory claims about the relationship between credence and action.

For example, the Lockean thinks that someone in Blaise's situation satisfies all the antecedents and qualifications in the principle. They want the child to have a moment of happiness. They believe (i.e., have a very high credence that) taking the bet will bring about this outcome, will have no costs at all, and will not prevent them doing anything else. Yet they will not think that people in Blaise's situation will generally take the bet, or that it would be rational for them to take the bet, or that taking the bet is explained by these high credences.

That's what's bad about making the belief/non-belief distinction arbitrary. It means that generalisations about belief are going to be not particularly explanatory, and are going to have systematic (and highly rational) exceptions. We should expect more out of a theory of belief.

8.4.2 Correctness

I've talked about this one a bit in Section 3.7.1, so I'll be brief here. Beliefs have correctness conditions. To believe p when p is false is to make a mistake. That might be an excusable mistake, or even a rational mistake, but it is a mistake. On the other hand, having an arbitrarily high credence in p when p turns out to be false is not a mistake. So having high credence in p is not the same as believing p.

Matthew Lee (2017a) argues that the versions of this argument by Jacob Ross and Mark Schroeder (2014) and Jeremy Fantl and Matthew McGrath (2009) are incomplete because they don't provide a conclusive case for the premise that having a high credence in a falsehood is not a mistake. But this gap can be plugged. Imagine a scientist, call her Marie, who knows the correct theory of chance for a given situation. She knows that the chance of p obtaining is 0.999. (If you think the belief/non-belief threshold is greater than 0.999, just increase this number, and change the resulting dialogue accordingly.) And her credence in p is 0.999, because her credences track what she knows about chances. She has the following exchange with an assistant.

> ASSISTANT: Will p happen?
> MARIE: Probably. It might not, but there is only a one in a thousand chance of that. So p will probably happen.

To their surprise, p does not happen. But Marie did not make any kind of mistake here. Indeed, her answer to the assistant's question was exactly right. But if the Lockean theory of belief is right, and false beliefs are mistakes, then Marie did make a mistake. So the Lockean theory of belief is not right.

8.4.3 Moorean Paradoxes

The Lockean says other strange things about Marie. By hypothesis, she believes that p will obtain. Yet she certainly seems sincere when she says it might not happen. So she believes both p and it might not be that p. This looks like a Moore-paradoxical belief, yet in context it seems completely banal.

The same thing goes for Chamira. Does she believe the Battle of Agincourt was in 1415? Yes, say the Lockeans. Does she also believe that it might not have been in 1415? Yes, say the Lockeans, that is why it was rational of her to play Red-True, and it would have been irrational to play Blue-True. So she believes both that something is the case, and that it might not be the case. This seems irrational, but Lockeans insist that it is perfectly consistent with her being a model of rationality.

Back in Section 2.3.1 I argued that this kind of thing would be a problem for any kind of orthodox theory. And in some sense all I'm doing here is noting that the Lockean really is a kind of orthodox theorist. But the argument that the Lockean is committed to the rationality of Moore-paradoxical claims doesn't rely on those earlier arguments; it's a direct consequence of their view applied to simple cases like Marie and Chamira.

8.4.4 Closure and the Lockean Theory

The Lockean theory makes an implausible prediction about conjunction.[9] It says that someone can believe two conjuncts, yet actively refuse to believe the conjunction. Here is how Stalnaker puts the point.

> Reasoning in this way from accepted premises to their deductive consequences (p, also q, therefore r) does seem perfectly straightforward. Someone may object to one of the premises, or to the validity of the argument, but one could not intelligibly agree that the premises are each acceptable and the argument valid, while objecting to the acceptability of the conclusion. (Stalnaker, 1984: 92)

On the Lockean view, this happens all the time, and is intelligible. According to the Lockeans, it is easy to find triples $\langle S, A, B \rangle$ such that:

- S is a rational agent.
- A and B are propositions.
- S believes A and believes B.

---

9   This subsection draws on material from Weatherson (2016a).

- S does not believe $A \land B$.
- S knows that she has all these states, and consciously reflectively endorses them.

One argument against the Lockean is that there are no such triples, at least when S is rational. That's what I think. Even if I'm wrong, there is a separate argument against the Lockean. The Lockean doesn't just think these triples are possible, they think they are common. That's because for any $t \in (0, 1)$ you care to pick, triples of the form $\langle S, C, D \rangle$ are common.

- S is a rational agent.
- C and D are propositions.
- S's credence in C is greater than t, and her credence in D is greater than t.
- S's credence in $C \land D$ is less than t.
- S knows that she has all these states, and reflectively endorses them.

David Christensen (2005) argues from considerations about the preface paradox to the conclusion that triples like $\langle S, A, B \rangle$ are possible. His argument is non-constructive; he doesn't state a particular triple that clearly satisfies all the constraints, just argues that one must exist. I'm sceptical about that argument, but even if it worked, it wouldn't show what's needed. What's needed is that triples satisfying the constraints I set out for $\langle S, A, B \rangle$ are just as common as triples satisfying the constraints I set out for $\langle S, C, D \rangle$, for at least some value t. Considerations about esoteric cases like the preface paradox can't show that, and I haven't seen any other argument that even attempts to show it.

8.5 Solving the Challenges

Critiquing other theories for their inability to meet a challenge that one's own theory cannot meet is unfair. So I'll conclude this chapter by showing that the six problems I have presented for Lockeans do not pose a problem for my interest-relative theory of (rational) belief. I've already discussed the points about correctness in Section 3.7.1, and about closure in Chapter 4 and Chapter 6, and there isn't much to be added. However, I would like to briefly touch upon the remaining four problems.

8.5.1 Coins

To believe p, one must have a disposition to take it for granted. A rational person prefers to bet on logically weaker propositions instead of logically stronger ones in the coin case. They would not take the logically stronger propositions for granted because if they did, they would be indifferent between the bets. Therefore, they would not believe that one of the coin tosses after the second will land heads or even that one of the coin tosses after the first will land heads. This is the correct outcome. The rational person assigns probability one to these propositions but does not believe them.

8.5.2 Games

In the Up-Down game, if the rational person believed that the other player would play *up*, they would be indifferent between UP and DOWN. But it's irrational to be indifferent between those options, so they wouldn't have the belief. They will think the probability that the other person will play UP/*up* is one—what else could it be? But they will not believe it on pain of incoherence.

8.5.3 Arbitrariness

According to IRT, the difference between belief and non-belief is the difference between willingness and unwillingness to take something as given in inquiry. This is far from an arbitrary difference. Moreover, it is a difference that supports lawlike generalisations. If someone believes that p, and believes that given p, A is better than B, they will prefer A to B. This isn't a universal truth; people make mistakes. But nor is it merely a statistical generalisation. Counterexamples to it are things to be explained, while instances are explained by the underlying pattern.

8.5.4 Moore

In many ways the guiding aim of this project was to avoid the kind of Moore-paradoxicality the Lockean falls into. So it shouldn't be a surprise that we avoid it here. If someone shouldn't do something because p might be false, that's conclusive evidence that they don't know that p. And it's conclusive evidence that either they don't rationally believe p, or they are making some very serious mistake in their reasoning. In the latter case, the reason they are making a mistake is not that p might be false, but that they have a seriously mistaken belief about the kind of choice they are facing. So we can never say that someone knows, or rationally believes, p, but their choice is irrational because p might be false.

9. Evidence

9.1 A Puzzle about Evidence

In Section 2.3.4, I argued that evidence can be interest-relative. The key example involved someone I called Parveen. Recall that she's in a restaurant and notices an old friend, Rahul, across the restaurant. The conditions for detecting people aren't perfect, and she's surprised Rahul is here. Still, we'd ordinarily say it is part of her evidence that Rahul is in this restaurant. She doesn't infer this from other facts, and she would not be called on to defend it if she relies on it in ordinary circumstances. She then plays the Red-Blue game, with these sentences.

- The red sentence is: *Two plus two equals four.*
- The blue sentence is: *Rahul is in this restaurant.*

The key premises for the argument that evidence is interest-relative are:

- The unique rational play for Parveen is Red-True.
- If evidence is interest-invariant, it is rational for Parveen to play Blue-True.

That argument shows that evidence is interest-relative. But it raises, without answering, two big questions:

1. When do interests matter for evidence?
2. When do interests matter for knowledge?

I used to think that there was an easy answer to the second question. A change in interest causes one to lose knowledge that p iff one becomes interested in a question which, given one's evidence, is rationally answered differently depending on whether or not one answers the question conditional on p. This answer is true as far as it goes, but it isn't particularly explanatory unless one holds fixed the evidence between the earlier and later set of interests. And that is just what I said should not be held fixed.

The aim of this chapter is to answer both questions simultaneously.

9.2 A Simple, but Incomplete, Solution

To keep things relatively simple, I'll assume in this chapter that Parveen is an expected utility maximiser. More carefully, I'll assume that the reasons covered in Chapter 6 about why expected utility theory is only an approximation to the correct theory of rational choice are not relevant. From here on, we'll assume we're in a situation where expected utility theory is close enough to the true theory of rational choice.

At a very high level of abstraction, we can think about the problem facing Parveen (or anyone else whose evidence might be interest-sensitive), as follows. They have some option o, and given their interests it matters whether the expected value of o is above or below x. I'll write $v(\bullet)$ for the function from options to their expected value, so the question here is whether or not $v(o)$ us at least x.

There is some background K that is uncontroversially in Parveen's evidence. There is some further proposition p which might or might not be in her evidence; that's what the change of interests calls into question. It is uncontroversial that her evidence includes some background K, and controversial whether it includes some contested proposition p. For any q in K, $v(o \mid q) = v(o)$. That is, expected values are conditional on evidence.

A common idealisation helps capture this last idea. Assume there is a prior value function v^*, with a similar metaphysical status to the prior probability function. Then for any choice c, $v(c) = v^*(c \mid E)$, where E is the evidence Parveen has.

Now I can offer a simple, but incomplete, solution to question 2, assuming p is the only proposition whose status as evidence is put into question by the interests-shift, and the only shift in interests is that the question of whether $v(o) \geq x$ is now relevant. Then she knows p only if $[v^*(o|K) + v^*(o|K \wedge p)]/2 \geq x$. That is, if p's status as evidence is questionable, the relevant 'value' for o is the average of its expected value with and without p being evidence.

That gets the right answer about what Parveen should do. Her evidence may or may not include that Rahul is in the restaurant. If it does, then Blue-True has a value of $50. If it does not, then Blue-True's value is somewhat lower. Even if the evidence includes that someone who looks a lot like Rahul is in the restaurant, the value of Blue-True might only be $45. Averaging them out, the value is less than $50. It would only be rational to play Blue-True if was worth $50. So she shouldn't play Blue-True.

Great! Well, great except for two monumental problems. The first is that it only handles this very special case. The second is that the formula used, take the arithmetic mean of the values with and without the evidence, is barely better than arbitrary. It gets one thing right, in that it says Parveen shouldn't play Blue-True, but it's hardly alone in having that virtue.

Pragmatic encroachment starts with a very elegant, very intuitive, principle: you only know the things you can reasonably take to be settled for the purposes of current deliberation. This arbitrary averaging formula is not elegant or intuitive.

Happily, the two problems have a common solution. Setting it out requires going over recent work on coordination games.

9.3 The Radical Interpreter

William Harper (1986) pointed out that many decision problems are really better thought of as games. For instance, Newcomb's problem can be represented by the game in Table 9.1, with the human as Row and the demon as Column.

Table 9.1 Newcomb's problem as a game.

	Predict 1 Box	Predict 2 Boxes
Choose 1 Box	1000, 1	0, 0
Choose 2 Boxes	1001, 0	1, 1

There is a unique equilibrium of this game: the bottom right corner. The reason it's the unique equilibrium is similar to the reason that two-boxers say to take two boxes: no other option is ratifiable for both players.

This section will be centred around a game that is only slightly more complicated. I call it The Interpretation Game. The game has two players. As in Newcomb's problem, they are a human and a mythical creature. Here the mythical creature is The Radical Interpreter.

In any game, the payouts are a function of what will happen to the players in each situation, and the players' values over those outcomes. To turn a physical situation into a game, we need to know the players' goals. Here are the goals I'll assume our players have:

- The Radical Interpreter assigns mental states to Human with the aim of making the action Human actually chooses the rational choice. I assume here that the 'mental states' include Human's evidence. Indeed, the main thing I'll have The Radical Interpreter do is assign evidence to Human.

- Human aims to maximise expected utility given their evidence. That last phrase, 'their evidence', should be read *de re*. More precisely, they aim to do the thing that is expected utility maximising given the evidence they actually have. (So their own views about their evidence don't matter; all that matters is what their evidence really is.)

Given these aims, The Radical Interpreter and Human often play coordination games. They will both achieve their aims if they act the 'same' way. That is, when it is uncertain whether p is part of Human's evidence, the coordination outcomes are:

- The Radical Interpreter says that p is part of Human's evidence, and Human maximises expected utility given $K \wedge p$.

- The Radical Interpreter says that p is part of Human's evidence, and Human maximises expected utility given K.

Coordination games typically have multiple equilibria, and that will also be the case here.

Let's focus on one example. Human is offered a bet on p. If the bet wins, it wins 1 util; if the bet loses, it loses 100 utils. Human's only choice is to Take or Decline the bet. The proposition p, the subject of the bet, is like the claim that Rahul is in the restaurant. That is, it is unclear whether it is in Human's evidence. Again, let K be the rest of Human's evidence, and stipulate that $\Pr(p \mid K) = 0.9$. Each party now faces a choice.

- The Radical Interpreter has to choose whether p is part of Human's evidence or not.
- Human has to decide whether to Take or Decline the bet.

The payouts for the game are given in Table 9.2.

Table 9.2 The Radical Interpreter game.

	$p \in E$	$p \notin E$
Take the Bet	1, 1	-9.1, 0
Decline the Bet	0, 0	0, 1

Why is this the right table? Let's start with The Radical Interpreter.

The Radical Interpreter achieves their aim iff the following biconditional obtains: Human takes the bet iff p is part of their evidence. That's why they get payout 1 in the cells where that obtains, and 0 otherwise.

Most of Human's payouts are obvious. In the bottom row, they are guaranteed 0, since the bet is declined. In the top left, the bet wins with probability 1, so their expected return is 1. In the top right, the bet wins with probability 0.9, so the expected return of taking it is $1 \times 0.9 - 100 \times 0.1 = -9.1$.

There are two Nash equilibria for the game—the top left and the bottom right. We could stop here and say that according to IRT it is indeterminate whether p is part of Human's evidence. But we can do better.

But to do that, I need to survey more contested areas of game theory. In particular, I need to introduce some work on equilibrium choice. To do that, it helps to think about a game that is inspired by an example of Jean-Jacques Rousseau's.

9.4 Risk-Dominant Equilibria

Table 9.3 is the abstract version of a two-player, two-option game.

Table 9.3 A generic 2 by 2 by 2 game.

	a	b
A	r_{11}, c_{11}	r_{12}, c_{12}
B	r_{21}, c_{21}	r_{22}, c_{22}

What are usually called Stag Hunt games have the following eight characteristics.

1. $r_{11} > r_{21}$
2. $r_{22} > r_{12}$
3. $c_{11} > c_{12}$
4. $c_{22} > c_{21}$
5. $r_{11} > r_{22}$
6. $c_{11} \geq c_{22}$
7. $r_{21} + r_{22} > r_{11} + r_{12}$
8. $c_{12} + c_{22} \geq c_{11} + c_{21}$

The first four conditions say that the game has two (strict) Nash equilibria: *Aa* and *Bb*. The next two conditions say that the *Aa* equilibrium is *Pareto-optimal*: neither player prefers *Aa* to *Bb*. In fact it says something a bit stronger: one of the players strictly prefers the *Aa* equilibrium, and the other player does not prefer *Bb*. The last two conditions say that the *Bb* equilibrium is *risk-optimal*.

Hans Carlsson and Eric van Damme (1993) offer an argument that in any such game, rational players will end up at *Bb*. The game that Human and The Radical Interpreter are playing fits these eight conditions, and The Radical Interpreter is perfectly rational. So if Carlsson and van Damme are right, The Radical Interpreter will say that $p \notin E$. Indeed, if Carlsson and van Damme are right, the toy theory I offered in Section 9.2 will be correct in all cases where it applies.

The rest of this chapter would be much simpler if I thought Carlsson and van Damme's argument worked in full generality. Unfortunately, I don't think it does. In particular, I think it fails in the important case where it is common knowledge that both players are rational, and both players know precisely the values of each of the eight payoffs. But I think it does work in the special case where one player has imperfect access to what the payouts are. And that, it turns out, is the special case that matters to us. That's getting ahead of the story though; let's start with their argument.

I said games satisfying these conditions are called Stag Hunt games. The name comes from a thought experiment in Rousseau's *Discourse on Inequality*.

> They were perfect strangers to foresight, and were so far from troubling themselves about the distant future, that they hardly thought of the morrow. If a deer was to be taken, every one saw that, in order to succeed, he must abide faithfully by his post: but if a hare happened to come within the reach of any one of them, it is not to be doubted that he pursued it without scruple, and, having seized his prey, cared very little, if by so doing he caused his companions to miss theirs. (Rousseau, 1913: 209–210)

Brian Skyrms (2001) has argued that these Stag Hunt games are important across philosophy; they are good models for many real-life situations that are often (incorrectly) modelled as Prisoners' Dilemmas. But going over why that is would be a needless digression. Our focus is on Carlsson and van Damme's argument that Rousseau was right: a "stranger to foresight", who is just focussing on this game, should take the rabbit.

To make matters a little easier, we'll focus on a very particular instance of Stag Hunt, the one in Table 9.4.

Table 9.4 A simple version of Stag Hunt.

	a	b
A	4, 4	0, 3
B	3, 0	3, 3

The equilibrium *Aa* is Pareto-optimal: it is the best outcome for each individual. But it is risky, and Carlsson and van Damme suggest a way to turn that risk into an argument for choosing *Bb*.

Embed Table 9.4 game in what they call a *global game*. Our first version of a global game is that each player knows that they will play Table 9.5, with x to be selected at random from a flat distribution over $[-1, 5]$.

Table 9.5 The global game.

	a	b
A	4, 4	0, x
B	x, 0	x, x

There isn't much to say about Table 9.5 with this prior knowledge. Let's give the players a little more knowledge. (And we'll call the players Row and Column to make it easier to refer to each of them.)

Before they play the game, each player will get a noisy signal about the value of x. There will be signals s_R and s_C chosen (independently) from a flat distribution over $[x - 0.25, x + 0.25]$, and shown to Row and Column respectively. So each player will know the value of x to within ¼, and know that the other player knows it to within ¼ as well. This is a margin of error model, and in those models there is very little that is common knowledge. That, Carlsson and van Damme argue, makes a huge difference.

They go on to prove that iterated deletion of strictly dominated strategies (almost) removes all but one strategy pair. (I'll go over the proof of this in the next subsection.) Each player will play A/a if the signal is greater than 2, and B/b otherwise.[1] Surprisingly, this shows that players should play the risk-optimal strategy even when they know the other strategy is Pareto-optimal. When a player gets a signal in (2, 3.75), then they know that $x < 4$, so *Bb* is the Pareto-optimal equilibrium. But the logic of the global game suggests the risk-dominant equilibrium is what to play.

---

1   Strictly speaking, we can't rule out various mixed strategies when the signal is precisely 2, but this makes little difference, since that occurs with probability 0.

Carlsson and van Damme go on to show that many of the details of this case don't matter. Most importantly, it doesn't matter that the margin of error in the signal was ¼; as long as it is positive the argument goes through.

Now what does this show about the game where players know precisely what the value of x is? Equivalently, what does it show about the game where the margin of error is 0?

Carlsson and van Damme argue that it shows that the risk-dominant choice is the right choice there as well. After all, the game where there is perfect knowledge just is a margin of error game, where the margin of error is 0. In previous work I'd endorsed this argument (Weatherson, 2018). I now think this was a mistake. The limit case, where the players know the value of x, is special. But, I'll argue, this doesn't actually undermine the argument that in the game between Human and The Radical Interpreter, both parties should choose the risk-dominant equilibria.

If the game between Human and The Radical Interpreter is meant to model a real situation, Human won't know precisely what the payoffs are. That's because real humans don't know precisely what their evidence is. They only know precisely what their evidence is if both positive and negative introspection hold for evidence, and that's no more plausible than that positive and negative introspection hold for knowledge. As Humberstone (2016: 380–402) shows, that's not particularly plausible, even if one doesn't accept the arguments in Williamson (2000) against positive introspection.

If Human doesn't know precisely what their evidence is, they don't know the payoffs in games like Table 9.5, because those payoffs are expected values. It turns out that's enough for the iterated dominance argument that Human should play the risk-dominant equilibrium to go through.

To be sure, The Radical Interpreter, who is just an idealisation, presumably does know the payouts in the different states of the game. It turns out, as I'll go over in Section 9.4.2, that Carlsson and van Damme's result only needs one player to be uncertain of the payouts. Given the failure of at least negative introspection (and, I'd say, positive introspection), that's something we can assume.

If Human should play the risk-dominant strategy in Table 9.2, they should decline the bet. So The Radical Interpreter, who can figure this out, should say that p is not part of their evidence. Since one's evidence just is what The Radical Interpreter says it is, that means that in Table 9.2, p is not part of Human's evidence.

Applied to the case of Parveen and Rahul, that means that The Radical Interpreter is best off saying it is no part of Parveen's evidence that Rahul is in the restaurant. More generally, in the simple cases described in Section 9.2, The Radical Interpreter should say that p is not part of Human's evidence just in case the equation used there holds.

The result is an interest-relative theory of evidence that is somewhat well motivated. At least, it can be incorporated into a broader theory of rational action.

This model keeps what was good about the pragmatic encroachment theory developed in the previous chapters, while also allowing that evidence can be interest-relative. It does require a considerably more complex theory of rationality than was previously used. Rather than just model rational agents as utility maximisers, they are modelled as playing risk-dominant strategies in coordination games under uncertainty about what the payouts are. Still, it turns out that this is little more than assuming that they maximise evidential expected utility, and they expect others (at least perfectly rational abstract others) to do the same, and they expect those others to expect they will maximise expected utility, and so on.

The rest of this section goes into more technical detail about Carlsson and van Damme's example. Readers not interested in these details can skip ahead to Section 9.5. In Section 9.4.1 I summarise their argument that we only need iterated deletion of strictly dominated strategies to get the result that rational players will play the risk-dominant strategies. Then in Section 9.4.2 I offer a small generalisation of their argument, showing that it still goes through when one of the players gets a precise signal, and the other gets a noisy signal.

9.4.1 The Dominance Argument for Risk-Dominant Equilibria

Two players, Row (or R) and Column (or C) will play the game depicted in Table 9.5. They won't be told what x is, but they will get a noisy signal of x, drawn from an even distribution over $[x - 0.25, x + 0.25]$. Call these signals s_R and s_C. Each player must then choose A, getting either 4 or 0 depending on the other player's choice, or choose B, getting x for sure.

Before getting the signal, the players must choose a strategy. In this context, a strategy is a function from signals to choices. Since the higher the signal is, the better it is to play B, we can more or less equate strategies with 'tipping points', where the player plays B if the signal is above the tipping point, and A below the tipping point.[2]

Call the tipping points for Row and Column respectively T_R and T_C. Since this game is symmetric, we'll just have to show that in conditions of common knowledge of rationality, $T_R = 2$. It follows by symmetry that $T_C = 2$ as well. The only rule that will be used is iterated deletion of strictly dominated strategies.

The return to a strategy is uncertain, even given the other player's strategy. But given the strategies of each player, each players' expected return can be computed. That will be treated as the return to the strategy pair.

Note first that $T_R = 4.25$ strictly dominates any strategy where $T_R = y > 4.25$. If $s_R \in (4.25, y)$, then T_R is guaranteed to return above 4, and the alternative strategy is guaranteed to return 4. In all other cases, the strategies have the same return. There is some chance that $s_R \in (4.25, y)$. So we can delete all strategies $T_R = y > 4.25$, and similarly all strategies $T_C = y > 4.25$. By similar reasoning, we can rule out $T_R < -0.25$ and $T_C < -0.25$.

If $s_R \in [-0.75, 4.75]$, then it is equally likely that x is above s_R as it is below it. Indeed, the posterior distribution of x is flat over $[s_R - 0.25, s_R + 0.25]$. From this it follows that the expected return of playing B after seeing signal s_R is just s_R.

Now comes the important step. For arbitrary $y > 2$, assume we know that $T_C \leq y$. Consider the expected return of playing A given various values for $s_R > 2$. Given that the lower T_C is, the higher the expected return is of playing A, we'll just work on the simple case where $T_C = y$, realising that this is an upper bound on the expected return of A given $T_C \leq y$. The expected return of A is 4 times the probability that

---

[2] I'm ignoring mixed strategies here, and strategies that differ in cases where the signal is right at the tipping point. It's trivial but tedious to extend the proof to cover these cases.

Column will play a, i.e., 4 times the probability that $s_C < T_C$. Given all the symmetries that have been built into the puzzle, we know that the probability that $s_C < s_R$ is 0.5. So the expected return of playing A is at most 2 if $s_R \geq y$. But the expected return of playing B is, as we showed in the last paragraph, sR, which is greater than 2. So it is better to play B than A if $s_R \geq y$. And the difference is substantial, so even if s_R is epsilon less than that y, it will still be better to play B. (This is rather hand-wavy, but I'll go over the more rigorous version presently.)

So for any $y > 2$ if $T_C \leq y$ we can prove that T_R should be lower still, because given that assumption it is better to play B even if the signal is just less than y. Repeating this reasoning over and over again pushes us to it being better to play B than A as long as $s_R > 2$. The same kind of reasoning from the opposite end pushes us to it being better to play A than B as long as $s_R < 2$. So we get $s_R = 2$ as the uniquely rational solution to the game.

Let's make that a touch more rigorous. Assume that $T_C = y$, and s_R is slightly less than y. In particular, we'll assume that $z = y - s_R$ is in $(0, 0.5)$. Then the probability that $s_C < y$ is $0.5 + 2z - 2z^2$. So the expected return of playing A is $2 + 8z - 8z^2$. And the expected return of playing B is, again, sR. These will be equal iff $s_R = y + ((145 - 32y)^{\frac{1}{2}} - 9)/16$. So if we know that $T_C \geq y$, we know that $T_R \geq y + ((145 - 32y)^{\frac{1}{2}} - 9)/16$, which will be less than y if $y > 2$. Then by symmetry, we know that T_C must be at most as large as that as well. Then we can use that fact to derive a further upper bound on T_R and hence on T_C, and so on. And this will continue until we push both down to 2. It does require quite a number of steps of iterated deletion. Table 9.6 shows the upper bound on the threshold after n rounds of deletion of dominated strategies. (The numbers in Table 9.6 are precise for the first two rounds, and correct to three significant figures after that.)

Table 9.6 How the threshold moves towards 2.

Round	Upper Bound on Threshold
1	4.250
2	3.875
3	3.599
4	3.378
5	3.195
6	3.041
7	2.910
8	2.798
9	2.701
10	2.617

That is, $T_R = 4.25$ dominates any strategy with a tipping point above 4.25. And $T_R = 3.875$ dominates any strategy with a higher tipping point than 3.875, assuming $T_C \leq 4.25$. And $T_R \approx 3.599$ dominates any strategy with a higher tipping point than 3.599, assuming $T_C \leq 3.875$. And so on.

Similar reasoning shows that at each stage not only are all strategies with higher tipping points dominated, but so are strategies that assign positive probability (whether it is 1 or less than 1), to playing A when the signal is above the 'tipping point'.[3]

So it has been shown that iterated deletion of dominated strategies will rule out all strategies except the risk-optimal equilibrium. The possibility that x is greater than the maximal return for A is needed to get the iterated dominance going. We also need the signal to have an

---

3 If we're careful about how we state this, we can use this to rule out all mixed strategies except those that respond probabilistically to $s_R = 2$.

error bar to it, so that each round of iteration removes more strategies. But that's all that was needed; the particular values used are irrelevant to the proof.

9.4.2 Making One Signal Precise

So far I've just been setting out Carlsson and van Damme's results. It's time to prove something just slightly stronger. I'll show that the result in Section 9.4.1 did not require that both parties receive a noisy signal. It's enough that just one party does.

More precisely, I'll change the game so that it is common knowledge that the signal Column gets, s_C, equals x. Since the game is no longer symmetric, I can't just appeal to the symmetry of the game as frequently as in the previous subsection. This slows the proof down, but doesn't stop it.

This change actually helps us at the first stage of the argument. Since Column could not be wrong about x, Column knows that if $s_C > 4$ then playing b dominates playing a. So one round of deleting dominated strategies rules out $T_C > 4$, as well as ruling out $T_R > 4.25$.

At any stage for any $y > 2$ such that we know $T_C \leq y$, the strategy $T_R = y$ dominates $T_R > y$. That's because if $s_R \geq y$, and $T_C \leq y$, the probability that Column will play a (given Row's signal) is less than 0.5. After all, the signal is just as likely to be above x as below it.[4] So if s_R is at or above T_C, the probability that Column's signal is above Column's tipping point is at least 0.5. So the probability that Column will play b is at least 0.5. So the expected return to Row of playing A, which is 4 times the probability that Column will play a, is at most 2. Since the expected return to Row of playing B equals the value of the signal,[5] that means that if the signal is above 2, they should play B.

Summing up, if Row knows $T_C \leq y$, for any $y > 2$, Row also knows it is better to play B if $s_R \geq y$. That is, if Row knows $T_C \leq y$, for any $y > 2$, Row's tipping point should be at most y.

---

[4] This isn't strictly true if the signal is close enough to 5, but in that case we have an independent reason to think Column will play a.

[5] Unless the signal is very close to 5, in which case they should play B anyway.

Assume now that it is common knowledge that $T_R \leq y$, for some $y > 2$. Assume Column's signal, which we'll call x, is just a little less than y. In particular, define $z = y - x$, and assume $z \in (0, 0.25)$. We want to work out the upper bound on the expected return to Column of playing a. (The return of playing b is known, it is x.)

The expected return to Column of playing a will be highest when T_R is highest. So we can work out an upper bound on that expected return by assuming that $T_R = y$. Given that assumption, the probability that Row plays A is $(1 + 2z)/2$. (That's the probability that Row's signal, which is a random draw from $[x - ¼, x + ¼]$, is above y.) So the expected return of playing a is $2 + 4z$, i.e., $2 + 4(y - x)$. That will be greater than x only when $x < (2 + 4y)/5$.

So if it is common knowledge that $T_R \leq y$, then it is best for Column to play b unless $x < (2 + 4y)/5$. That is, if it is common knowledge that $T_R \leq y$, then TC must be at most $(2 + 4y)/5$.

The rest of the proof proceeds in a zig-zag fashion. At one stage, we show that T_R must be no greater than T_C. So whatever value we've shown to be an upper bound for T_C is also an upper bound for T_R. At the next stage, we show that given any upper bound on T_R greater than 2, we can derive a new upper bound on T_C which is lower still. This process will eventually rule out all values for T_R and T_C greater than 2. So just using iterated deletion of dominated strategies, we eventually rule out all strategies that involve tipping points above 2.

There is one last point to be careful about. It takes infinitely many steps to rule out all tipping points above 2. Since it isn't obviously sound to have infinitely many steps of iterated deletion, one might worry about the soundness of the proof at this point. The key thing to note is that for any tipping point above 2, it is ruled out in a finite number of steps. So purely finitary reasoning rules out all tipping points above 2. It's just that there is no upper bound to the (finite!) number of steps needed.

This completes the mathematical part of the argument; I'll return to discussing whether this result matters for thinking about evidence and rational action, and reply to some objections to thinking that it does.

9.5 Objections and Replies

Objection: The formal argument requires that in the 'global game' there are values for x that make A the dominant choice. These cases serve as a base step for an inductive argument that follows. But in Parveen's case, there is no such setting for x, so the inductive argument can't get going.

Reply: What matters is that there are values of x such that A is the strictly dominant choice, and Human (or Parveen) doesn't know that they know that they know, etc., that those values are not actual. And that's true in our case. For all Human (or Parveen) knows that they know that they know that they know..., the proposition in question is not part of their evidence under a maximally expansive verdict on The Radical Interpreter's part. So the relevant cases are there in the model, even if both players know that they know that they know ... that the models don't obtain, for a high but finite number of repetitions of 'that they know'.

Objection: This model is much more complex than the simple motivation for pragmatic encroachment.

Reply: Sadly, this is true. I would like to have a simpler model, but I don't know how to create one. I suspect any such simple model will just be incomplete; it won't say what Parveen's evidence is. In this respect, any simple model will look just like applying tools like Nash equilibria to coordination games. So more complexity will be needed, one way or another. I think paying this price in complexity is worth it overall, but I can see how some people might think otherwise.

Objection: Change the case involving Human so that the bet loses 15 utils if p is false, rather than 100. Now the risk-dominant equilibrium is that Human takes the bet, and The Radical Interpreter says that p is part of Human's evidence. But note that if it was clearly true that p was not part of Human's evidence, then this would still be too risky a situation for them to know p. So whether it is possible that p is part of Human's evidence, and not just part of their knowledge, matters.

Reply: This is all true, and it shows that the view I'm putting forward is incompatible with some programs in epistemology. In particular, it is incompatible with E=K, since what it takes to be evidence in this story is slightly different from what it takes to be knowledge. The next section argues that this is independently plausible.

9.6 Evidence, Knowledge, and Cut-Elimination

In the previous section I noted that my theory of evidence is committed to denying Williamson's E=K thesis. This is the thesis that says one's evidence is all and only what one knows. What I say is consistent with, and arguably committed to, one half of that thesis. Nothing I've said here provides a reason to reject the implication that if p is part of one's evidence, then one knows p. Indeed, the story I'm telling would have to be complicated even further if that fails. But I am committed to denying the other direction. According to my view, there can be cases where someone knows p, but p is not part of their evidence.

My main reason for this comes from the kind of cases that Shyam Nair (2019) describes as failures of "cut-elimination". I'll quickly set out what Nair calls cut-elimination, and why it fails, and then look at how it raises problems for E=K.

Start by assuming that we have an operator $\models$ such that $\Gamma \models A$ means that A can be rationally inferred from Γ. I'm following Nair (and many others) in using a symbol usually associated with logical entailment here, though this is potentially misleading. A big plotline in what follows will be that $\models$, so understood, behaves very differently from familiar notions of entailment.

For the purposes of this section, I'm staying somewhat neutral on what it means to be able to rationally infer A from Γ. In particular, I want everything that follows to be consistent with the interpretation that an inference is rational only if it produces knowledge. I don't think that's true; I think folks with misleading evidence can rationally form false beliefs, and I think the traveller in Dharmottara's example rationally believes there is a fire. But there is a dialectical reason for staying neutral here. I'm arguing against one important part of the 'knowledge first' program, and I don't want to do so by assuming the falsity of other parts of it. So for this section (only), I'll write in a way that is consistent with saying rational belief requires knowledge.

Given that, one way to interpret $\Gamma \models A$ is that A can be known on the basis of Γ. What can be known on the basis of what is a function of, among other things, who is doing the knowing, what their background evidence is, what their capacities are, and so on. Strictly speaking, that suggests we should have some subscripts on $\models$ for who is the knower, what their background evidence is, and so on. In the interests of readability, I'm going to leave all those implicit. In the next section it will be important to come back and look at whether the force of some of these arguments is diminished if we are careful about this relativisation.

That's our important notation. The principle *Cut* that Nair focuses on is that if 1 and 2 are true, so is 3.

9. $\Gamma \models A$
10. $\{A\} \cup \Delta \models B$
11. $\Gamma \cup \Delta \models B$

The principle is intuitive. Indeed, it is often implicit in a lot of reasoning. Here is one instance of it in action.

> I heard from a friend that Jack went up the hill. This friend is trustworthy, so I'm happy to infer that Jack did indeed go up the hill. I heard from another friend that Jack and Jill did the same thing. This friend is also trustworthy, so I'm happy to infer that Jill did the same thing as Jack, i.e., go up the hill.

Normally we wouldn't spell out the 'happy to infer' steps, but I've included them in here to make the reasoning a bit more explicit. But note what I didn't need to make explicit, even in this laborious reconstruction. I didn't need to note a change of status of the claim that Jack went up the hill. That goes from being a conclusion to being a premise. What matters for our purposes is that there doesn't seem to be a gap between the rationality of inferring that Jack went up the hill, and the rationality of using that as a premise in later reasoning. The idea that there is no gap here just is the idea that the principle *Cut* is true.

While *Cut* seems intuitive in cases like this, Nair argues that it can't be right in general. (If that's right we have a duty, one Nair takes up, to explain why cases like Jack and Jill seem like cases of good reasoning.) For my purposes, it is helpful to divide the putative counterexamples to *Cut* into two categories. I'll call them *monotonic* and *non-monotonic* counterexamples. The categorisation turns on whether $\Gamma \cup \Delta \models A$ is true assuming that $\Gamma \models A$ is true. I'll call cases where it is true monotonic instances of *Cut*, and cases where it is false non-monotonic instances.

That *Cut* fails in non-monotonic cases is fairly obvious. We can see this with an example that was hackneyed a generation ago.

Γ = {Tweety is a bird}
Δ = {Tweety is a penguin}
A = B = Tweety can fly

From Tweety is a bird we can rationally infer that Tweety flies. And given that Tweety is a flying penguin, we can infer that she flies. But given that Tweety is a penguin and a bird, we cannot infer this. So principles 1 and 2 in *Cut* are true, but 3 is false. And the same pattern will recur any time Δ provides a defeater for the link between Γ and A.

These cases will matter in what follows, but they are rather different from the monotonic examples. The monotonic example I'll set out (in the next three paragraphs) is very similar to one used in an argument against E=K by Alvin Goldman (2009). In many ways the argument against E=K I'm going to give is just a notational variant on Goldman's, but I think the notation I'm borrowing from Nair helps bring out the argument's strength.

Here is the crucial background assumption for the example. (I'll come back to how plausible this is after setting the example up.) The nature of F around here varies, but it varies very slowly. If we find a pattern in common to all the F within distance (in miles) d of here, we can rationally infer that the pattern extends another mile. That's just boring induction. But we can't infer that it extends to infinity, that would be a radical step. If we can't infer that the pattern goes to infinity, there must be a point beyond which we can't infer the pattern goes. Let's say that's one mile. So if we know the pattern holds within distance d of here, we can infer that it holds within distance $d + 1$, but no more.[6]

To see a case like this, imagine we're doing work that's more like working out the diet of local wildlife than working out the mass of an electron. If you know the mass of electrons around here, and what pigeons around here eat, there are some inferences you can make. You can come to know what the mass of electrons will be in the next town over, and what pigeons eat in the next town over. But there is a difference between the cases. You can also infer from this evidence what the mass of electrons will be on the other side of the world. But you can't make very confident inferences about what pigeons eat on the other side of

---

6   In any remotely realistic case, it would make more sense to say we can infer it holds in some multiple of d rather than adding some value to d. But I'm simplifying a lot to make a point, and this is just one more simplification.

the world; they may have adapted their diet to local conditions. In our case F and G concern things more like pigeon diets than electron masses.

Now here is the counterexample.

$\Gamma = \Delta = \{$Every F within 3 miles of here is $G.\}$
$A = $ Every F between 3 and 4 miles of here is G.
$B = $ Every F between 4 and 5 miles of here is G.

If what I said was right, then this is a counterexample to *Cut*. $\Gamma \models A$ is true because it says given evidence about all the F within 3 miles of here, we can infer that all the F within 4 miles are like them. And $\{A\} \cup \Delta \models B$ is true because it says that given evidence about all the F within 4 miles of here, we can infer that all the F within 5 miles are like them. But $\Gamma \cup \Delta \models A$ is false, because it purports to say that given evidence about the F within 3 miles of here, we can infer that all the F within 5 miles are alike. And that's an inductive bridge too far.

This particular example involving distances was an extreme idealisation. But all we need for the larger argument is that there is some similarity metric such that inductive inference is rational across short jumps in that similarity metric, but not across long jumps. One kind of similarity is physical distance from a salient point. That's not the only kind of similarity, and rarely the most important kind.

As long as there is some 'inductive margin of inference', the argument works. What I mean by an inductive margin of inference is that given that all the F that differ from a salient point (along this metric) by amount d are G, it is rational to infer that all the F that differ from that salient point by amount $d + m$ are G, but not that all the F that differ from that salient point by amount $d + 2m$ are G. And it seems very plausible to me that there are some metrics, and values of F, G, d, m such that that's true.

For example, given what I know about Miami's weather, I can infer that it won't snow there for the next few hundred Christmases. Indeed, I know that. But I can't know that it won't snow there for the next few million Christmases. There is some point, and I don't know what it is, where my inductive knowledge about Miami's snowfall (or lack thereof) gives out.

While it is plausible that such cases are possible, any particular case fitting this pattern is weird. Here's what is weird about them. It will be easier to go back to the case where the metric is physical distance to set this out, but the weirdness will extend to all cases. Imagine we investigate the area within 3 miles of here thoroughly, and find that all the *F* are *G*s. We infer, and now know, that all the *F* within 4 miles of here are *G*s. We keep investigating, and keep observing, and after a while we've observed all the *F* within 4 miles. And they are all *G*, as we knew they would be. But now we are in a position to infer that all the *F* within 5 miles are *G*. Observing something that we knew to be true gives us a reason to do something, i.e., make a further inference, that we couldn't do before. That's weird, and I'm going to come back in the next section to how it relates to the story I told about knowledge in Chapter 4.

The key point now is that this possibility undermines E=K. There is a difference between knowing *A* and being able to use *A* to support further inductive inferences. It is very natural to call that the difference between knowing *A* and having *A* as evidence.

The reasoning that I've been criticising violates a principle Jonathan Weisberg calls "No Feedback" (Weisberg, 2010: 533–534). This principle says that if a conclusion is derived from some premises, plus some intermediary conclusions, then it is only justified if it could, at least in principle, be derived from those premises alone. A natural way to read this is that we have some evidence, and things that we know on the basis of that evidence have a different functional role from the evidence. They can't do what the evidence itself can do, even if known. This looks like a problem for E=K, as Weisberg himself notes (2010: 536).

If any monotonic instances of failures of Cut exist, we need to distinguish between things the thinker knows by inference, and things they know by observation, in order to assess their inferences. That's to say, some knowledge will not play the characteristic role of evidence. T suggests that E=K is false.

9.7 Basic Knowledge and Non-Inferential Knowledge

It would be natural to conclude from the examples I've discussed that evidence is something like non-inferential knowledge. This is very similar to a view defended by Patrick Maher (1996). And it is, I will argue, close to the right view. But it can't be exactly right, for reasons Alexander Bird (2004) brings out.

I will argue that evidence is not non-inferential knowledge, but rather basic knowledge. The primary difference between these two notions is that *being non-inferential* is a diachronic notion—it depends on the causal source of the knowledge—while being basic is a synchronic notion—it depends on how the knowledge is currently supported. In general, non-inferential knowledge will be basic knowledge, and basic knowledge will be non-inferential. But the two notions can come apart, and when they do, the evidence is what is basic, not what is non-inferential.

The following kind of case is central to Bird's objection to the idea that evidence is non-inferential knowledge. Assume that our inquirer sees that A and rationally infers B. On the view that evidence is non-inferential knowledge, A is evidence but B is not. Now imagine that at some much later time, the inquirer remembers B, but has forgotten that it is based on A. This isn't necessarily irrational. As Gilbert Harman (1986) stresses, an obligation to remember our evidence is wildly unrealistic. The inquirer learns C and infers $B \land C$. This seems perfectly rational. But why is it rational?

If evidence is non-inferential knowledge, then this is a mystery. Since B was inferred, that can't be the evidence that justifies $B \land C$. So the only other option is that the evidence is the, now forgotten, A. It is puzzling how something that is forgotten can now justify. But a bigger problem is that if A is the inquirer's evidence, then they should also be able to infer $A \land C$. But this would be an irrational inference.

So I agree with Bird that we can't identify evidence with non-inferential knowledge, if by that we mean knowledge that was not originally gained through inference. (And what else could it mean?) But a very similar theory of evidence can work. The thing about evidence is that it can play a distinctive role in reasoning—it provides a distinctive kind of reason. In particular, it provides basic reasons.

Evidence stops regresses. That's why we can say that our fundamental starting points are self-evident. Now there is obviously a controversy about what things are self-evident. I don't find it particularly likely that claims about the moral rights we were endowed with by our Creator are self-evident. But I do think it is true that a lot of things are self-evident. (Even including, perhaps, that we have moral rights.) We should take this notion of self-evidence seriously. Sometimes a piece of knowledge is a basic reason; it is evidence for itself, and not something that is grounded in further evidence.

What is it for a reason to be basic? It isn't that it was not originally inferred. Something that was once inferred from long forgotten premises may now be a basic reason. Rather, it is something that needs no further reason given as support. (Its support is itself, since it is self-evident.) What makes a reason need further support? I'm an interest-relative epistemologist, so I think this will be sensitive to the agent's interests. For example, I think facts reported in a reliable history book are pieces of basic evidence when we are thinking about history, but not when we are thinking about the reliability of that book. But this kind of interest-relativity is inessential to the story. What is essential is that evidence provides a reason that does not in turn require more justification.

This picture suggests an odd result about cases of forgotten evidence. There is a much-discussed puzzle about forgotten evidence that was set in motion by Harman (1986). He argued that if someone irrationally believes p on the basis of some evidence, then later forgets the evidence but retains the belief, the belief may now be rational. It would not be rational if they remembered both the evidence, and that it was the evidence for p. But, and this is what I want to take away from the case, there is no obligation for thinkers to keep track of why they believe each of the things they do.

There is a large literature now on this case; Sinan Dogramaci (2015) both provides a useful guide to the debate and moves it forward by considering what we might aim to achieve by offering one or other evaluation of the believer in this case. The view I'm offering here is, as far as I can tell, completely neutral on Harman's original case. But it has something striking to say about a similar case.

Imagine an inquirer, call him Jaidyn, believes p for the excellent reason that he read it in a book from a reliable historian H. Six months later, he has forgotten that that's where he learned that p, though he still believes that p. In a discussion about historians, a friend of Jaidyn's says that H is really unreliable. Jaidyn is a bit shocked, and literally can't believe it. This is for the best since H is in fact reliable, and his friend is suffering from a case of mistaken identity. But he is moved enough by the testimony to suspend judgment on H's reliability, and so he forms a disposition to not believe anything H says without corroboration. Since he doesn't know that he believes p because H says so, he doesn't do anything about this belief. What should we say about Jaidyn's belief that p?

Here's what I want to say. I don't claim this is particularly intuitive, but I'm not sure there is anything particularly intuitive; it's best to just see what a theory says about the case. My theory says that Jaidyn still knows that p. This knowledge was once based on H's testimony, but it is no longer based on that. Indeed, it is no longer based on anything. Presumably, if Jaidyn is rational, the knowledge will be sensitive to the absence of counter-evidence, or to incoherence with the rest of his worldview. But these are checks and balances in Jaidyn's doxastic system, they aren't the basis of the belief. Since the belief is knowledge, and is a basic reason for Jaidyn, it is part of his evidence.

Note three things about that last conclusion. First, this is a case where a piece of inferential knowledge can be in someone's evidence. By (reasonably) forgetting the source of the knowledge, it converts to being evidence. Second, almost any knowledge could make this jump. Whenever someone has no obligation to remember the source or basis of some knowledge, they can reasonably forget the source, and the basis, and the knowledge will become basic. And then it is evidence. The picture I'm working with is that pieces of knowledge can easily move in and out of one's evidence set; sometimes all it takes is forgetting where the knowledge came from. But third, if Jaidyn had done better epistemically, and remembered the source, he would no longer know that p.

It is somewhat surprising that knowledge can be dependent on forgetting. Jaidyn knows that p, but if he'd done better at remembering why he believes p, he wouldn't know it. Still, the knowledge isn't grounded in forgetting. It's originally grounded in testimony from an actually reliable source, and Jaidyn did as good a job as he needed to in checking the reliability of the source before accepting the testimony. Now since Jaidyn is finite, he doesn't have any obligation to remember everything. It seems odd to demand that Jaidyn adjust his beliefs on the basis of where they are from if he isn't even required to track where they are from. It would be very odd to say that Jaidyn's evidence now includes neither p (because it is undermined by his friend's testimony), nor the fact that someone said that p. That suggests any p-related inferences Jaidyn makes are totally unsupported by his evidence, which doesn't seem right.

So the picture of evidence as basic knowledge, combined with a plausible theory of when forgetting is permissible, suggests that the forgetful reader knows more than the reader with a better memory. I suspect the same thing will happen in versions of Goldman's explosive inductive argument. Imagine a thinker observes all the Fs within 3 miles, sees they are all G, and rationally infers that all the Fs within 4 miles are G. Some time later they retain the belief, the knowledge actually, that all Fs within 4 miles are G. But they forget that this was partially inferential knowledge, like Jaidyn forgot the source of his knowledge that p. They then make the seemingly sensible inductive inference that all Fs within 5 miles are G. Is this rational, and can it produce knowledge? I think the answer is yes; if they (not unreasonably) forget the source of their knowledge that the Fs 3 to 4 miles away are G, then this knowledge becomes basic. If it's basic, it is evidence. And if it is evidence, it can support one round of inductive reasoning.

I've drifted a fair way from discussing interest-relativity. And a lot of what I say here is inessential to defending IRT. So I'll return to the main plotline with a discussion of how my view of evidence helps respond to a challenge Ram Neta issues to IRT, and implies a rejection of a key principle in Jeremy Fantl and Matthew McGrath's theory of knowledge.

9.8 Holism and Defeaters

The picture of evidence I've outlined here grounds a natural response to a nice puzzle case outlined by Ram Neta (2007).[7]

> Kate needs to get to Main Street by noon: her life depends upon it. She is desperately searching for Main Street when she comes to an intersection and looks up at the perpendicular street signs at that intersection. One street sign says "State Street" and the perpendicular street sign says "Main Street." Now, it is a matter of complete indifference to Kate whether she is on State Street—nothing whatsoever depends upon it. (Neta, 2007: 182)

---

7 This section draws Weatherson (2011: §5).

Neta argues that IRT implies Kate knows that she is on State Street, but does not know that she is on Main Street. He suggests this is intuitively implausible. I think I agree with that intuition, so let's take it for granted and ask whether IRT has this problematic implication.

Let's also assume that it is not rational for Kate to take the street sign's word for it. I'm not sure that's true actually, but let's assume it to get the argument going. I think Neta is reasoning that since Kate's life depends on it, then IRT must say that she can't trust street signs, because the stakes are so high.

That claim about the relation between stakes and what one can take for granted can't be right. I often take actions that my life depends on going by the say so of signs. For example, I often turn onto the freeway ramp labelled 'on ramp', and not the ramp labelled 'off ramp', without really double checking. If I was wrong about this there is a very high chance I'd be very quickly killed. (Wrong-way crashes on freeways are a very common kind of fatal collisions.) If Kate can't take the sign for granted, it isn't just because her life is at stake; somewhat disconcertingly, that doesn't make the case any different from everyday driving.

But maybe Kate has some other way of checking where she is—like a map on a phone in her pocket—and it would be irrational to take the sign for granted and not check that other map. So I'm not going to push on this assumption.

So what evidence should The Radical Interpreter assign to Kate? It doesn't seem to be at issue that Kate sees that the signs say State and Main. The big question is whether she can simply take it as evidence that she is on State and Main. That is, do the contents of the sign simply become part of Kate's evidence? (Assume that the signs are accurate and there is no funny business going on, so it is plausible that the signs contribute to this evidence.) There are three natural options.

1. Both signs supply evidence directly to Kate, so her evidence includes that she is on State and that she is on Main.
2. Neither sign contributes evidence directly to Kate, so her evidence includes what the signs say, but nothing directly about her location.
3. One sign contributes evidence directly to Kate, but the other does not.

Option 1 implies that Kate is rational to not check further whether she is on Main Street. And that's irrational, so option 1 is out.

Option 3 implies that the signs behave differently, and that The Rational Interpreter will assign them different roles in Kate's cognitive architecture. But this will be true even though the signs are equally reliable, and Kate's evidence about their reliability is identical. So Kate treating them differently would be irrational, and The Radical Interpreter does not want to make Kate irrational if it can be helped. So option 3 is out.

That leaves option 2. Kate's evidence does not include that she is on State, and does not include that she is on Main. The latter 'non-inclusion' is directly explained by pragmatic factors. The former is explained by those factors plus the requirement that Kate's evidence is what The Radical Interpreter says it is, and The Radical Interpreter's desire to make Kate rational.

So Kate's evidence doesn't distinguish between the streets. It does, however, include that the signs say she is on State and that she is on Main. Could she be justified in inferring that she is on State, but not that she is on Main?

It is hard to see how this could be so. Street signs are hardly basic epistemic sources. They are the kind of evidence we should be 'conservative' about in the sense of James Pryor (2004). We should only use them if we antecedently believe they are correct. So for Kate to believe she's on State, she'd have to believe the street signs she can see are correct. If not, she'd incoherently be relying on a source she doesn't trust, even though it is not a basic source. But if she believes the street signs are correct, she'd believe she was on Main, and that would lead to practical irrationality. So there's no way to coherently add the belief that she's on State Street to her stock of beliefs. So she doesn't know, and can't know, that she's either on State or on Main. This is, in a roundabout way, due to the practical situation Kate faces.

Neta thinks that the best way for IRT to handle this case is to say that the high stakes associated with the proposition that Kate is on Main Street imply that certain methods of belief formation do not produce knowledge. And he argues, plausibly, that such a restriction will lead to implausibly sceptical results.

What to say about this suggestion turns on how we understand what a 'method' is. If methods are individuated very finely, like *Trust street signs right here*, then it's plausible that Kate should restrict what methods she uses, but implausible that this is badly sceptical. If methods are individuated very coarsely, like *Trust written testimony*, then it's plausible that this is badly sceptical, but implausible that Kate should give up on methods this general. I can rationally treat some parts of a book as providing direct evidence about the world, and other, more speculative, parts as providing direct evidence about what the author says, and hence indirect evidence about the world. Similarly, Kate can treat these street signs as indirect evidence about her location, while still treating other signs around her as providing direct evidence. So there is no sceptical threat here.

But while the case doesn't show IRT is false, it does tell us something interesting about the implications of IRT. When a practical consideration defeats a claim to know that p, it will often also knock out nearby knowledge claims. Some of these are obvious, like that the practical consideration defeats the claim to know $0=0 \to p$. But some of these are more indirect. When the inquirer knows what her evidence is, and knows that she has just the same evidence for q as for p, then if a practical consideration defeats a claim to know p, it also defeats a claim to know q. In practice, this makes IRT a somewhat more sceptical theory than it may have first appeared. It's not so sceptical as to be implausible, but it's more sceptical than is immediately obvious. This kind of result, where IRT ends up being somewhat sceptical but not implausibly so, has been a theme of many different cases throughout the book.

9.9 Epistemic Weakness

The cases where cut-elimination fails raise a problem for the way that Fantl and McGrath spell out their version of IRT. Here is a principle they rely on in motivating IRT.

> When you know a proposition p, no weaknesses in your epistemic position with respect to p—no weaknesses, that is, in your standing on any truth-relevant dimension with respect to p—stand in the way of p justifying you in having further beliefs. (Fantl and McGrath, 2009: 64)

And a few pages later they offer the following gloss on this principle.

> We offer no analysis of the intuitive notion of 'standing in the way'. But we do think that, when Y does not obtain, the following counterfactual condition is sufficient for a subject's position on some dimension d to be something that stands in the way of Y obtaining: whether Y obtains can vary with variations in the subject's position on d, holding fixed all other factors relevant to whether Y obtains. (Fantl and McGrath, 2009: 67)

This gloss suggests that the difference between knowledge and evidence is something that stands in the way of an inference. The inquirer who knows that nearby Fs are Gs, but does not know that somewhat distant Fs are Gs, has many things standing in the way of this knowledge. One of them is, according to this test, that her evidence does not include that all nearby Fs are Gs. Yet this is something she knows. So a weakness in her epistemic position with respect to the nature of nearby Fs, that it is merely evidence and not knowledge, stands in the way of it justifying further beliefs.

The same thing will be true in the monotonic cases of cut-elimination failure. The thinker whose evidence includes $\Gamma \cup \Delta$, and whose inferential knowledge includes A, cannot infer B. But if they had A as evidence, and not merely as knowledge, then they could infer B. So the weakness in their epistemic position, the gap between evidence and knowledge, stands in the way of something.

I didn't endorse the principle of Fantl and McGrath's quoted above, but I did endorse very similar principles, and one might wonder whether they are subject to the same criticism. The main principle I endorsed was that if one knows that p, one is immune from criticism for using p on the grounds that p might be false, or is too risky to use. Equivalently, if the use of p in an inference is defective, but p is known, the explanation of why it is defective cannot be that p is too risky. But now won't the same problem arise? Our inquirer in the monotonic cut-elimination example can't use A in reasoning to B. If A was part of their evidence, then it wouldn't be risky, and they would be able to use it. So the risk is part of what makes the use of it mistaken.

I reject the very last step in that criticism. The fact that something is wrong, and that it wouldn't have been wrong if X, does not mean the non-obtaining of X is part of the ground, or explanation, for why it is wrong. If I break a law, then what I do is illegal. Had the law in question been struck down by a constitutional court, then my action wouldn't have been illegal. Similarly, if the law had been repealed, my action would not have been illegal. But that doesn't imply that the ground or explanation of the illegality of my action is the court's not striking the law down, or the later legislature not repealing the law. That is to put too much into the notion of ground or explanation. No, what makes the act illegal is that a particular piece of legislation was passed, and this act violates it. This explanation is defeasible—it would be defeated if a court or later legislature had stepped in—but it is nonetheless complete.

The same thing is true in the case of knowledge and evidence. Imagine an inquirer who observes all the Fs within 3 miles being G, and infers both that all the Fs within 4 miles are G, and, therefore, that all the Fs within 5 miles are G. The intermediate step is, in a sense, risky. And the final step is bad. And the final step wouldn't have been bad if the intermediate step hadn't been risky. But it's not the riskiness that makes the second inference bad. No, what makes the second inference bad is that it violates Weisberg's No Feedback principle. That's what the reasoner can be criticised for, not for taking an epistemic risk.

There are two differences then between the core principle I rely on—using reasons that are known provides immunity to criticism for taking epistemic risks—and the principle Fantl and McGrath rely on. I use a concept of epistemic risk where they use a concept of strength of epistemic position. I don't think these are quite the same thing, but they are clearly similar. But the bigger difference is that they endorse a counterfactual gloss of their principle, and I reject any such counterfactual gloss. I don't say that the person who uses known p is immune to all criticisms that would have been vitiated had p been less risky. I just say that the risk can't be the ground of the criticism; something else must be. In some cases, including this one, that 'something else' might be correlated with risk. But it must be the explanation.

Of course, this difference between my version of IRT and Fantl and McGrath's is tiny compared to how much our theories have in common. And indeed, it's tiny compared to how much my theory simply borrows from theirs. But it's helpful I think to highlight the differences to understand the choice points within versions of IRT.

10. Power

Knowledge is power. That is, knowledge grounds our ability to do things. What things? Not, typically, bodily movements. If Lupin knows the passcode for the phone, he can unlock the phone. But even without that knowledge, he could make the bodily movement of typing in 220348 or whatever the passcode was. What power does he get from knowing the code is 220348? He gets the ability to deliberately unlock the phone. He gets the ability to unlock the phone by typing 220348, and for this to not be a lucky guess, but a rational action. Knowledge makes rational action possible. That's why it is powerful. That's what its power consists in. That's why the Nyāya philosophers were right to base anti-sceptical arguments on the possibility of rational action. Knowledge matters in everyday life; it explains why we have the power to act rationally.[1]

But it turns out to be surprisingly hard to articulate the magnitude of that power. One might want to say that the actions which knowing that p makes rational include all the actions whatsoever that make sense if p can be taken as given. This, as we've seen many times over, can't be right. If it were right it would entail either that some actions that seem horribly reckless are in fact rational, or that an absurd form of scepticism is true, and almost no actions are in fact rational. If our pre-theoretic judgments of which actions are rational are even close to being right, there must be limits to the power of knowledge.

Are those limits sensitive to the interests of the would-be knower, or are they independent of those interests? I've argued that they are

---

[1] The story I'm telling in this paragraph deliberately echoes the view that ability modals do not express possibility but necessity (Mandelkern, Schultheis and Boylan, 2017). To say Lupin can unlock the phone is not to say he might unlock the phone—anyone might unlock it hitting random numbers—it's to say he has a method that would unlock the phone if deployed.

sensitive to the knower's interests, against what I called the orthodox view that they are not. There are two primary reasons I've given for this.

One reason is that the interest-relative answer, unlike the orthodox answer, clarifies why the boundary between knowledge and non-knowledge matters. From the interest-relative viewpoint, the boundary between knowledge and non-knowledge is philosophically and practically significant. In contrast, the orthodox view treats the boundary between knowledge and non-knowledge as analogous to the distinction between heavy things and non-heavy things. How heavy something is matters a lot; but which side of the heavy/non-heavy boundary it falls on does not.

According to orthodoxy, to know something is to have enough power to use that knowledge to act rationally in, you know, a wide enough range of cases. How wide? It's sort of wide enough. Why is it this range rather than some other? Oh, no good reason. We just talk that way, and it's the job of epistemologists to explain why we do. No, not explain—because it's arbitrary and inexplicable. It's to describe the limits, limits which are ultimately quite arbitrary. This is no good at all. The heterodox interest-relative view has a better answer. The limits are set just where they need to be to make it true that what this person knows rationalises the actions that it should in fact rationalise.

A second reason for favouring the interest-relative view is that it makes some core principles of action theory and decision theory turn out to be correct, while the orthodox view makes them not quite right. Here are the (versions of the) principles I have in mind.

Means-End Rationality
If X should be aiming for end E, and X knows both that action A is the only means to end E, and that A will indeed lead to end E, to then X should intend to perform A.

Strict Dominance Reasoning
If X has to choose between A and B, and there is some partition P of a space of possibilities such that X knows both that precisely one member of P is actual, that X's actions make no difference to which member is actual, and that conditional on each member of P, A is better than B, then X should prefer A to B.

Given orthodoxy, neither of these can be correct. In each case, X might know that A will lead to a good outcome, but it might also be probable enough that *A* will lead to a disastrous outcome for it to be irrational for *X* to choose *A*. That's absurd, and so we should reject orthodoxy. The interest-relative view makes these, and any number of related principles, turn out unrestrictedly true.[2]

If these are the two reasons for adopting an interest-relative view, the appeal of some kind of contextualist version of an interest-invariant view should be clear. The contextualist can, and does, say that there is something special about the boundary between knowledge and non-knowledge. When one says that someone knows something, one means (more or less) that their evidence for that thing is good enough for one's own purposes. Any speaker of the language can truly say, "When I use 'knows', it means what I need it to mean, neither more nor less". We could quibble here, but that's something like a solution to the problem of arbitrariness.

The problems come with principles like Means-End Rationality and Strict Dominance Reasoning. These are both false within standard, interest-invariant, contextualist views.[3] Contextualists are aware of this fact, and say that they have something nearly as good: a meta-linguistic replacement. Both principles are true if we replace talk about what *X* knows with talk about what *X* can truly self-predicate 'knowledge' of. It doesn't matter whether *X* knows that *A* will lead to end *E*, but whether *X* can say the words *I know that performing A will lead to end E*. But it's absurd to think that fundamental principles of rationality should make reference to a particular language, e.g., English, like this. So contextualism cannot get us out of this jam. This is not to say that contextualism is false. Maybe there are other reasons to believe in contextualism. It might be supported by general principles about the way that names behave in attitude ascriptions. Or it might be a consequence of the view that 'knows' is polysemous, a view I floated in a footnote in Section 2.7. Or it might be supported by reflection on cases where people talk about others with lower evidential needs than their own. I don't take a stance

---

2   Note that it's not much help to say that the principles are approximately true according to the orthodox picture. In game theory we want to be able to iterate principles like this, and approximately true principles can't be applied iteratively.

3   For the rest of this chapter, when I talk about contextualism, I mean the standard version of contextualism that does not entail that knowledge is interest-relative.

on these questions here; I'm just arguing that contextualism doesn't save orthodoxy.

All these benefits of the interest-relative view are of no use if the interest-relative view has even worse defects. And most of this book has involved pushing back against some of the alleged defects of the view. In some cases, I've avoided possible criticisms by adopting a form of interest-relative epistemology that doesn't allow the criticisms to take hold. Many existing critiques of interest-relative epistemology focus on forms of the view where being in a 'high-stakes' situation is relevant to what one knows. Since my version of the view does not say that interests matter iff they put the chooser in a high-stakes situation, those criticisms don't have any bite. Other critiques target a part-time version of interest-relative epistemology, where some but not all key notions are interest-relative. I used to endorse such a part-time interest-relative theory, but eventually decided that the criticisms of such a view were decisive.

Still, many criticisms do need replies, and much of this book has consisted in replying to them. In Chapter 3 I replied to (successful) criticisms of how I'd previously handled knowledge of propositions that are not relevant to the thinker's current inquiries. In Chapter 5 I replied to arguments that started with the observation that it sometimes seems right to double check things that we know. And in Chapter 6 I replied to arguments based on how some versions of interest-relative epistemology (including the version I'd previously endorsed) handled choices between nearly indistinguishable options.

Many criticisms of interest-relative epistemology do not turn on detailed engagement with how the view handles this or that case, but on the very idea of interests being relevant to epistemology. One way you see this is with arguments that just start from the implausibility of two people who are alike in evidence differing with respect to knowledge. But you also see it in the surprisingly common position in the literature that there is some extra-large burden of proof on defenders of interest-relativity. It seems to be a common presupposition that unless there is a super compelling argument that knowledge is interest-relative, we should reject the idea that it is, even if there is no equally compelling argument against the idea. I'm in general very sceptical of burden of proof arguments; it always looks like an attempt to win by bribing the umpires. But there is extra reason to be sceptical of these particular burden of proof arguments. It's hard to even state a principle about the (alleged) independence of knowledge and interests without saying something false about double luck cases, or variable reliability cases, or deviant causal chain cases.

We've known since 1963 (if not many centuries before) that knowledge depends on more than just the evidential basis of the thing purportedly known. Since then there has been a dizzying array of proposals about what else knowledge might depend on. And on reflection, many of these proposals have been very plausible. This book aims to defend one such proposal, that knowledge depends on interests. In particular, how much evidential support one needs to have knowledge depends on what inquiries one is, and should be, engaged in. Given the tight relationships between knowledge and rational action, adding this to the vast list of things knowledge is sensitive to should not be surprising.

References

Adamson, Peter. (2015). *Philosophy in the Hellenistic and Roman worlds: A history of philosophy without any gaps*, volume 2 (Oxford). Oxford University Press.

Adamson, Peter. (2019). *Medieval philosophy: A history of philosophy without any gaps*, volume 4. Oxford University Press.

Adamson, Peter, and Jonardon Ganeri. (2020). *Classical Indian philosophy: A history of philosophy without any gaps*, volume 5. Oxford University Press.

Anderson, Charity, and John Hawthorne. (2019a). Knowledge, practical adequacy, and stakes. *Oxford Studies in Epistemology*, 6, 234–257.

Anderson, Charity, and John Hawthorne. (2019b). Pragmatic encroachment and closure. In Brian Kim and Matthew McGrath (Eds.), *Pragmatic encroachment in epistemology* (107–115). Routledge.

Armour-Garb, B. (2011). Contextualism without pragmatic encroachment. *Analysis*, 71(4), 667–676. https://doi.org/10.1093/analys/anr083

Aumann, Robert J. (1999). Interactive epistemology I: Knowledge. *International Journal of Game Theory*, 28(3), 263–300. https://doi.org/10.1007/s001820050111

Basu, Rima, and Mark Schroeder. (2019). Doxastic wrongings. In Brian Kim and Matthew McGrath (Eds.), *Pragmatic encroachment in epistemology* (181–205). Routledge.

Bennett, Karen. (2017). *Making things up*. Oxford University Press.

Bhatt, Rajesh. (1999). Covert modality in non-finite contexts (PhD thesis). University of Pennsylvania.

Bird, Alexander. (2004). Is evidence non-inferential? *Philosophical Quarterly*, 54(215), 252–265. https://doi.org/10.1111/j.0031-8094.2004.00350.x

Blome-Tillmann, Michael. (2009). Contextualism, subject-sensitive invariantism, and the interaction of 'knowledge'-ascriptions with modal and temporal operators. *Philosophy and Phenomenological Research*, 79(2), 315–331. https://doi.org/10.1111/j.1933-1592.2009.00280.x

Boyd, Kenneth. (2016). Pragmatic encroachment and epistemically responsible action. *Synthese*, 193(9), 2721–2745. https://doi.org/10.1007/s11229-015-0878-y

Brittain, Charles, and Peter Osorio. (2021). Philo of Larissa. In Edward N. Zalta (Ed.), *The Stanford encyclopedia of philosophy* (Summer 2021). Metaphysics Research Lab, Stanford University. https://plato.stanford.edu/archives/sum2021/entries/philo-larissa/

Brown, Jessica. (2008). Subject-sensitive invariantism and the knowledge norm for practical reasoning. *Noûs*, 42(2), 167–189. https://doi.org/10.1111/j.1468-0068.2008.00677.x

Buchak, Lara. (2013). *Risk and rationality*. Oxford University Press.

Caplin, Andrew, Mark Dean, and Daniel Martin. (2011). Search and satisficing. *American Economic Review*, 101(7), 2899–2922. https://doi.org/10.1257/aer.101.7.2899

Carlsson, Hans, and Eric van Damme. (1993). Global games and equilibrium selection. *Econometrica*, 61(5), 989–1018. https://doi.org/10.2307/2951491

Chakravarti, Ashok. (2017). Imperfect information and opportunism. *Journal of Economic Issues*, 51(4), 1114–1136. https://doi.org/10.1080/00213624.2017.1391594

Chernev, Alexander, Ulf Böckenholt, and Joseph Goodman. (2015). Choice overload: A conceptual review and meta-analysis. *Journal of Consumer Psychology*, 25(2), 333–358. https://doi.org/10.1016/j.jcps.2014.08.002

Cherniak, Christopher. (1986). *Minimal rationality*. MIT Press.

Cho, In-Koo, and David M. Kreps. (1987). Signalling games and stable equilibria. *The Quarterly Journal of Economics*, 102(2), 179–221. https://doi.org/10.2307/1885060

Christensen, David. (2005). *Putting logic in its place*. Oxford University Press.

Christensen, David. (2007). Does Murphy's law apply in epistemology? Self-doubt and rational ideals. *Oxford Studies in Epistemology*, 2, 3–31.

Christensen, David. (2011). Disagreement, question-begging and epistemic self-criticism. *Philosophers' Imprint*, 11(6), 1–22. https://doi.org/2027/spo.3521354.0011.006

Christensen, David. (2019). Formulating independence. In Mattias Skipper and Asbjørn Steglich-Petersen (Eds.), *Higher-order evidence: New essays* (13–34). Oxford University Press.

Clark, Christopher. (2012). *The sleepwalkers: How Europe went to war in 1914*. Harper Collins.

Cohen, Stewart. (2002). Basic knowledge and the problem of easy knowledge. *Philosophy and Phenomenological Research*, 65(2), 309–329. https://doi.org/10.1111/j.1933-1592.2002.tb00204.x

Cohen, Stewart. (2004). Knowledge, assertion, and practical reasoning. *Philosophical Issues*, 14(1), 482–491. https://doi.org/10.1111/j.1533-6077.2004.00040.x

Conlisk, John. (1996). Why bounded rationality? *Journal of Economic Literature*, 34(2), 669–700.

Crisp, Roger. (2021). Well-being. In Edward N. Zalta (Ed.), *The Stanford encyclopedia of philosophy* (Winter 2021). Metaphysics Research Lab, Stanford University.

Cross, Charles, and Floris Roelofsen. (2018). Questions. In Edward N. Zalta (Ed.), *The Stanford encyclopedia of philosophy* (Spring 2018). Metaphysics Research Lab, Stanford University. https://plato.stanford.edu/archives/spr2018/entries/questions/

Das, Nilanjan. (2016). Epistemic stability (PhD thesis). MIT.

DeRose, Keith. (2002). Assertion, knowledge and context. *Philosophical Review*, 111(2), 167–203. https://doi.org/10.2307/3182618

Diab, Dalia L., Michael A. Gillespie, and Scott Highhouse. (2008). Are maximizers really unhappy? The measurement of maximizing tendency. *Judgment and Decision Making*, 3(5), 364–370. https://doi.org/10.1017/S1930297500000383

Dogramaci, Sinan. (2015). Forget and forgive: A practical approach to forgotten evidence. *Ergo*, 2(26), 645–677. https://doi.org/10.3998/ergo.12405314.0002.026

Dylan, Bob. (2016). *The lyrics: 1961-2012*. Simon and Schuster.

Eaton, Daniel, and Timothy Pickavance. (2015). Evidence against pragmatic encroachment. *Philosophical Studies*, 172, 3135–3143. https://doi.org/10.1007/s11098-015-0461-x

Egan, Andy. (2008). Seeing and believing: perception, belief formation and the divided mind. *Philosophical Studies*, 140(1), 47–63. https://doi.org/10.1007/s11098-008-9225-1

Elster, Jon. (1979). *Ulysses and the sirens: Studies in rationality and irrationality*. Cambridge University Press.

Falbo, Arianna. (2021). Inquiry and confirmation. *Analysis*, 81(4), 622–631. https://doi.org/10.1093/analys/anab037

Fantl, Jeremy, and Matthew McGrath. (2002). Evidence, pragmatics, and justification. *Philosophical Review*, 111(1), 67–94. https://doi.org/10.2307/3182570

Fantl, Jeremy, and Matthew McGrath. (2009). *Knowledge in an uncertain world*. Oxford University Press.

Foley, Richard. (1993). *Working without a net*. Oxford University Press.

Friedman, Jane. (2017). Why suspend judging? *Noûs*, 51(2), 302–326. https://doi.org/10.1111/nous.12137

Friedman, Jane. (2019a). Checking again. *Philosophical Issues*, 29(1), 84–96. https://doi.org/10.1111/phis.12141

Friedman, Jane. (2019b). Inquiry and belief. *Noûs*, 53(2), 296–315. https://doi.org/10.1111/nous.12222

Friedman, Jane. (2020). The epistemic and the zetetic. *Philosophical Review*, 129(4), 501–536. https://doi.org/10.1215/00318108-8540918

Friedman, Jane. (2024a). Suspension of judgment is a question-directed attitude. In Blake Roeber, Ernest Sosa, Matthias Steup, and John Turri (Eds.), *Contemporary debates in epistemology* (3rd ed., 66–78). Wiley Blackwell.

Friedman, Jane. (2024b). The aim of inquiry? *Philosophy and Phenomenological Research*, 108(2), 506–523. https://doi.org/10.1111/phpr.12982

Ganson, Dorit. (2008). Evidentialism and pragmatic constraints on outright belief. *Philosophical Studies*, 139(3), 441–458. https://doi.org/10.1007/s11098-007-9133-9

Ganson, Dorit. (2019). Great expectations: Belief and the case for pragmatic encroachment. In Brian Kim and Matthew McGrath (Eds.), *Pragmatic encroachment in epistemology* (10–34). Routledge.

Gao, Jie. (2023). Should credence be sensitive to practical factors? A cost-benefit analysis. *Mind and Language*, 38(5), 1238–1257. https://doi.org/10.1111/mila.12451

Gendler, Tamar Szabó, and John Hawthorne. (2005). The real guide to fake barns: A catalogue of gifts for your epistemic enemies. *Philosophical Studies*, 124(3), 331–352. https://doi.org/10.1007/s11098-005-7779-8

Gettier, Edmund L. (1963). Is justified true belief knowledge? *Analysis*, 23(6), 121–123. https://doi.org/10.1093/analys/23.6.121

Gigerenzer, Gerd, and Reinhard Selten. (2001). *Bounded rationality: The adaptive toolbox*. MIT Press.

Gillies, Anthony S. (2010). Iffiness. *Semantics and Pragmatics*, 3(4), 1–42. https://doi.org/10.3765/sp.3.4

Goldman, Alvin. (2009). Williamson on knowledge and evidence. In Patrick Greenough and Duncan Pritchard (Eds.), *Williamson on Knowledge* (73–91). Oxford University Press.

Hájek, Alan (2011). Conditional Probability. In Prasanta S. Bandyopadhyay and Malcolm R. Forster (Eds.), *Philosophy of Statistics* (99–135). North-Holland.

Harman, Gilbert. (1973). *Thought*. Princeton University Press.

Harman, Gilbert. (1986). *Change in view*. MIT Press.

Harper, William. (1986). Mixed strategies and ratifiability in causal decision theory. *Erkenntnis*, 24(1), 25–36. https://doi.org/10.1007/BF00183199

Hawthorne, John. (2004). *Knowledge and lotteries*. Oxford University Press.

Hawthorne, John. (2005). Knowledge and evidence. *Philosophy and Phenomenological Research*, 70(2), 452–458. https://doi.org/10.1111/j.1933-1592.2005.tb00540.x

Hawthorne, John, Daniel Rothschild, and Levi Spectre. (2016). Belief is weak. *Philosophical Studies*, 173, 1393–1404. https://doi.org/10.1007/s11098-015-0553-7

Hawthorne, John, and Amia Srinivasan. (2013). Disagreement without transparency: Some bleak thoughts. In David Christensen and Jennifer Lackey (Eds.), *The epistemology of disagreement: New essays* (9–30). Oxford University Press.

Hawthorne, John, and Jason Stanley. (2008). Knowledge and action. *Journal of Philosophy*, 105(10), 571–590. https://doi.org/10.5840/jphil20081051022

Hedden, Brian. (2012). Options and the subjective ought. *Philosophical Studies*, 158(2), 343–360. https://doi.org/10.1007/s11098-012-9880-0

Hieronymi, Pamela. (2013). The use of reasons in thought (and the use of earmarks in arguments). *Ethics*, 124(1), 114–127. https://doi.org/10.1086/671402

Hills, Alison. (2009). Moral testimony and moral epistemology. *Ethics*, 120(1), 94–127. https://doi.org/10.1086/648610

Holliday, Wesley H., and Matthew Mandelkern. (2024). The orthologic of epistemic modals. *Journal of Philosophical Logic*, 53, 831–907. https://doi.org/10.1007/s10992-024-09746-7

Hotelling, Harold. (1929). Stability in competition. *The Economic Journal*, 39(153), 41–57. https://doi.org/10.2307/2224214

Humberstone, I. L. (1981). From worlds to possibilities. *Journal of Philosophical Logic*, 10(3), 313–339. https://doi.org/10.1007/BF00293423

Humberstone, Lloyd. (2016). *Philosophical applications of modal logic*. College Publications.

Hunter, Daniel. (1996). On the relation between categorical and probabilistic belief. *Noûs*, 30, 75–98. https://doi.org/10.2307/2216304

Ichikawa, Jonathan. (2012). Knowledge norms and acting well. *Thought: A Journal of Philosophy*, 1(1), 49–55. https://doi.org/10.1002/tht3.7

Ichikawa, Jonathan. (2017). *Contextualising knowledge*. Oxford University Press.

Iyengar, Sheena S., Rachael E. Wells, and Barry Schwartz. (2006). Doing better but feeling worse: Looking for the 'best' job undermines satisfaction. *Psychological Science*, 17(2), 143–150. https://doi.org/10.1111/j.1467-9280.2006.01677.x

Jackson, Frank. (1987). *Conditionals*. Basil Blackwell.

Joyce, James M.. (2018). Deliberation and stability in Newcomb problems and pseudo-Newcomb problems. In Arif Ahmed (Ed.), *Newcomb's problem* (139–158). Cambridge University Press.

Joyce, James M. (1999). *The foundations of causal decision theory*. Cambridge University Press.

Keynes, John Maynard. (1936). Herbert Somerton Foxwell. *The Economic Journal*, 46(184), 589–619. https://doi.org/10.2307/2224674

Keynes, John Maynard. (1937). The general theory of employment. *Quarterly Journal of Economics*, 51(2), 209–223.

Kim, Brian. (2023). Pragmatic infallibilism. *Asian Journal of Philosophy*, 2(2), 1–22. https://doi.org/10.1007/s44204-023-00097-9

Kimball, Miles. (2015). Cognitive economics. *The Japanese Economic Review*, 66(2), 167–181. https://doi.org/10.1111/jere.12070

Knight, Frank. (1921). *Risk, uncertainty and profit*. University of Chicago Press.

Kohlberg, Elon, and Jean-Francois Mertens. (1986). On the strategic stability of equilibria. *Econometrica*, 54(5), 1003–1037. https://doi.org/10.2307/1912320

Kratzer, Angelika. (2012). *Modals and conditionals*. Oxford University Press.

Kripke, Saul. (2011). Nozick on knowledge. In *Philosophical troubles: Collected papers*, volume 1 (161–224). Oxford University Press.

Kroedel, Thomas. (2012). The lottery paradox, epistemic justification and permissibility. *Analysis*, 72(1), 57–60. https://doi.org/10.1093/analys/anr129

Lasonen-Aarnio, Maria. (2010). Unreasonable knowledge. *Philosophical Perspectives*, 24, 1–21. https://doi.org/10.1111/j.1520-8583.2010.00183.x

Lasonen-Aarnio, Maria. (2014). Higher-order evidence and the limits of defeat. *Philosophy and Phenomenological Research*, 88(2), 314–345. https://doi.org/10.1111/phpr.12090

Lederman, Harvey. (2018). Two paradoxes of common knowledge: Coordinated attack and electronic mail. *Noûs*, 52(4), 921–945. https://doi.org/10.1111/nous.12186

Lee, Matthew. (2017a). Credence and correctness: In defense of credal reductivism. *Philosophical Papers*, 46(2), 273–296. https://doi.org/10.1080/05568641.2017.1364142

Lee, Matthew. (2017b). On the arbitrariness objection to the threshold view. *Dialogue*, 56(1), 143–158. https://doi.org/10.1017/S0012217317000154

Lewis, David. (1969). *Convention: A philosophical study*. Harvard University Press.

Lewis, David. (1976). Probabilities of conditionals and conditional probabilities. *Philosophical Review,* 85(3), 297–315. https://doi.org/10.2307/2184045

Lewis, David. (1982). Logic for equivocators. *Noûs,* 16(3), 431–441. https://doi.org/10.1017/cbo9780511625237.009

Lewis, David. (1986). Probabilities of conditionals and conditional probabilities II. *Philosophical Review,* 95(4), 581–589. https://doi.org/10.2307/2185051

Lewis, David. (1988). Desire as belief. *Mind,* 97(387), 323–332. https://doi.org/10.1093/mind/xcvii.387.323

Lewis, David. (1996). Desire as belief II. *Mind,* 105(418), 303–313. https://doi.org/10.1093/mind/105.418.303

Lewis, David. (2004). Causation as influence. In John Collins, Ned Hall, and L. A. Paul (Eds.), *Causation and counterfactuals* (75–106). MIT Press.

Lipsey, R. G., and Kelvin Lancaster. (1956–1957). The general theory of second best. *Review of Economic Studies,* 24(1), 11–32. https://doi.org/10.2307/2296233

Littlejohn, Clayton. (2018). Stop making sense? On a puzzle about rationality. *Philosophy and Phenomenological* Research, 96(2), 257–272. https://doi.org/10.1111/phpr.12271

MacFarlane, John. (2005). The assessment sensitivity of knowledge attributions. *Oxford Studies in Epistemology,* 1, 197–233.

Machamer, Peter, Lindley Darden, and Carl F. Craver. (2000). Thinking about mechanisms. *Philosophy of Science,* 67(1), 1–25. https://doi.org/10.1086/392759

Maher, Patrick. (1996). Subjective and objective confirmation. *Philosophy of Science,* 63(2), 149–174. https://doi.org/10.1086/289906

Maier, John. (2022). Abilities. In Edward N. Zalta and Uri Nodelman (Eds.), *The Stanford encyclopedia of philosophy* (Fall 2022). Metaphysics Research Lab, Stanford University. https://plato.stanford.edu/archives/fall2022/entries/abilities/

Maitra, Ishani, and Brian Weatherson. (2010). Assertion, knowledge and action. *Philosophical Studies,* 149(1), 99–118. https://doi.org/10.1007/s11098-010-9542-z

Mandelkern, Matthew, Ginger Schultheis, and David Boylan. (2017). Agentive modals. *Philosophical Review,* 126(3), 301–343. https://doi.org/10.1215/00318108-3878483

Mangan, Jean, Amanda Hughes, and Kim Slack. (2010). Student finance, information and decision making. *Higher Education,* 60(5), 459–472. https://doi.org/10.1007/s10734-010-9309-7

Manski, Charles F. (2017). Optimize, satisfice, or choose without deliberation? A simple minimax-regret assessment. *Theory and Decision*, 83(2), 155–173. https://doi.org/10.1007/s11238-017-9592-1

McGrath, Matthew. (2021). Being neutral: Agnosticism, inquiry and the suspension of judgment. *Noûs*, 55(2), 463–484. https://doi.org/10.1111/nous.12323

McGrath, Matthew, and Brian Kim. (2019). Introduction. In Brian Kim and Matthew McGrath (Eds.), *Pragmatic encroachment in epistemology* (1–9). Routledge.

Melchior, Guido. (2019). *Knowing and checking: An epistemological investigation*. Routledge.

Mercier, Hugo. (2020). *Not born yesterday: The science of who we trust and what we believe*. Princeton University Press.

Nagel, Jennifer. (2010). Epistemic anxiety and adaptive invariantism. *Philosophical Perspectives*, 24(1), 407–435. https://doi.org/10.1111/j.1520-8583.2010.00198.x

Nagel, Jennifer. (2013). Motivating Williamson's model Gettier cases. *Inquiry*, 56(1), 54–62. https://doi.org/10.1080/0020174X.2013.775014

Nagel, Jennifer. (2014). *Knowledge: A very short introduction*. Oxford University Press.

Nair, Shyam. (2019). Must good reasoning satisfy cumulative transitivity? *Philosophy and Phenomenological Research*, 98(1), 123–146. https://doi.org/10.1111/phpr.12431

Neta, Ram. (2007). Anti-intellectualism and the knowledge-action principle. *Philosophy and Phenomenological Research*, 75(1), 180–187. https://doi.org/10.1111/j.1933-1592.2007.00069.x

Newman, David B., Joanna Schug, Masaki Yuki, Junko Yamada, and John B. Nezlek. (2018). The negative consequences of maximizing in friendship selection. *Journal of Personality and Social Psychology*, 114(5), 804–824. https://doi.org/10.1037/pspp0000141

North, Jill. (2010). An empirical approach to symmetry and probability. *Studies in History and Philosophy of Science Part B: Studies in History and Philosophy of Modern Physics*, 41(1), 27–40. https://doi.org/10.1016/j.shpsb.2009.08.008

Nozick, Robert. (1981). *Philosophical explorations*. Harvard University Press.

Odell, John S. (2002). Bounded rationality and world political economy. In David M. Andrews, C. Randall Henning, and Louis W. Pauly (Eds.), *Governing the world's money* (168–193). Cornell University Press.

Ogaki, Masao, and Saori C. Tanaka. (2017). *Behavioral economics: Toward a new economics by integration with traditional economics*. Springer.

Papi, Mario. (2013). Satisficing and maximizing consumers in a monopolistic screening model. *Mathematical Social Sciences*, 66(3), 385–389. https://doi.org/10.1016/j.mathsocsci.2013.08.005

Pasnau, Robert. (2017). *After certainty: A history of our epistemic ideals and illusions*. Oxford University Press.

Pingle, Mark. (2006). Deliberation cost as a foundation for behavioral economics. In Morris Altman (Ed.), In *Handbook of contemporary behavioral economics: foundations and developments* (340–355). Routledge.

Pryor, James. (2004). What's wrong with Moore's argument? *Philosophical Issues*, 14(1), 349–378. https://doi.org/10.1111/j.1533-6077.2004.00034.x

Quiggin, John. (1982). A theory of anticipated utility. *Journal of Economic Behavior & Organization*, 3(4), 323–343. https://doi.org/10.1016/0167-2681(82)90008-7

Quong, Jonathan. (2018). Public Reason. In Edward N. Zalta (Ed.), *The Stanford encyclopedia of philosophy* (Spring 2018). Metaphysics Research Lab, Stanford University. https://plato.stanford.edu/archives/spr2018/entries/public-reason/

Railton, Peter. (1984). Alienation, consequentialism and the demands of morality. *Philosophy and Public Affairs*, 13(2), 134–171.

Ramsey, Frank. (1990). General propositions and causality. In D. H. Mellor (Ed.), *Philosophical papers* (145–163). Cambridge University Press.

Reutskaja, Elena, Rosemarie Nagel, Colin F. Camerer, and Antonio Rangel. (2011). Search dynamics in consumer choice under time pressure: An eye-tracking study. *American Economic Review*, 101(2), 900–926. https://doi.org/10.1257/aer.101.2.900

Roberts, Craige. (2012). Information structure in discourse: Towards an integrated formal theory of pragmatics. *Semantics and Pragmatics*, 5(6), 1–69. https://doi.org/10.3765/sp.5.6

Ross, Jacob, and Mark Schroeder. (2014). Belief, credence, and pragmatic encroachment. *Philosophy and Phenomenological Research*, 88(2), 259–288. https://doi.org/10.1111/j.1933-1592.2011.00552.x

Rousseau, Jean-Jacques. (1913). *Social contract & discourses* (G. D. H. Cole, Trans.). J. M. Dent and Sons.

Russell, Gillian, and John M. Doris. (2009). Knowledge by indifference. *Australasian Journal of Philosophy*, 86(3), 429–437. https://doi.org/10.1080/00048400802001996

Russell, Stuart J. (1997). Rationality and intelligence. *Artificial Intelligence*, 94(1–2), 57–77. https://doi.org/10.1016/S0004-3702(97)00026-X

Savage, Leonard. (1967). Difficulties in the theory of personal probability. *Philosophy of Science*, 34(4), 305–310. https://doi.org/10.1086/288168

Scheibehenne, Benjamin, Rainer Greifeneder, and Peter M. Todd. (2010). Can there ever be too many options? A meta-analytic review of choice overload. *Journal of Consumer Research*, 37(3), 409–425. https://doi.org/10.1086/651235

Schmidt, Eva. (forthcoming). Reasons, attenuators, and virtue: A novel account of pragmatic encroachment. *Analytic Philosophy*. https://doi.org/10.1111/phib.12314

Schoenfield, Miriam. (2013). Permission to believe: Why permissivism is true and what it tells us about irrelevant influences on belief. *Noûs*, 47(1), 193–218. https://doi.org/10.1111/nous.12006

Schroeder, Mark. (2009). Means-end coherence, stringency, and subjective reasons. *Philosophical Studies*, 143(2), 223–248. https://doi.org/10.1007/s11098-008-9200-x

Schroeder, Mark. (2012). Stakes, withholding and pragmatic encroachment on knowledge. *Philosophical Studies*, 160(2), 265–285. https://doi.org/10.1007/s11098-011-9718-1

Schwartz, Barry. (2004). *The paradox of choice: Why more is less*. Harper Collins.

Schwartz, Barry, Andrew Ward, John Monterosso, Sonja Lyubomirsky, Katherin White, and Darrin R. Lehman. (2002). Maximizing versus satisficing: Happiness is a matter of choice. *Journal of Personality and Social Psychology*, 83(5), 1178–1197. https://doi.org/10.1037/0022-3514.83.5.1178

Skyrms, Brian. (2001). The stag hunt. *Proceedings and Addresses of the American Philosophical Association*, 75(2), 31–41. https://doi.org/10.2307/3218711

Sosa, Ernest. (1999). How to defeat opposition to Moore. *Philosophical Perspectives*, 13, 141–153. https://doi.org/10.1111/0029-4624.33.s13.7

Sperber, Dan, Fabrice Clément, Christophe Heintz, Olivier Mascaro, Hugo Mercier, Gloria Origgi, and Deirdre Wilson. (2010). Epistemic vigilance. *Mind and Language*, 25(4), 359–393. https://doi.org/10.1111/j.1468-0017.2010.01394.x

Staffel, Julia. (2019). How do beliefs simplify reasoning? *Noûs*, 53(4), 937–962. https://doi.org/10.1111/nous.12254

Stalnaker, Robert. (1975). Indicative conditionals. *Philosophica*, 5(3), 269–289. https://doi.org/10.1007/bf02379021

Stalnaker, Robert. (1984). *Inquiry*. MIT Press.

Stalnaker, Robert. (1994). On the evaluation of solution concepts. *Theory and Decision*, 37(1), 49–73. https://doi.org/10.1007/BF01079205

Stalnaker, Robert. (1996). Knowledge, belief and counterfactual reasoning in games. *Economics and Philosophy*, 12, 133–163. https://doi.org/10.1017/S0266267100004132

Stalnaker, Robert. (1998). Belief revision in games: Forward and backward induction. *Mathematical Social Sciences*, 36(1), 31–56. https://doi.org/10.1016/S0165-4896(98)00007-9

Stalnaker, Robert. (1999). Extensive and strategic forms: Games and models for games. *Research in Economics*, 53(3), 293–319. https://doi.org/10.1006/reec.1999.0200

Stanley, Jason. (2005). *Knowledge and practical interests*. Oxford University Press.

Stanley, Jason. (2011). *Know how*. Oxford University Press.

Steglich-Petersen, Asbjørn. (2024). An instrumentalist explanation of pragmatic encroachment. *Analytic Philosophy*, 65(3), 374–392. https://doi.org/10.1111/phib.12283

Strevens, Michael. (2020). *The knowledge machine: How irrationality created modern science*. Liveright.

Tucker, Chris. (2016). Satisficing and motivated submaximization (in the philosophy of religion). *Philosophy and Phenomenological Research*, 93(1), 127–143. https://doi.org/10.1111/phpr.12191

Unger, Peter. (1975). *Ignorance: A case for scepticism*. Oxford University Press.

Weatherson, Brian. (2005a). Can we do without pragmatic encroachment? *Philosophical Perspectives*, 19(1), 417–443. https://doi.org/10.1111/j.1520-8583.2005.00068.x

Weatherson, Brian. (2005b). True, truer, truest. *Philosophical Studies*, 123(1–2), 47–70. https://doi.org/10.1007/s11098-004-5218-x

Weatherson, Brian. (2011). Defending interest-relative invariantism. *Logos & Episteme*, 2(4), 591–609. https://doi.org/10.5840/logos-episteme2011248

Weatherson, Brian. (2012). Knowledge, bets and interests. In Jessica Brown and Mikkel Gerken (Eds.), *Knowledge ascriptions* (75–103). Oxford University Press.

Weatherson, Brian. (2016a). Games, beliefs and credences. *Philosophy and Phenomenological Research*, 92(2), 209–236. https://doi.org/10.1111/phpr.12088

Weatherson, Brian. (2016b). Reply to Eaton and Pickavance. *Philosophical Studies*, 173(12), 3231–3233.

Weatherson, Brian. (2017). Interest-relative invariantism. In Jonathan Ichikawa (Ed.), *The Routledge handbook of epistemic contextualism* (240–253). Routledge.

Weatherson, Brian. (2018). Interests, evidence and games. *Episteme*, 15(3), 329–344.

Weatherson, Brian. (2019). *Normative externalism*. Oxford University Press.

Weisberg, Jonathan. (2010). Bootstrapping in general. *Philosophy and Phenomenological Research*, 81(3), 525–548. https://doi.org/10.1111/j.1933-1592.2010.00448.x

Weisberg, Jonathan. (2013). Knowledge in action. *Philosophers' Imprint*, 13(22), 1–23. https://doi.org/2027/spo.3521354.0013.022

Weisberg, Jonathan. (2020). Belief in psyontology. *Philosophers' Imprint*, 20(11), 1–27. https://doi.org/2027/spo.3521354.0020.011

White, Roger. (2005). Epistemic permissiveness. *Philosophical Perspectives*, 19, 445–459. https://doi.org/10.1111/j.1520-8583.2005.00069.x

Williams, Bernard. (1976). Persons, character and morality. In Amélie Oksenberg Rorty (Ed.), *The identities of persons* (197–216). University of California Press.

Williamson, Timothy. (1994). *Vagueness*. Routledge.

Williamson, Timothy. (2000). *Knowledge and its limits*. Oxford University Press.

Williamson, Timothy. (2005). Contextualism, subject-sensitive invariantism and knowledge of knowledge. *The Philosophical Quarterly*, 55(219), 213–235. https://doi.org/10.1111/j.0031-8094.2005.00396.x

Williamson, Timothy. (2007). How probable is an infinite sequence of heads? *Analysis*, 67(295), 173–180. https://doi.org/10.1093/analys/67.3.173

Williamson, Timothy. (2013). Gettier cases in epistemic logic. *Inquiry*, 56(1), 1–14. https://doi.org/10.1080/0020174X.2013.775010

Williamson, Timothy. (forthcoming). Knowledge, credence, and the strength of belief. In Amy Flowerree and Baron Reed (Eds.), *Towards an expansive epistemology: Norms, action, and the social world*. Routledge.

Wittgenstein, Ludwig. (1953). *Philosophical investigations*. Macmillan.

Woodard, Elise. (2024). Why double-check. *Episteme*, 21(2), 644–667. https://doi.org/10.1017/epi.2022.22.

Wright, Crispin. (2002). (Anti-)sceptics simple and subtle: G.E. Moore and John McDowell. *Philosophy and Phenomenological Research*, 65(2), 330–348. https://doi.org/10.1111/j.1933-1592.2002.tb00205.x

Wright, Crispin. (2018). *A plague on all your houses: Some reflections on the variable behaviour of 'knows'.* In Annalisa Coliva, Paolo Leonardi and Sebastiano Moruzzi (Eds.), *Eva Picardi on Language, analysis and history* (357–383). Palgrave Macmillan.

Wu, Jenny Yi-Chen. (forthcoming). A defense of impurist permissivism. *Episteme*. https://doi.org/10.1017/epi.2023.22

Yalcin, Seth. (2018). Belief as question-sensitive. *Philosophy and Phenomenological Research*, 97(1), 23–47. https://doi.org/10.1111/phpr.12330

Yalcin, Seth. (2021). Fragmented but rational. In Christina Borgoni, Dirk Kindermann, and Andrea Onofori (Eds.), *The fragmented mind* (156–179). Oxford University Press.

Ye, Ru. (2024). Knowledge-action principles and threshold-impurism. *Erkenntnis*, 89, 2215–2232. https://doi.org/10.1007/s10670-022-00626-7

Zweber, Adam. (2016). Fallibilism, closure, and pragmatic encroachment. *Philosophical Studies*, 173(10), 2745–2757. https://doi.org/10.1007/s11098-016-0631-5

List of Tables

2.1	Darja's choice between answering the question, and checking Google.	p. 48
3.1	Betting on the Red Sox.	p. 64
4.1	Ragnar's trip to work.	p. 90
4.2	Payouts in the Hotelling game.	p. 95
4.3	The Hotelling game after one iteration.	p. 96
4.4	What the Red-Blue game looks like if Anisa assumes that the Battle of Agincourt was in 1415.	p.102
8.1	An underspecified decision problem.	p.203
8.2	A simple game.	p.204
8.3	Death in Damascus as a game.	p.205
8.4	The Up-Down game.	p.206
9.1	Newcomb's problem as a game.	p.219
9.2	The Radical Interpreter game.	p.221
9.3	A generic 2 by 2 by 2 game.	p.222
9.4	A simple version of Stag Hunt.	p.223
9.5	The global game.	p.224
9.6	How the threshold moves towards 2.	p.228

Index

action and knowledge 9, 13, 14, 19, 102, 141, 145, 153, 154, 226, 247, 248, 251. *See also* K-Nec; *See also* K-Suff; *See also* rational action
action theory 12, 57–58, 248
Adamson, Peter 9–10, 12–13, 74
Anderson, Charity 5, 27, 46, 48, 80, 113, 123, 125, 153
Armour-Garb, Bradley 27, 36
assertion 36–38, 42, 150–152, 157
  norms of 150
Austin, J. L. 16

basic knowledge. *See* evidence
Basu, Rima 107, 146
belief. *See also* rational belief
  and correctness 22, 76–77, 200, 212, 215, 233
  and maps 58–62
  relation to knowledge 10–11, 14–15, 18, 23, 56–57, 89, 144, 169, 195, 200
  weak belief 56, 58
Bennett, Karen 181, 188–189
Bird, Alexander 237–238
Blome-Tillmann, Michael 179
Boyd, Kenneth 198
Brittain, Charles 9
Brown, Jessica 4–5, 22, 48, 53, 94, 125, 141–144
Buchak, Lara 162
Buridan, Jean 10–12, 57, 74

Carlsson, Hans 222–226, 230
certainty 7, 10–11, 36, 39, 50, 53, 101, 104
  moral 10–11
Cherniak, Christopher 170
Cho, In-Koo 205
Christensen, David 138–139, 167, 214
Clark, Christopher 182–186

close calls 22, 125–126
closure 21–22, 87, 111–114, 116–117, 119, 122–123, 153, 157–158, 166, 178, 213, 215
  multiple premise 112, 116–117, 123
  single premise 112–113, 116, 123
Cohen, Stewart 5, 36, 129
Conlisk, John 167–169, 171–172, 175
contextualism 27, 36–38, 52–53, 126–127, 144, 249–250
Craver, Carl 17
credence 4, 40, 42, 43, 56, 75, 76, 77, 81, 84, 86, 100, 155, 195, 199, 200, 201, 206, 208, 209, 211, 212, 214. *See also* probability
  relation to belief 84, 195
cut-elimination 149, 233, 244–245

Darden, Lindley 17
Das, Nilanjan 21, 23, 181, 191–192
decision tables 64–65, 90, 94, 98–99, 101–102
decision theory 64, 90, 92, 126, 153, 178, 205, 248
deliberation costs 91, 126, 167–169, 177
DeRose, Keith 36
Descartes, René 45
Dogramaci, Sinan 239
dominance reasoning 2, 42–43, 63–64, 77–78, 207–209
  strict dominance 248–249
  weak dominance 63, 83, 207–209
Doris, John M. 179, 190
double checking 104, 125, 139–143, 242, 250
Dylan, Bob 154

Eaton, Daniel 4, 179
Egan, Andy 133, 139

Elster, Jon 173
epistemicism 29–34, 146, 210
epistemicist 31
equilibrium 2, 94–95, 140, 204–205, 220–222, 224–226, 229, 232
   risk-dominant 222, 224–226, 232
Euclid 106
evidence 21, 23, 43–45, 47, 51, 100, 105, 126, 135, 180, 217–246
   as knowledge 180–181, 232–237
   higher-order 138–141

Falbo, Arianna 13–14, 136
false belief. *See* belief: and correctness
Fantl, Jeremy 8, 23, 49, 76, 103, 137–138, 145, 187, 212, 241, 244–246
Foley, Richard 210
Friedman, Jane 13–14, 22, 127–128

game theory 2, 63–64, 203–205, 221, 249
Ganson, Dorit 41, 55, 64
Gendler, Tamar Szabó 5, 191
Gettier, Edmund L. 180, 183, 200
Gigerenzer, Gerd 169
Gillies, Anthony 68, 81–82
given, taken as 60, 62, 65, 67, 74–75, 89, 247
Goldman, Alvin 235, 241
grounding of knowledge 13, 16, 25, 147, 177, 188–189, 239–240, 247

Harman, Gilbert 97, 149, 170, 184, 188, 238–239
Harper, William 219
Hawthorne, John 5, 8, 27, 46, 48, 56, 79–80, 103, 112–113, 123, 125, 128, 131, 153, 191
Hedden, Brian 92
Hieronymi, Pamela 103
Hills, Alison 131–132
Hotelling, Harold 94–96
Humberstone, Lloyd 64, 93, 173, 225
Hunter, Daniel 210

Ichikawa, Jonathan 4–5, 37, 106, 142

inquiry. *See also* double checking; *See also* settled attitude
   aim of 14
   practical 2–3, 20, 90
   starting points 2, 7, 14, 20, 22, 45, 56–57, 105, 107, 125, 128, 147, 149–150, 187, 238
   theoretical 20, 90

Jackson, Frank 130, 173–174
Joyce, James M. 162, 176
JTB, theory of knowledge 126, 181–183, 187–188, 190

Keynes, John Maynard 91, 94
Kimball, Miles 169, 175–176
Kim, Brian 8, 79
K-Nec 53–54
Knight, Frank 131, 167–168, 170
Kohlberg, Elon 203
Kratzer, Angelika 81
Kreps, David 205
Kripke, Saul 130
Kroedel, Thomas 119
K-Suff 53, 94

Lancaster, Kelvin 16
Lasonen-Aarnio, Maria 30
learning modality (face-to-face vs. online) 275
Lederman, Harvey 5, 97, 171
Lee, Matthew 210, 212
Lewis, David 8, 68, 96–97, 133, 180, 197–198
libraries 275
Lipsey, R. G. 16
Littlejohn, Clayton 139
Lockean thesis 23, 76, 201–203, 209–214, 216

MacFarlane, John 38
Machamer, Peter 17
Maher, Patrick 237
Maitra, Ishani 5, 35, 151
Manski, Charles 163–164

McGrath, Matthew 5, 8, 23, 49, 76, 79, 103, 128, 137–138, 145, 187, 212, 241, 244–246
Melchior, Guido 13–14, 129, 136, 140
Mercier, Hugo 15
Mertens, Jean-Francois 203
Moore's Paradox 34–36, 105, 157, 212–213, 216
moral encroachment 109–110, 146

Nagel, Jennifer 5, 37, 61, 184, 200
Nair, Shyam 5, 233–235
Neta, Ram 241–243
Newcomb's problem 42, 166, 219–220
North, Jill 206
Nozick, Robert 8, 18, 41
Nyāya 2, 12–13, 247

orthodox theory 11, 30–39, 42–46, 91, 146, 213, 248–250

Papi, Mauro 163
Pasnau, Robert 10–11, 15, 57
Philo of Larissa 9–10, 12, 15
Pickavance, Timothy 4, 179
pragmatic encroachment 3, 5, 226, 232
pragmatist theory 30–32, 34, 146
Prisoners' Dilemma 223
Pritchard, Duncan 8
probability 17, 20, 33, 42–45, 50–51, 56, 62, 67–68, 80, 82–83, 85, 90–91, 99, 101, 155, 161, 164, 176–178, 199, 202–203, 205–206, 208, 215, 218, 221, 224, 227–231
Pryor, James 243

questions 70–74
  conditional 67–70, 75–76, 89, 114
  unconditional 68, 89, 158
Quiggin, John 162
Quong, Jonathan 134

Radical Interpreter, The 23, 219–222, 225–226, 232, 242–243
Railton, Peter 90
Ramsey, Frank 58–59, 82

rational action 9, 145, 153–154, 226, 231, 247, 251
rational belief 3, 23, 50, 62, 149, 188, 193, 195–201, 233
Red-Blue game 25–26, 28, 43–45, 59, 61–62, 65, 78, 84, 102, 104, 113, 117, 121, 202, 206, 217
Reutskaja, Elena 163, 167
Roberts, Craige 70
Ross, Jacob 5, 62, 76, 78, 83–87, 212
Rousseau, Jean-Jacques 221, 223
Russell, Gillian 179, 190
Russell, Stuart 170

safety 8–9, 187–188, 191, 193
Savage, Leonard 164
scepticism 9, 12–14, 19–20, 22, 29, 31–33, 41, 45, 50, 53, 99, 119, 123, 146, 148, 153, 156–159, 177–178, 214, 243–244, 247, 250
Schoenfield, Miriam 206
Schroeder, Mark 5, 20, 58, 62, 76, 78, 83–87, 107, 146, 212
Schwartz, Barry 165–166
Selten, Reinhard 169
sensitivity 8–9, 14, 18, 61, 129–130, 136–138, 142–143, 186, 191
settled attitude 18, 19, 20, 55, 70, 127, 128, 151, 219. *See also* inquiry
Skyrms, Brian 223
Sosa, Ernest 5, 8–9
Sperber, Dan 176, 198
Srinivasan, Amia 131
Staffel, Julia 55–56
Stag Hunt game 222–223
stakes 1–2, 10, 19–21, 27, 29, 46–48, 55, 60, 62, 126, 139, 146, 178, 242–243, 250
Stalnaker, Robert 5, 133, 203, 205, 207–208, 210, 213
Stanley, Jason 5, 8, 20, 46, 49–50, 73–74, 103, 128, 180
Strevens, Michael 14, 133–134, 136

Tucker, Chris 163

Unger, Peter 29

Up-Down game 206, 208, 215
utility 2–3, 22, 42–43, 47–48, 68, 74–76, 79–80, 83, 85, 90–91, 126, 142, 153, 155–156, 158–159, 161–165, 167, 170–171, 173, 198–199, 207, 209, 218, 220, 226
  maximising expected 2–3, 22, 42–43, 47–48, 68, 74–75, 80, 126, 142, 153, 158, 162–163, 165, 171, 173–174, 198, 207, 209, 218, 220, 226

van Damme, Eric 222–226, 230
Vātsyāyana 12–13
vigilance 198–199
  epistemic 198

Weisberg, Jonathan 55, 109, 237, 246
White, Roger 206
Wilkins, John 11–12, 15
Williams, Bernard 190
Williamson, Timothy 8, 18, 42, 50, 57, 100, 185, 195, 200–202, 209–210, 225, 233
Wittgenstein, Ludwig 170
Woodard, Elise 13–14, 21, 128, 136
Wright, Crispin 108–109, 179–180, 187–188

Yalcin, Seth 58

Zweber, Adam 80, 113, 123, 125, 153

About the Team

Alessandra Tosi was the managing editor for this book.

Sophia Bursey and Adèle Kreager proof-read this manuscript. Adèle compiled the index.

Jeevanjot Kaur Nagpal designed the cover. The cover was produced in InDesign using the Fontin font.

Cameron Craig typeset the book in InDesign and produced the paperback and hardback editions. The main text font is Tex Gyre Pagella and the heading font is Californian FB.

Cameron also produced the PDF and HTML editions. The conversion was performed with open-source software and other tools freely available on our GitHub page at https://github.com/OpenBookPublishers.

Jeremy Bowman created the EPUB.

Raegan Allen was in charge of marketing.

This book was peer-reviewed by Jonathan Ichikawa, Professor of Philosophy, University of British Columbia, and two anonymous referees. Experts in their field, these readers give their time freely to help ensure the academic rigour of our books. We are grateful for their generous and invaluable contributions.

This book need not end here...

Share

All our books — including the one you have just read — are free to access online so that students, researchers and members of the public who can't afford a printed edition will have access to the same ideas. This title will be accessed online by hundreds of readers each month across the globe: why not share the link so that someone you know is one of them?

This book and additional content is available at
https://doi.org/10.11647/OBP.0425

Donate

Open Book Publishers is an award-winning, scholar-led, not-for-profit press making knowledge freely available one book at a time. We don't charge authors to publish with us: instead, our work is supported by our library members and by donations from people who believe that research shouldn't be locked behind paywalls.

Join the effort to free knowledge by supporting us at
https://www.openbookpublishers.com/support-us

We invite you to connect with us on our socials!

BLUESKY	MASTODON	LINKEDIN
@openbookpublish.bsky.social	@OpenBookPublish@hcommons.social	open-book-publishers

Read more at the Open Book Publishers Blog
https://blogs.openbookpublishers.com

You may also be interested in:

Basic Knowledge and Conditions on Knowledge
Mark McBride

https://doi.org/10.11647/obp.0104

Knowledge and the Norm of Assertion
An Essay in Philosophical Science
John Turri

https://doi.org/10.11647/obp.0083

Forms of Life and Subjectivity
Rethinking Sartre's Philosophy
Daniel Rueda Garrido

https://doi.org/10.11647/obp.0259

www.ingramcontent.com/pod-product-compliance
Lightning Source LLC
Chambersburg PA
CBHW051050230426
43666CB00012B/2633